# The WORKING WOMAN'S Guide to MANAGING TIME

TAKE CHARGE OF YOUR JOB AND YOUR LIFE
WHILE TAKING CARE OF YOURSELF

## ROBERTA ROESCH

Foreword by Alec Mackenzie
Author of *The Time Trap* and *Time for Success*

**PRENTICE HALL**
Englewood Cliffs, New Jersey 07632

**Library of Congress Cataloging-in-Publication Data**

Roesch, Roberta.
    The working woman's guide to managing time : take charge of your
job and your life while taking care of yourself / by Roberta Roesch
foreword by Alec Mackenzie.
      p.  cm.
    Includes bibliographical references and index.
    ISBN 0-13-097437-4—ISBN 0-13-097429-3 (pbk.)
    1. Women—Time management.   2. Women—Employment.
3. Work and family.   I. Title.
HQ1221.R677   1995                    95-37227
640′.43′082—dc20                     CIP

*Printed in the United States of America*

*10  9  8  7  6  5  4  3  2*

**ISBN 0-13-097437-4    ISBN 0-13-097429-3(PBK)**

---

**ATTENTION: CORPORATIONS AND SCHOOLS**

Prentice Hall books are available at quantity discounts with bulk purchase for educational,
business, or sales promotional use. For information, please write to: Prentice Hall Career &
Personal Development Special Sales, 113 Sylvan Avenue, Englewood Cliffs, NJ 07632. Please
supply: title of book, ISBN number, quantity, how the book will be used, date needed.

---

**PRENTICE HALL**
Career & Personal Development
Englewood Cliffs, NJ 07632
A Simon & Schuster Company

**On the World Wide Web at http://www.phdirect.com**

Prentice-Hall International (UK) Limited, *London*
Prentice-Hall of Australia Pty. Limited, *Sydney*
Prentice-Hall Canada Inc., *Toronto*
Prentice-Hall Hispanoamericana, S.A., *Mexico*
Prentice-Hall of India Private Limited, *New Delhi*
Prentice-Hall of Japan, Inc., *Tokyo*
Simon & Schuster Asia Pte. Ltd., *Singapore*
Editora Prentice-Hall do Brasil, Ltda., *Rio de Janeiro*

# OTHER BOOKS BY ROBERTA ROESCH

*How to Be Organized in Spite of Yourself*
*(Co-authored with Sunny Schlenger)*

*Smart Talk: The Art of Savvy Business Conversation*

*You Can Make It Without a College Degree*

*Jobs for Weekends*

*There's Always a Right Job for Every Woman*

*Money, Jobs, and Futures*

*Women in Action*

*The Encyclopedia of Depression*

*Anyone's Son*

*World's Fairs*

# ABOUT THE AUTHOR

Roberta Roesch is an award-winning author who has specialized in writing about jobs and careers, time management and organization, and women's personal development for more than 25 years. During that time she has interviewed thousands of working women and experts on women's issues and written more than 5,000 newspaper columns, ten previous books, and hundreds of articles in leading magazines, including *Reader's Digest, Good Housekeeping, Family Circle, McCall's, Glamour, Parents, Working Woman, USA Weekend, New Woman,* and many others.

Roesch has appeared on radio and television in major cities, lectured extensively, and conducted seminars and workshops on working women for businesses and organizations, colleges, churches, malls, and book and department stores. She's a former member of the adjunct faculty at Bergen Community College and a graduate of Centenary College from which she received the 1993 Van Winkle Achievement Award, an honorary Doctorate of Humane Letters, and a citation as one of the college's 125 Distinguished Graduates. She's a member of the Authors Guild and American Society of Journalists and Authors and lives with her husband and family in Westwood, New Jersey.

# CONTENTS

# PART ONE

## MANAGING YOUR TIME ON THE JOB: A 7-POINT PROGRAM FOR GAINING CONTROL OF YOUR 9 TO 5 HOURS—1

### POINT ONE:
#### *Recognize and Conquer Women's Nine Greatest Time Problems—3*

### POINT TWO:
#### *Jump-Start Your Day by Using Six Tested Time Tools—17*

### POINT THREE:
#### *Use Short- and Long-Range Planning to Keep Time from Slipping Away—37*

## POINT SEVEN:
### *Be the Mistress of Your Own Time by Working at Home—121*

# PART TWO

## MANAGING YOUR TIME AWAY FROM THE JOB:
## A 3-POINT PROGRAM FOR DAWN-TO-DUSK AND BEYOND—147

## POINT EIGHT:
### *Balance the Work/Home Time Crunch and Feel Good About Yourself—149*

# 𝒫ART THREE

## MANAGING YOUR PERSONAL TIME: A 3-POINT PROGRAM FOR MAKING TIME FOR YOURSELF AND TIME FOR OTHERS—205

### POINT ELEVEN:

*Set Aside Personal Time for Yourself to Recharge Your Batteries—207*

## POINT TWELVE:
### *Stay Focused and You Can Almost "Have It All" Your Way—227*

## POINT THIRTEEN:
### *Let Your Individual Situation Guide Your Time Management Choices—243*

## WHO'S WHO:
### *A Quick-Check Guide to the Women in the Book—257*

## INDEX—273

# CKNOWLEDGMENTS

In that time management is a key issue for every working woman, I'm deeply indebted to the working women everywhere in the country who have taken time from their juggling-act lives to answer my questions on time problems and solutions. Many spent hours in personal evaluation sessions to give me the in-depth answers and advice they share throughout this book. A few asked for anonymity, so in these infrequent instances I haven't used real names.

I owe another thank you to the thousands of additional working women I've interviewed through the years for my books, articles, and newspaper columns. Whether they know it or not, they've contributed to this book. So have my working-women family and friends.

Time management consultants, career counselors, psychologists, psychotherapists and other professionals who provided research and suggestions also played a significant role in the writing of this book. Their names are noted throughout the text, but special thanks are due to Alec Mackenzie, who so generously shared experiences and information from the hundreds of seminars on time management he has given throughout the world; Ted Rose who supplied me with helpful material from the The Prodigy Services Company Report on Women prepared by the The Roper Organization; and John J. Gauthier who provided research and surveys from Priority Management.

Other individuals and organizations who gave me valuable assistance are The Bureau of National Affairs; Sheila Wellington of Catalyst; Entrepreneur Magazine Group; Families and Work Institute; Leonard LoPinto and the staff of the Westwood Public Library; Linda Marks of New Ways to Work; Barbara Schryver of Manpower Temporary Services; and the Women's Bureau of the U. S. Department of Labor.

I'm especially grateful to my editor, Ellen Schneid Coleman, for her editorial expertise and perception, and to my agent, Bert Holtje, for his counsel and encouragement.

And, always and forever, I thank my family—Phil, Meredith, Bonnie, and Jeff—for their constant and ongoing support.

**Roberta Roesch**

# FOREWORD

When I wrote *About Time! A Woman's Guide to Time Management* at the beginning of the 1980s, I stressed that women's conditioning, perceptions, expectations, and needs make time management different for women than for men.

Today this book reaffirms that.

I also mentioned that women's most difficult choices were "A career is fulfilling," "Homemaking is satisfying," "More education is intriguing," and "A social life is fun."

Today none of this has changed, as Roberta Roesch reports.

The things that *have* changed are the number of women who work. According to the latest statistics from the U. S. Department of Labor, women accounted for 62% of the total labor force growth between the '80s and '90s. Moreover, as today's working women try to balance work, home, family, relationships, *and* values, our high-tech era—with devices undreamed of at the start of the '80s—speeds up the pace of their lives.

In addition, our information explosion accelerates this pace by offering women an overabundance of options and things to do. Their pressures mount. Their expectations get higher. And as their lives grow busier and busier, they feel they have less and less time.

As a result of these changes from the early '80s, priorities and time management problems are more important than ever today.

Roberta Roesch cuts through these issues with hundreds of wide-ranging interviews with working women and time management professionals. As she reports on her research—and her own experience and knowledge—the wealth of time-saving techniques that evolve adds up to a point-by-point plan any woman can follow to learn to manage time.

From my 20 years of studying time management—and working all over the world with approximately 50,000 people in almost every field—I *know* that people who want to *can* learn to manage time. In fact, my studies consistently show that, on the average, people can save two hours every day through improving their time management habits.

This stimulating, practical, and *workable* book shows women how to do this, as the author and legions of working women discuss what works for them in stretching their 24-hour days.

It's right on target for all working women who have too little time but who want to make the best use of that time in their working and personal lives.

**Alec Mackenzie**—*President, Alec Mackenzie and Associates, Inc.*
*International Speaker and Seminar Leader*

# $\mathcal{I}$NTRODUCTION

Is the story of your life "Too much to do and too little time to do it?"

And are you bogged down by the daily tasks of trying to handle and juggle an overcommitted life?

As one of the 57 million women in the working world your answer to both questions is probably an instant "Yes" as you struggle to find time for *everything*. You also face time problems that are *different* from men's since most working women do two jobs—one at work and one at home.

"At work I deal with crises from the time I begin till I leave," a nurse supervisor told me, "and then I switch to home chores and driving the children around. I've read every time management book I can find and try to do what they say.

"But I *still* don't have enough hours for all I want to do. I need some more ideas!"

For the past 25 years I've spent my work life interviewing working women—and writing about their jobs and careers, their day-to-day balancing acts, and their special time management problems.

Personally, I've faced time problems ranging from A to Z as I've merged raising a family, taking care of a home, and either commuting to 40-hour-a-week jobs or sometimes working 60-hour weeks in my office at home.

From my own job-and-life experiences—and the job-and-life stories I hear—I see on an ongoing basis that how we manage our hours while trying to balance our lives is one of the crucial measuring rods for determining our success. It's also the key to enjoying life rather than hurrying through it.

The way to make our juggling act work—and lead a less breathless life—is managing time *women's way* which, by definition, means taking practical action steps specifically geared to women who want to take charge of their jobs and their lives and, also, take care of themselves.

This book will show you how.

# *W*HAT THIS BOOK WILL DO FOR YOU

First, you'll note immediately that this book is a different time management book because it (1) focuses *exclusively* on women's day-to-day problems and solutions to them, (2) provides time-saving strategies custom-tailored to women's needs, and (3) goes well beyond list-making and other tried-and-true, but tired, approaches to time management. Those things are still important, but for today's woman, the really *essential* tool for managing time is the ability to decide what's vital and valuable to you so you can use time in a meaningful way and touch and live life as you go.

Second, you'll learn how to use time to do this—and achieve immediate and lasting benefits—through a 13-Point Program for managing your nine-to-five hours, your before-and-after work life, and your personal time for yourself and others.

Third, you'll receive expert advice from time management consultants, career counselors, psychologists, other professionals, and working women of different ages from all walks of life with different types of jobs and levels of responsibility.

Fourth, you'll gain perspective on *what* you need to do to improve your use of time through worksheets, exercises, self-analysis tests, questionnaires, checklists, and charts.

Fifth, you'll get solutions to your problems from the easy-to-apply *how*-to-do-it Quick Starts, Time Boosters, and What Successful Women Say features.

Sixth, at the end of the book you'll find a Who's Who so you can do a quick-check on the names and jobs of women in the book when you want to refresh your memory.

# NINE BENEFITS THIS BOOK WILL HELP YOU ACHIEVE

As your ability to manage time improves you will be able to:

1. Simplify your life and cut back on non-necessary things so you won't be stretched-out and stressed-out. Today's "voluntary simplicity" movement is attracting many women who want a better quality of life before time runs out.

2. Gain better control of your day-to-day life to produce this quality of life because you will know how to match your realistic goals and priorities to your available time.

3. Advance your career through greater productivity by keeping on top of what to do in the days, weeks, months, and years ahead.

4. Stay away from detouring main-road destinations to less-important side-road temptations.

5. Decrease the rush hours and continuous "Hurry up" of your home life.

6. Increase your time for family and friends.

7. Double hours for yourself.

8. Maximize the self-esteem and sense of self that, along with earning a salary for your own achievements, is one of the greatest pleasures of being a working woman.

9. Remain in constant touch with how to blend the work, home, family, personal, physical, emotional, and spiritual segments of your life into a more satisfying and simpler whole.

# ℛEAL-LIFE ANSWERS FROM REAL-LIFE WORKING WOMEN

One question women always ask me is "How do other women manage?" In the points that follow you'll hear how more than a hundred *real-life* working women handle the time dilemmas that plague them. As you hear their voices, you'll (1) discover the day-to-day hints these "hands-on experts" use to resolve the multidemands of their lives and (2) learn how to apply these practical solutions to your own time management dilemmas.

The voices of working women are becoming increasingly important; so important, as a matter of fact, that in 1994 the U. S. Labor Department initiated a survey to find out from working women themselves what they think about their work. Launched by Hillary Rodham Clinton, this survey calls working women the "experts"—just as this book does.

# 𝒯HE POSITIVES OF THE JUGGLING ACT

Though *all* working women have to deal with multicommitment roles, this juggling need *not* be negative. Instead, with the right priorities and attitude, it can be positive. As Dr. Kathleen Gerson, professor of sociology at New York University, an expert in gender and family issues, and author of *Hard Choices: How Women Decide About Work, Careers and Motherhood* stresses, "The process can be satisfying and meaningful, and women definitely benefit from having multiple roles. Research has shown that if you compare working women with nonworking women you generally find working women are happier and have a higher sense of self-esteem."

In my years of writing about women and work I've also discovered this. For instance, one woman who uses the time boosts in this book balances her job as an assistant actuary with caring for her home and family, volunteering for school and community projects, making Halloween and Christmas costumes for her children, shopping for and visiting her mother in a nursing home, vacationing with her husband and children, and indulging in her passions for gourmet cooking, entertaining, and gardening.

"I've worked all my life and would miss a job's intellectual demands," she says. "So by mixing an interesting job life with a fulfilling home and personal life I have the best of all worlds."

*Your* mix-and-match needs are unique to you since every woman is different. But if "Too much to do and too little time" is the story of your life, this book will give you ideas that will help turn those negatives into positives.

As you see how other working women stretch their 24 hours you'll learn to balance what you *need* to do and what you *want* to do and, like the assistant actuary, have the best of all worlds.

## HOW TO GET THE MOST FROM THIS BOOK

- For instant ideas to start saving time right away, flip through the pages rapidly to pull out *Quick-Start* and *Time-Booster* solutions to your specific problems.

- Next go back and thoroughly read each point and make notes on how you can apply each suggestion to your life.

- Copy the blank self-analysis quizzes, questionnaires, checklists, and worksheets. Fill them in as you go along and put copies of each completed exercise (along with other notes you make) in a looseleaf notebook you set up for this purpose. If you do this you'll have your own personal time management book by the time you finish the book.

- Review this personal guide regularly to track how you're progressing with and maintaining your time management goals.

- As you progress repeat the exercises and worksheets and continue to track your development.

# $\mathcal{T}$UNE INTO THE GENDER DIFFERENCES:

## *Making Your Strengths Work for You*

*You bet my time problems are different!*
—**A mathematics teacher**

When Barbara Brabec, a publisher of home business reports and newsletters, asked her readers to submit their tips for managing time only one man responded.

"Generally when I ask for contributions I get a nice balance of material from both men and women," reported Barbara, "so in this instance I think we're simply dealing with a problem that's different for women and men."[1]

In talking to Barbara and other women about time management I hear "My problems are different from men's" over and over again. But, for some reason, most working women still feel they should manage their time on the job exactly like men do instead of managing time *women's* way and making their strengths work for them.

At the end of this section you will see how to benefit from those strengths. You'll also fill out a questionnaire that will test your attitude toward time. But first we'll take a hard look at some of the key gender differences affecting your time management.

# WOMEN JUGGLE MORE ROLES THAN MEN

Most women are much more torn than men as they try—in 24 hours—to meet all their commitments and keep track of all they need to do.

"Simply look around you whenever you walk down the street," says Judith Moncrieff Baldwin, an inventor of time management products. "Notice that the majority of men are either carrying nothing—or carrying only *one* hard-sided case with no easy access to the inside. Conversely, most of the women look like pack mules with briefcases or totes that have openings at the top for easy access to the inside and soft sides for plenty of room to expand.

"This difference is not because men have pockets and we don't. It's because most women carry around *all* their important information and sources so they can connect to anyone or anything at any time. On the other hand, the only two sources to which many men need connections are their secretaries and their wives. These two can connect them with anyone or anything they require."

## T I M E   B O O S T E R S

Tie your various roles together by using your carry-along bag as a portable office wherever you happen to be. Information, sources, and supplies to keep in it (and what I carry in mine) are:

- your appointment book (ideally one with a calendar for daily commitments and a section for addresses and phone numbers of people you may need to contact)
- a to-do list for work and home
- paperwork you can do away from your desk
- pens, pencils, highlighter, and small pad
- index cards for writing notes and ideas
- envelopes, stamps, and Post-it notes
- postcards for quick correspondence
- birthday and greeting cards
- paper clips, small stapler, scissors

# WOMEN STILL HAVE A HEAVIER WORKLOAD AT HOME

Though men with working wives often are doing more these days, most working couples still have different workloads at home. In fact, a study by the New York-based Families and Work Institute shows clearly that employed women are much more likely than employed men to have the main responsibility for the most demanding household chores—cooking, cleaning, shopping, and child care.[2] (See Figure 1: Comparison of Women and Men in Dual-Earner Families with Respect to Who Takes the Greater Responsibility for Household Work.)

"Child care arrangements take up *my* time, rather than my husband's," says a wife whose husband is so unfamiliar with such arrangements that he thinks it's possible to get a New Year's Eve baby-sitter on two days' notice.

While talking with female audiences about child-care arrangements, I hear most women say that even though they partially succeed in getting their husbands involved *they* are still the ones who rearrange their schedules if the nanny calls in sick or the day-care center closes unexpectedly. And they are the ones who communicate with their children's schools, attend school functions, and participate in everything from fundraisers to class trips, even though *both* parents work.

## QUICK STARTS

 Get over the feeling that you should (or can) do everything yourself. If you send out this feeling—even unconsciously—partners are less likely to come through with assistance.

 Discuss the tasks that need to be done and consider what chores you can rotate or alternate with other people who live with you.

**FIGURE 1:** Comparison of Women and Men in Dual-Earner Families with Respect to Who Takes the Greater Responsibility for Household Work

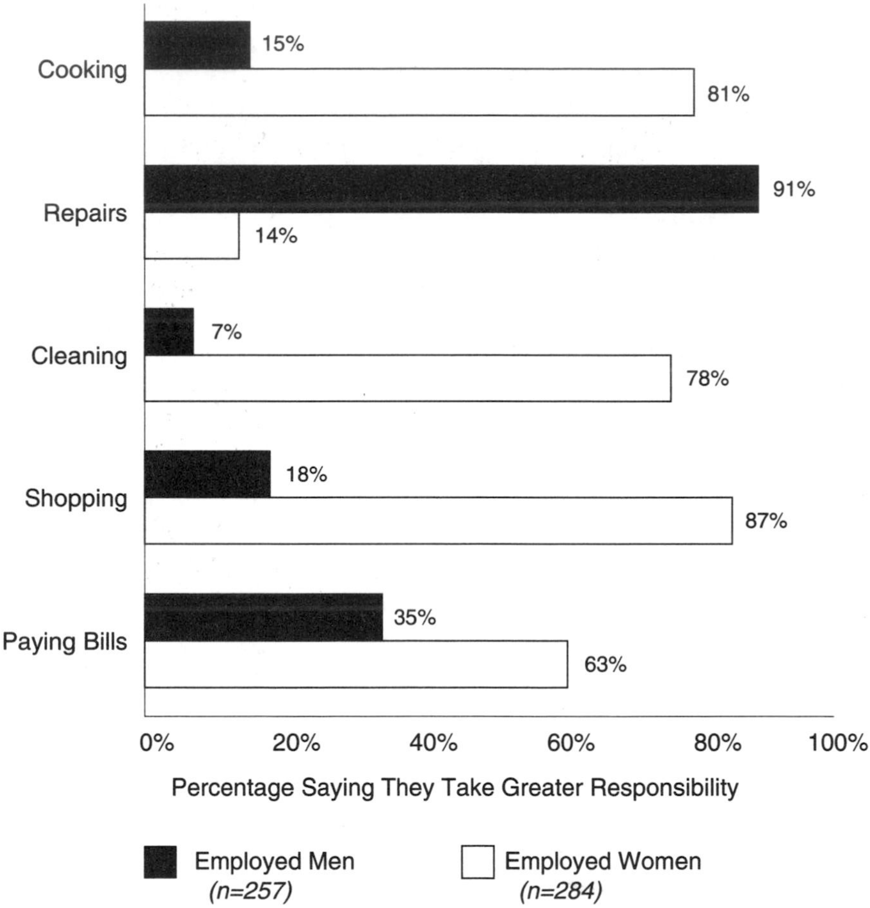

Cooking
15%
81%

Repairs
91%
14%

Cleaning
7%
78%

Shopping
18%
87%

Paying Bills
35%
63%

0%    20%    40%    60%    80%    100%

Percentage Saying They Take Greater Responsibility

■ Employed Men
(n=257)

☐ Employed Women
(n=284)

*All comparisons were significant at the p < .0001 level*

*Source: Families and Work Institute, 1993*

# WOMEN ARE THE PRIMARY CAREGIVERS FOR FAMILY HEALTH NEEDS

With America's aging population, the need to spend extra time caring for a parent (or other family member) is becoming such a growing time problem that almost 25% of employees nationwide are caregivers.[3] Some do this over and above their hours on a full-time job. Others have to put their jobs on hold and take a leave of absence.

Since 1993 the Family and Medical Leave Act has provided workers with the right to take unpaid job-protected time off for family health needs, their own illnesses, or maternity leave. However, when a poll conducted by the Bureau of National Affairs asked 694 employed persons how they would make use of the Family and Medical Leave Act, the results showed clearly that women would more likely become the caregivers than men.

Forty-six percent of the women said they would take the full 12-weeks allowance of unpaid leave to care for a gravely ill parent or spouse. But only 26 percent of the men said they'd do likewise. The poll also found an enormous difference between men and women in their willingness to take long leaves without pay to care for newborns or newly adopted children.[4]

## TIME BOOSTERS

- Handle the tough times in which your hours can be swallowed up by another person's needs with as much composure as possible. One woman who cares for her mother leaves for her job at 8:30 A.M. and returns at 7:00 P.M. She spends two hours caring for her mother before she goes to work and even more time in the evening. For the hours she's at work she hires a home health aide.

- To save meal preparation and medication time she prepares 21 meals for the freezer each weekend. She also divides a week's supply of pills into separate bottles. To save her sanity she hires a sitter for her mother a few hours on Saturdays and Sundays so she can pursue a life of her own. And she keeps herself going calmly in her time-pressured life by working around her caregiving role rather than letting it defeat her.

# WOMEN ARE "LEARNED" OR "INBORN" NURTURERS

I can't wait to start work in the morning—but, still, some inner voice commands that I take some nurturing time to dash off a note to a sick relative, put chicken and veggies for my family's favorite soup into a slow cooker, or browse through my bookshelves for a book a colleague wants to borrow. Other women hear this voice, too, because whenever I talk with them about their use of time the subject of nurturing comes up. Some take the "It's learned" view and feel nurturing is taught from an early age. Others believe "It's inborn" and something for which they want to take time, no matter how busy their working lives are.

## The Learned View

"My first grade son has difficulty paying attention at school and is often on the wrong page in his book," says Sandra Sharp, a bank manager. "So what do you think the teacher did? Her solution was to seat him between two girls so they could look after him and help him find the right place. Already these six-year-old girls are learning to be nurturers!"

## The Inborn View

"Nurturing has to do with just being a woman," stresses Dr. Violet Master, an internist in private practice. "You see all that needs to be done and always have the subconscious concern 'Will this be taken care of?' In my earlier medical days when my first son was very young—and when I'd be on night duty and work 36 or more hours at a stretch—I'd see something to take care of as soon as I came home, not because I had to do it but because I wanted to do it."

## The Workplace View

According to management consultant Carol Painter Campi, "Women are more comfortable than men implementing the nurturing quality at work. Some men will do this also," she observes. "But they'll call it mentoring, or being somebody's 'rabbi' or 'godfather.'"

## QUICK STARTS

 Build your nurturing instincts into your "women's way" of managing time—but keep it under control. If you feel like doing a favor for someone at work, put a time limit on it and stick to your allotted time frame.

If you enjoy nurturing at home don't let it spill over into your time at work. Especially if you work at home, do your nurturing during nonwork time (maybe for a 30-minute stint in the morning), then get going on your job.

# *W*OMEN ARE RELUCTANT TO DELEGATE

We don't have time to do everything and handle every detail, so delegating certain jobs to people who can give you a hand is a major way to gain time. It's essential for women like Elizabeth Randall, who as New Jersey banking commissioner, *has* to delegate and who stresses the need for *all* working women to learn to delegate regardless of their job level.

"Even without an assistant, most working women have *someone* who will help with a task if, when circumstances reverse, they reciprocate," she says.

## QUICK START

 Stop doing routine work that you can delegate. No matter how small the task is it will save you time if somebody else can do it. (See Point 4 for more tips on delegating.)

# *W*OMEN WORRY MORE ABOUT DETAILS

Men (more often than women) have other people to handle details, so men are not as prone to becoming caught up in them. Similarly, most men concentrate, first, on the hands-on details on their desk—the words, facts, numbers, and tangibles.

On the other hand, women tend to hold back and look at the overview. As they consider all the details leading to the end result, they shy away from getting started if their end goal is perfection. But since *every* job needn't be perfect, always aiming for perfection is a tremendous time waster.

### QUICK START

Evaluate the importance of each job and then get moving within the time frame that the desired result justifies rather than getting bogged down by details and perfection anxiety.

## WOMEN ARE MORE INCLINED TO FEEL THEY SHOULD HELP OTHERS

Because of their nurturing and caretaking natures, women can be more inclined than men to (1) feel they should go above and beyond their normal job responsibilities to help their boss operate and (2) say "Yes" to coworkers' requests for answering their phones or filling in for them at meetings.

"As I consult at corporations I see women with the problem of not only managing their own time but also believing they should help their boss function," says Sunny Schlenger, a consultant on personal management techniques and my coauthor of *How To Be Organized in Spite of Yourself.*

"This is a female sort of thing because I can't see a guy in their positions thinking in the same way."

In some cases, it may be the nature of your job to have to help out in areas outside your regular duties. That's fine, and of course, you don't want to butt heads with your boss over what you should be asked to do. The key is to not let yourself feel that you *have* to always help out. When you let that happen, your time will be lost and you will fall behind.

## QUICK STARTS

 Avoid conveying the impression you're the person who's always willing to pitch in and take over tasks that other people can't finish on time.

 Refrain from looking for extra ways to help your boss operate when the extras are time-consuming tasks that you don't have to do and that interfere with your own work time.

 When coworkers ask you to help with something you don't have time to do, say graciously but firmly "I'd like to help out, but I'm completely bogged down."

# WOMEN SPEND MORE TIME ON PERSONAL BUSINESS

Invariably I hear women say they're the "designated driver" for their family's personal affairs—buying gifts, writing thank-you notes, arranging play dates for their children, and preserving the couple's contacts with others.

"I have a darling, caring husband," says Sherry Suib Cohen, a journalist. "But I spend far more time on personal business—such as making social engagements and listening to a friend's problems—than he does. In fact, he spends almost no time on things like that."

## QUICK START

 Handling the personal business in your family circle is generally one of your multiple roles that's not easy to delegate. However, one working woman has her youngest daughter keep track of everyone's birthday and send the birthday cards she purchases a year in advance. Since you'll be doing most of these jobs, use some of the time you'll save by following the tips in this book. Some personal business is fun business too, so be positive rather than negative about your need to take time for it.

## MOST WOMEN WANT TIME FOR "LITTLE THINGS" AT HOME

Along with being working women, most of us tend to be nesters who generally care more than men about "little things" in the house. Even feminist Betty Freidan has said her favorite therapy is re-arranging furniture. Other women are drawn to arranging flowers, centering a vase on a table, grouping photographs on a picture wall, and color-coordinating bathroom towels—all things a man could walk right by and never even see!

"And what about dinner parties," asks Diane Hahnel, a health-screening nurse who enjoys cooking and entertaining so much she carried her cookbooks with her (instead of shipping them) when she moved across the country. "In most cases it's the woman who cares enough to take the time to get out the good china and special serving plates."

### QUICK START

Regard the time you spend on little things that give you pleasure as time to be good to yourself. Consider caring for and using accoutrements you've worked for as time off for savoring the moment or moments.

## WOMEN AND MEN EXPERIENCE DIFFERENT LIFE CYCLES

Women's approach to managing time relates to the cycle in which we're living and, because we have more cycles than men, we come to time management in a different way. As Warren Leight wrote in *Mademoiselle*: "Why Can't a Man Tell Time Like a Woman?" men can consistently lurch forward, from moment to moment, because for them speed and motion take the place of ritual and closure.

"Women's bodies experience various biological cycles: 28 days, nine months, and so on" wrote Leight. "They innately know how to juggle careers, relationships, and domestic responsibility while simultaneously keeping an eye on the future and acknowledging the past."5

## QUICK START

Accept the fact that how you arrange your 24 hours will be influenced by such cycles and stages as childbearing, child-rearing, caretaking, working full-time, working part time, or working at home. As you move through each cycle deal with time in the best way you can.

# *T*URN THESE SIX WOMEN'S STRENGTHS INTO TIME-SAVING BENEFITS

As a woman, you bring special strengths to your job that can work to your advantage—though some can be disadvantages if you let them get out of hand. (For example, your people accessibility can make you lose time if you let it.) The important thing is to control the strengths and use them as positive time-gaining techniques.

Here are six of your primary strengths.

**(1)** *You're people-oriented.* You have a sensitivity to connecting with other persons and being accessible for responding to their needs. In a survey that examined the sensitivity of women executives vs. male executives to the environment and employee relations, most of the women surveyed believed employee relations would improve under their management, and more than one-third of the men agreed that women would do a better job in employee relations and the environment. The survey, conducted by Brouillard Communications, included 416 men and 90 women executives selected from the largest United States firms.6

**(2)** *You take time to listen.* Your intuition and understanding for people's feelings and your capacity for nurturing relationships can pay off in ultimately solving problems and making decisions. "Men may move through their work with emphasis on the immediate solution of a problem and save hours as a result," says time management consultant Donna Goldfein, author of *Every Woman's Guide to Time Management.* "However, the methods women often use in listening to and acting on people's suggestions can result in higher morale and a more efficient work force. Thus, in the long-run, overall time-saving is often directly related to the assets women bring to the workplace in their ability to listen and draw a consensus."

(**3**) *You're able to talk out problems.* Women generally are more comfortable in opening up to others and expressing and sharing their own feelings. Men, as a whole, tend not to share as many close revelations. This two-way communication and interaction is a plus in keeping human contacts smooth and pleasant and avoiding lost time because of misunderstandings, arguments, and unresolved complaints.

(**4**) *You have a natural bent for planning.* As a child you were subjected to your mother's plans. Later you probably adhered to a female teacher's plans. But women are creative and resourceful in getting things done, so once on your own you made your own plans, both in and out of the workplace. If you married you made plans for your husband (or at least *tried* to make them), and if you expanded to a household you took on the task of planning home and family needs, entertaining, vacations, and volunteer activities. All of this natural ability to plan is beneficial in the workplace.

(**5**) *You can handle more than one person and/or situation at a time.* Most women have daily practice in handling multiple demands simultaneously. As Sunny Schlenger says, "You can't compartmentalize your lives into separate isolated categories and take care of one category at a time in the same way a man can. You have to be able to work on several tasks at once in order to survive."

(**6**) *You're flexible.* You don't always have the same kind of flexibility as a man to work overtime and long hours or pursue the same pattern of lifelong uninterrupted employment, but you are often better able than men to adjust to changing situations so you have a capacity to be flexible in many day-to-day matters. Naturally you don't welcome interruptions and unexpected changes any more than your male peers do. But, still, you're geared to going with the flow while men have greater problems switching from their focus.

## SELF-TEST:
### *Determine Your Attitude Toward Time*

Check the "Always," "Sometimes," and "Never" responses that follow as they apply to you.

|   |   | Always | Sometimes | Never |
|---|---|--------|-----------|-------|
| 1. | Do you feel you have more roles to fill and more to do in a day than most of the men you know? | ____ | ____ | ____ |
| 2. | Are you the primary caregiver— child care, elder care, whatever? | ____ | ____ | ____ |
| 3. | Do you juggle caregiving around your schedule rather than your partner's schedule? | ____ | ____ | ____ |
| 4. | Do you spend more time on personal business and squeeze in home responsibilities at lunch or during coffee breaks to a greater extent than men? | ____ | ____ | ____ |
| 5. | Are you so detail-oriented you procrastinate and delay starting a job till you get all the details in order? | ____ | ____ | ____ |
| 6. | Does your husband or partner depend on you to make all plans for home, family, and social life? | ____ | ____ | ____ |
| 7. | Do you believe the male in your life considers it "your job" to remind him of (or *ask* him to do) anything beyond his usual routine? | ____ | ____ | ____ |
| 8. | Do you think nurturing is your province? | ____ | ____ | ____ |
| 9. | Do you delegate tasks as much as men do? | ____ | ____ | ____ |
| 10. | Do you care more than most men about "little things" you wouldn't *have* to do but like and want to do? | ____ | ____ | ____ |

|  | **Always** | **Sometimes** | **Never** |
|---|---|---|---|
| 11. Do you ask yourself "How perfectly does this job have to be done?" when you're over-whelmed? | ____ | ____ | ____ |
| 12. Do you think of time as gender-based? | ____ | ____ | ____ |
| **TOTAL NUMBER** | ____ | ____ | ____ |

**Scoring:** Add up your "Always," "Sometimes," and "Never" answers. If you checked primarily "Always," you share the attitude—*and* experience—of many working women. If you checked mostly "Sometimes" and occasional "Nevers," you're ahead in the time game. Wherever you stand, you'll gain more time by being aware of these attitudes and the time drain they can create.

*Quick Check/Recheck* You're now ready, once and for all, to acknowledge the differences in men and women's time management and stop trying to manage your time like a man. You've seen how to benefit from making your women's strengths work for you. Along with putting them to good use in your job, apply them to the other aspects of your life that you value as a woman. Don't waste time on unnecessary details and don't waste energy on too much perfection-anxiety. Give up the feeling you should (or can) do everything yourself and rotate or alternate tasks with others.

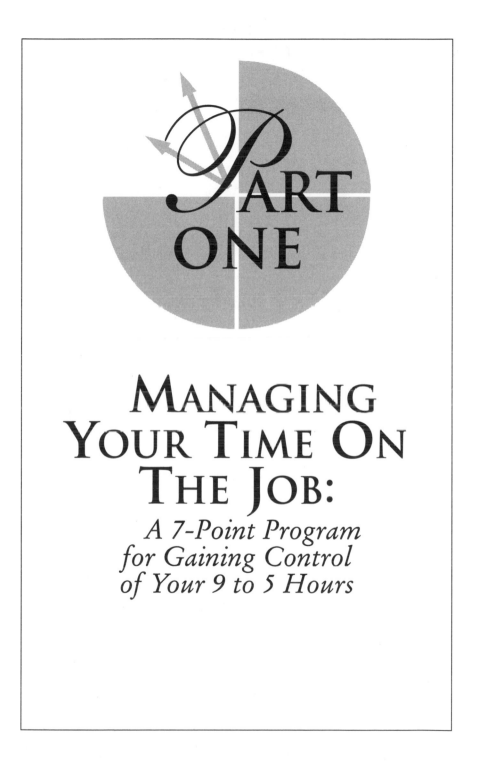

# PART ONE

# MANAGING YOUR TIME ON THE JOB:

*A 7-Point Program for Gaining Control of Your 9 to 5 Hours*

# Recognize and Conquer Women's Nine Greatest Time Problems

*I feel I can't run any faster, but I don't dare slow down.*
**—An office manager**

What are your greatest time problems during your 9:00 A.M. to 5:00 P.M. day?

When I give out index cards to workshop audiences and ask them to write what concerns them most about time management, card after card contains some version of "I never feel caught up."

I could easily write "Never feeling caught up" on my own index cards. But whenever I mention this problem to a male friend who experiences it too, his response is invariably, "Join the club!" And then, while I hurry faster to do some catch-up work, he shoves his stress aside and leaves for a game of golf.

Most working women identify in a woman's way to "Never feeling caught up" and many also cite the other problems that follow in the Self-Test. As you take this quiz, circle beside each of the statements, a 0 if you don't have the problem, or a 1, 2, or 3 to rate how much the problems you have affect your time on the job. The higher the number the more that problem relates to your working life.

3

Here, in their own words, is what working women say.

### SELF-TEST:
### *What Time Problems Do You Have on the Job?*

| | | | | |
|---|---|---|---|---|
| "I live with the haunting feeling I should be doing more." | 0 | 1 | 2 | 3 |
| "I take on too many jobs." | 0 | 1 | 2 | 3 |
| "I always feel under the gun." | 0 | 1 | 2 | 3 |
| "My whole life is full of loose ends." | 0 | 1 | 2 | 3 |
| "I'm forever running late." | 0 | 1 | 2 | 3 |
| "I'm drowning in paperwork." | 0 | 1 | 2 | 3 |
| "I'm pulled in too many directions at once." | 0 | 1 | 2 | 3 |
| "I get caught short by the unexpected." | 0 | 1 | 2 | 3 |
| "I'm never on time with deadlines." | 0 | 1 | 2 | 3 |
| "I never feel caught up." | 0 | 1 | 2 | 3 |

**TOTALS** __  __  __  __

**Scoring:** Mostly "0s" puts you at the head of the class in being in control of your time. Mostly "1s" indicates you're on the right track but can still improve. A majority of "2s" shows you're somewhere in the middle of being fairly in control and way out of control. Primarily "3s" tells you clearly you're *not* in control of your time.

You'll find the solutions to the problems you've circled in the subsequent sections in this book. But first we'll examine more day-to-day problems that plague working women.

# HANDLING THE "BIG NINE" TIME PROBLEMS

The following Big Nine time management problems are the ones I hear not only from working women but also from time management consultants, career counselors, psychologists, psychotherapists, and other professionals. In this section, you'll receive Quick Start and Time Booster tips for immediate help with these problems. Then in upcoming points, you'll get more Big Nine solutions. Here are the "Big Nine" problems.

## (1) No Matter How Hard You Try You Can't Get Everything Done

In this variation of "Never feeling caught up," Suzanne Frisse, a seminar leader and trainer who has seen close to 40,000 people (85% women, compared to 15% men), finds that whenever she asks "What challenges do you face at work?" the most common response is "Not enough time to get everything done." Moreover, a study by *USA Today* also found that time pressures affect women more directly than men. In the study, 27% of women vs. 17% of men described their lives as "on the run from the time I get up until the time I go to bed."[1]

In another spin on the problem, Diane Wolverton, editor of "Home Office Opportunities," talks about how, in her earlier life, she would feel so guilty if she wasn't working on some project that she put off doing things she liked to do because she thought she'd better get her "should's" done first.

But reflecting on what she'd learned from looking back, she says, "As long as I believed I did not have enough time, I didn't. When I'd wake up saying 'I've got too much to do today, I'll never get it all done,' I didn't get it done. Now my affirmation is 'There's always enough time for the things that are important to me.' And the magic part is that when I believe I have time, I get more done."[2]

### QUICK STARTS

Ask yourself what you can immediately weed out of your agenda to gain time. Naturally, you can't eliminate all the mundane, unrewarding office chores. But generally there's *something* that can go to give you more time to accomplish the really essential things.

Develop a positive outlook for doing the best you can with your daily allotment of time because the reality is there will *never* be enough time to get *everything* done!

## (2) You're Never Able to Complete One Job Before You're Interrupted by Another

"Interruptions are *my* main problem" says Paula Baum, an assistant buyer for a large department store. "In fact, my days have so many of them that I can't complete a task in an orderly fashion before I have to leave that job to take care of something else."

Since women, by nature, are accessible, we're easy prey for interruptions when people at work need something from us that they want "yesterday." Realistically, we can't ever hope for long stretches without interruptions, particularly if our supervisor/boss is the one who interrupts or if—on top of our job demands—we're also the person on call for family necessities.

But *many* interruptions simply aren't necessary. When you allow them to occur, your time gets lost in external circumstances and your desk becomes a depot for half-started, incomplete jobs.

Hyrum W. Smith, whose Franklin Time Management System trains 4,000 to 6,000 people each week, told me about a secretary who started one Monday by outlining 15 things she wanted to accomplish that day. At 9:30 A.M. her boss interrupted with "I have something urgent to be done right now."

Normally the secretary would have dropped what she was working on and pushed that and her other 14 jobs aside, but this time she tried a different approach.

"Wait a minute," she said to her boss. "This is what I had planned to do today. Since all of these tasks are for you, please help me set priorities."

The boss was completely dumbfounded by all the tasks she had to do. In fact, he saw several items he admitted were more important than his "urgent" job.

"When can you get to this other job?" he asked.

And when the secretary said "Thursday" he said "Okay" and returned to his office.

## TIME     BOOSTERS

- Avoid nonurgent phone calls—both work-related calls and unnecessary personal ones. If a spouse, child, parent, or friend calls for no specific reason, be firm about when you're available to receive calls and ask them to call you only at that time.

- When coworkers interrupt you for something they want—and your day is full of tasks you need to do—ask "Can it wait?"

## (3) You Take Too Long to Make Decisions

Sometimes women, more than men, hold back from making decisions and waste time waffling back and forth about what action to take. This lack of confidence may have its roots in our not-too-distant history when many women were job-cast in supportive roles.

But each day you're faced with countless decisions on what you ought to do next. And if you're too indecisive you end up as the loser when your time management and productivity are tallied.

### SELF-TEST:
### *Check Your Decision-Making Skills*

The following quiz will show you what you need to do to save time through faster and better decisions. Circle "Y" (Yes) or "N" (No) to the questions as they apply to you.

1. Do you decide quickly on low-level choices—such as what color file folders to use for certain projects?     **Y     N**

2. Do you clarify the reasons for and define the issues involved in high-level decisions?     **Y     N**

### SELF-TEST:
#### *Check Your Decision-Making Skills*
#### *(continued)*

3.  Do you look at the resources you have for making
    those decisions?                                                  Y     N

4.  Do you obtain additional facts (if necessary) before
    making high-level decisions?                                      Y     N

5.  Are you realistic about how much you can do with
    the time, resources, and facts you have?                          Y     N

6.  Do you identify the possible decisions—or
    alternatives—you could make?                                      Y     N

7.  Do you evaluate what you would gain or lose by
    each decision or alternative?                                     Y     N

8.  Do you set deadlines for making major decisions?                  Y     N

9.  Do you have confidence in your abilities to meet a
    deadline or make a decision?                                      Y     N

10. Do you act on a decision once it is made?                         Y     N

                                                    **TOTALS**    __    __

**Scoring:** If the number of questions to which you answered "Yes" is:

9–10:       You have a good handle on the way you make decisions.

7–8:        You're doing fairly well—but you could do better.

5–6:        You take too long to make large or small decisions.

4 or fewer  Get to work and start turning each "No" into a time-gaining
            "Yes."

## Q U I C K   S T A R T S

 Be willing to take some risks. Not every decision will be flawless;
but even when you make mistakes, the learning experience of a
wrong decision will help you upgrade your decision-making skills
in the future.

 Be aware of—and prepared for—the small or large risks most decisions involve.

## (4) You Have Too Many Added Duties Because of Company Cutbacks

As companies downsize and eliminate jobs people who remain are frequently asked to take on tasks from eliminated jobs. Often it's a woman who's expected to pick up the slack not only because of our reputations for being willing to take on added responsibilities, but also because of our demonstrated ability to juggle many tasks.

"When your responsibilities triple," says Joanne Frangides, an advertising-space saleswoman, "it's hard to concentrate on building up and maintaining the work to which you're already committed as effectively as you'd like to. We do what we can as well as we can, but we end up with the added problem of dealing with the frustration of not being able to balance it all."

### QUICK STARTS

 Make employers aware of your current commitments and how much work you're already doing when they begin distributing the duties of eliminated jobs.

 Say "I feel I should mention I'm really bogged down with other urgent jobs right now. Maybe someone who's not doing quite so much would be better able to handle these extra duties."

## (5) You Procrastinate

There are many reasons for procrastination. Two main ones that apply to women are (1) our penchant for perfection, and (2) our belief that we need more information before we dig into a job.

This "I-need-more-information" thinking sometimes gets in my way as it did when a colleague and I were asked to give a series of Saturday seminars on "Fiction vs. Nonfiction Writing." Neither he nor I had been a fiction writer for the past few years. However, he immediately went into action preparing his talk with material he had.

I, on the other hand, delayed getting started with "I need new information." I could have "winged it" as readily as he did, but because of my procrastination I put off preparing my talks to the zero hour. In the end, I used no new information in my seminars.

"I have a little reminder on my computer which says, 'Procrastination prevents results,'" reveals Barbara Hemphill, an organizer and time management expert, author of *Taming the Paper Tiger* and past president of the National Association of Professional Organizers.

"Every time I'm tempted to slip something aside and say 'I'll do it later' I stop and say 'What am I going to know tomorrow that I don't know today?' Then if I wait till tomorrow, it's procrastination."

## QUICK STARTS

 Get a task started and get it out! Don't put off jobs that must be done till you're suddenly overwhelmed by crisis time management.

Put a "Do it Now" (or something similar) sign on your desk or computer—and take the message seriously.

## (6) You're Asked to Attend Too Many Meetings

"Long meetings with rambling discussions are *my* time bugaboo," reports a marketing director. "Yet there's hardly a day that someone doesn't buttonhole me and ask me to come to a meeting he or she is planning."

Meetings are *everyone's problem*—and sometimes the people who plan them want you to attend because they expect, as a woman, you'll be more sensitive to their issues than some of the men in the group. But you have to be tough about meetings (whenever you possibly can) if you want to avoid fracturing your time. Make a copy of the following Time Boosters to clip to your calendar.

## TIME BOOSTERS

When you're asked to attend meetings . . .

- First, determine if it's truly necessary for you to attend.
- If you must attend, be prepared with your contribution.
- Avoid arriving ahead of the scheduled time.
- Stay only for as long as you're really needed.

When you're asked to plan meetings . . .

- Decide whether it's really essential to have the meeting at all.
- Stick to three or four important points during the meeting.
- Steer clear of getting sidetracked.
- Begin and end on time.

## (7) You Have Trouble Saying "No"

Although there are many times in your life when you need to say "Yes" (more about this later) a feeling of false obligation—and a fear of displeasing others—can make many women answer "Yes" when they really should say "No." "No" could save them enormous chunks of time and make their life easier.

"Men, as a rule, were trained early on to say 'No,' thus freeing up their time for leisure or more challenging opportunities," says Dr. Mary Frame, a consultant on leadership and time management and dean of South Carolina's Columbia College Leadership Center for Women.

"But women I've run into in my work have a compulsion to say 'okay' to every task that comes along because they (1) don't want to miss out on being seen as a team player, (2) don't want anyone to get mad at them, (3) don't have a clue on how to say 'No,' and (4) don't want to appear incompetent.

"Because of what they think they *ought* to do instead of thinking 'What's the best use of my time at the moment?' they get on merry-go-rounds."

## TIME   BOOSTERS

Alec Mackenzie, internationally known time management expert, recommends this basic plan for saying "No" when you *should* say "No."

- Listen—to show interest and understanding of the request.
- Say "No" immediately to avoid building up false hopes.
- Give reasons so your refusal will be understood.
- Offer alternatives (if possible) to show good faith.

### (8) You Let the Telephone Become a Time Trap

As a woman, you try to show your concern for other people's needs. But if you spend too long on the phone talking about situations that have nothing to do with your job, you allow Mr. Bell's invention to be the time robber it can be. You shortchange yourself on the time you can spend on more productive work.

"I find I'm vulnerable to that," admits Dixie Darr, publisher of a newsletter, *The Accidental Entrepreneur.* "All too often I receive calls from persons who like to recite all their problems—most of which don't concern my work. This can really become a problem."

### QUICK   STARTS

Set the stage for brief calls by saying immediately, "I've only got three minutes," "You just caught me—I'm on my way out," or "I'm sorry I can't talk right now—I'm in the middle of something."

If you have an assistant, have your incoming calls screened. Let your assistant know which calls to put through—say a child is suddenly sick. Provide a list of people to put through at all times plus a list of persons who never should be put through. Whenever possible, have the assistant return calls for you with the requested information and answers.

 If you have no assistant to screen calls, use an answering machine or voice mail. When you do get on the phone, offer to call back—or time the call and stick to its purpose.

 Keep an egg timer or minute timer by your phone to remind you to be brief. Sometimes when callers hear a timer go off they think you have another call and hurry up and finish their call.

 Terminate as quickly as possible nonurgent work-related calls and unnecessary calls from children, spouse, parents, and others. Some beneficial phrases to use are "I have to go now," "I can't talk much longer," and "I have someone in my office."

## (9) You Get Diverted from Your Main Tasks

Another major problem for women is getting diverted from essential tasks by less important distractions. Men are often totally engrossed in one pursuit at a time, while women are accustomed, by necessity, to getting involved in first one thing, and then going on to another. Though this usually is a "women's-way" strength, it can become a time-stealing negative when you're distracted by too many small things first, rather than starting your main tasks.

For example, a purchasing agent with a piled-high desk plans to spend an afternoon sorting out the paperwork and setting priorities. But while she's out of the office for lunch a colleague drops off a purchasing magazine and several books on related topics. As soon as the purchasing agent returns, she gets engrossed in looking at this reading material for the next half hour. She would maintain a much better grip on her time management by jumping right into her main task after lunch and leaving the reading for some other time, maybe later on at home.

Even the *best* time managers have moments of getting diverted by less important tasks. However, as a bottom-line principle, unless you eliminate trivia and the small things first distraction, you lose too much time for the important work that provides better benefits.

## TIME   BOOSTER

- Make copies of the following test. As you fill it in and see your distractions, your greater awareness of them will help you cut down on these time-wasting diversions.

### THE TRIVIA-AND-SMALL-THINGS TIME-WASTER TEST

1.  Describe three occasions in which you—in retrospect—let yourself get distracted by doing "small things first." Note when a distraction happened and how it held you back from having a productive working day. In what kind of situation did each occur? Use extra paper or the back of each sheet if you need it.

    **Distraction 1:** _____

    _____

    _____

    _____

    **Distraction 2:** _____

    _____

    _____

    _____

    **Distraction 3:** _____

    _____

    _____

    _____

2. Assess the underlying reasons for the distractions you listed.

   **Distraction 1:** _____

   _____

   _____

   _____

   **Distraction 2:** _____

   _____

   _____

   _____

   **Distraction 3:** _____

   _____

   _____

   _____

3. Write possible ways of how you might cut down on each diversion you listed.

   **Distraction 1:** _____

   _____

   _____

   _____

   **Distraction 2:** _____

   _____

   _____

   _____

   **Distraction 3:** _____

   _____

   _____

   _____

***Quick Check/Recheck*** By being aware of the Big Nine time management problems working women encounter, you can minimize the nagging sensation of "never feeling caught up." One of the main solutions for reducing this problem is to determine each day what nonessentials you can weed out of your agenda. Realistically, there's no way to eliminate all mundane, unrewarding work chores—but there's generally something that can go to give you more time to accomplish the essentials that really matter. Above all, develop a positive outlook for doing your best with the time you have because you'll never get everything done at one time. As a wise working woman once said to me, "When everything is done, your life is done." *That's* no alternative!

# Jump-Start Your Day by Using Six Tested Time Tools

*I came in and had coffee and people stopped by—
and suddenly the whole day got blown.*

**—A graphic artist**

The best way to get a good start—and work your way through the whole day—is to overcome the Slow-Start Syndrome and its power to steal your time. When you succumb to a slow-motion start, your work day becomes a time management problem in every sense of the word.

You'll find solutions to the slow-start problem later in this section. But first evaluate if you're falling victim to this syndrome and why. Take the following Quiz and mark "Yes" or "No" to each question.

18                                                    POINT TWO

## SELF-TEST:
### *Are You Plagued by the Slow-Start Syndrome?*

|  | Yes | No |
|---|---|---|
| 1. Do you spend too much time in the restroom fixing your hair and make-up when you first arrive at your job? | ___ | ___ |
| 2. Do you feel like you need to take a breather before you get down to work? | ___ | ___ |
| 3. Do you let external factors—personal phone calls or drop-in visitors—steal your time and delay you from starting to work? | ___ | ___ |
| 4. Do you get hung up on reading and replying to E-mail messages that could wait? | ___ | ___ |
| 5. Do you waste time deciding what to do first? | ___ | ___ |
| 6. Do you fall into the trap of wanting to get little tasks out of the way before you begin "real" work? | ___ | ___ |
| 7. Do you fear you won't do a perfect job on what you need to do that day? | ___ | ___ |
| 8. Do you spend too much time stewing about a task and trying to figure out how to do it? | ___ | ___ |
| **TOTALS** | ___ | ___ |

**Scoring:** Count the check marks in the "Yes" and "No" columns. If the "Yes" answers outweigh the "No's," you're a victim of the Slow-Start Syndrome. If the two columns are equal you're a partial victim. If you mark mostly "No" you're on your way to a good A.M. start. Whatever your score is, however, keep on top of these start-up Quick Starts.

## Q U I C K   S T A R T S

 Allow time for personal grooming before you leave home. This puts you in a better mental state when you get to work.

 Catch your breath if you must upon arrival, but for no more than 10 minutes. Then get going! Any more than a 10-minute-breather will be counterproductive.

Cut phone distractions short by telling nonurgent callers "I have to get started on a project right now. I'll call you later?"

 Control in-person interruptions by standing up from your desk and moving to your files. Or say "I'm going to the copy machine. We'll have to walk and talk." You'll create a "busyness" atmosphere and prevent a sit-down "kaffee-klatsch."

 Look past the small insistent demands that tempt you and force yourself to move on to the larger, more important tasks.

 Accept the fact that many assignments don't *have* to be perfect. Getting to them—and producing acceptable results—is often more important in business than perfection.

 Ask for help when you don't know how to do something by finding someone you can trust who will willingly give you answers that enable you to proceed.

You can also jump-start your day with these six tested time tools.

## $\mathscr{T}$URN YOUR COMMUTE INTO PRODUCTIVE TIME

If you travel to a job away from your home use your between-home-and-work time resourcefully. For example:

**(1)** *If you commute by public transportation:* Make good use of your carry-along notepad by thinking through and roughing out your plans for the day. Write quick notes and memos. Catch up on your reading. Carry a laptop computer to get a head start on your work.

**(2)** *If you walk:* Combine exercise with contemplation. In an article in *New Woman* Kelly Good McGee quotes Karen Walden, an editor who walks to work, as saying, "I really think a lot about the problems of the day, the issues I have to deal with, what I want to say to people, what I want to accomplish, and I'm able to organize my thoughts without anyone interrupting me. So it's one pure hour of focused time and it takes care of transportation!"[1]

**(3)** *If you drive or carpool:* When you travel solo you can also use the time to get your thoughts together without anyone interrupting you. Listen to informative or motivational tapes and keep your carry-along bag accessible to use if you're stuck in traffic. If you carpool with compatible people suggest turning the ride-time into a networking session for bouncing off ideas and exchanging information. Or use the days you don't drive for catching up on reading and paperwork.

## ℊET TO WORK ON TIME

"Be on *time* for work," stresses management consultant Carol Painter Campi. "Better yet, get there ahead of time. That quiet time before phones ring and people come to your office can pay big dividends. Too many people arrive five, ten, or fifteen minutes late. Even though that's not a lot of time, it can set your whole day back. You find yourself playing 'catch up' for the rest of the day."

### Three Benefits of Getting to Work on Time

1. You increase your productivity for the day.
2. You keep up with your workload with less effort.
3. You're better prepared for crises because you aren't playing the "catch up" game simultaneously.

Marcia Yudkin, a creativity consultant, tells the story of a woman who could *never* get to work on time. Her problem? She buried herself in a book before she left home for work. Since reading was her passion, this was a way of nurturing herself with a simple pleasure for starting her day.

But the unpleasant aspect of her pleasurable start was the fact she was always late for work. While she had her nose in a book, she lost track of time and bus schedules.

She got back on track by leaving her home on an early bus, and then taking her book to a small cafe across the street from her office. When 9:00 A.M. came she closed her book, crossed the street to her office, and presto, she was at work on time!

If you have a problem arriving at work on time—no matter what the reason may be—try these solutions.

### Q U I C K    S T A R T S

 Set your alarm clock for the exact time you want to awaken and get up as soon as it rings.

Expect to have a good day at work. Have a positive mental attitude and think of things to look forward to—like finally finishing that special report and getting it off your desk.

 Eliminate anticipatory anxieties—the traffic tie-up you may encounter, the unpleasant phone call you may have to handle.

If you're in a position to take arbitrary time before work for something that brings you pleasure—like the nurturing we talked about in the Introduction or reading, crossword puzzles or whatever—allocate a limited time for it and strictly adhere to that schedule.

## $\mathcal{U}$SE A PERSONAL/WORK CALENDAR

Carrying a calendar with you is insurance against the problem one sales representative experienced when she made a commitment for "next Tuesday," another for the "first Tuesday in the month," and still another for "Tuesday the third" when all three were on the same day!

Along with avoiding this woman's fate, you benefit in other ways when you have a personal/work calendar to keep you on target and time. For example, (1) you make your life less stressful by eliminating the worry that you'll forget a commitment, and (2) you have a basic starting point for preparing the To-Do Lists and Planning Sheets we'll talk about later in this section.

Some women use one calendar for everything they need to do. Others use one calendar for work and a second for home. Still others use even more.

"I live by three calendars," says Barbara Brabec. "The first is for work dates and deadlines to remind me of what I'm to do each day. The second is for paying bills. On this one I mark the due date for payment as soon as each bill comes in and pay a few every week. This is a helpful time management tool since it avoids large bill-paying tasks at the end of the month. My third calendar is for personal appointments. And no, I don't get fouled up by having three calendars. It makes life less stressful for me."

On the other hand, Lisa Brandon, a full-time temporary worker, uses just one calendar—and she says the bigger the space for each day the better. Sheree Bykofsky, author of *500 Terrific Ideas for Organizing Everything* also uses a single calendar. Her portable daily calendar is *her* key to time management, she reports. She puts *everything* on it, including making time for preparations, follow-ups, and phone calls.

There's no set rule as to how many calendars to use, but a carry-along-for-everything, plus a back-up one for home works for many women. When the carry-along is with you wherever you happen to be your appointments are always in front of you—and with phone numbers next to people's names you can make calls from any place to replan, reschedule, or cancel appointments.

## QUICK STARTS

 Choose the number of calendars and a format (a page for each day or a week-at-a-glance divided into days) that fit your needs best.

 Write your commitments on your calendar as soon as you make them.

 Look at your calendar the first thing each day.

 Select from your calendar what needs to go on your To-Do List and Daily Planning Sheet.

# *G*ET ON TRACK WITH TO-DO LISTS

Along with calendars, a To-Do list or your own substitute, is a valuable tool to help you gain control of your time each day. This tool provides a quick look at what you need (or would like) to accomplish and lists everything from cashing a check to changing the tape on your answering machine.

## Four Ways a To-Do List Helps Solve Time Problems

- It minimizes cluttering your mind with odds and ends of things to do and people to see.

- It makes the trivia you need to take care of visible.

- It improves your ability to remember more because of the mental activity of writing everything down.

- It gives you a quick and clear focus on what to do immediately, what to do if possible, and what to do only if time permits.

Although these are first-rate benefits, women differ in their views of to-do lists. Some wouldn't be caught without one. Others say they've tried them and aren't convinced they work. Speaking personally, I always say "Take my pearls. Take my chocolate. Take my Mozart tapes. But don't *ever* take my lists!"

Suzanne Frisse shares this view and points out to women in her seminars that whenever she feels lazy about organizing a list she reminds herself that starting to work without one is like driving from Kansas City, where she lives, to Yellowstone Park without a roadmap. She would probably get there eventually, but she'll waste a lot of time and gasoline making the effort. "Working without a list leaves me without a clear direction to my day," she advises. "I end the day exhausted, scratching my head and saying 'I *know* I was busy, but I seem to have nothing to show for all that activity!'"

Other working women agree that making lists—or substitutes for lists—gets them started in the morning and gives them more to show for their day.

## What Successful Women Say About Lists

Here are seven ideas you may find helpful.

(1) "I keep a personal to-do book in my briefcase that includes not only all my daily work-related tasks and commitments but also all my personal commitments," says Elizabeth Randall. "Losing that to-do book would be like losing control of my life."

(2) "Every day I make a list of what needs to be done," says Pat Peters, a part-time hairdresser. "Then I number everything in the most logical order depending on its importance. I refer to my list throughout the day and cross off each item as it's completed. This gives me great satisfaction."

(3) "I keep my business to-do lists in a small looseleaf book on my desk," says Judith Moncrieff Baldwin. "As I think of tasks, I write one to-do item per page (with brief notes and pertinent information) and rearrange the entries in priority order. When I want to keep a permanent record I note the date and stick the entry on a sheet of paper for filing in the relevant project file. If the to-do is a one-shot thing I erase the entry once the task is completed."

(4) "I definitely need a daily to-do list for working on dresses and outfits and for bridal parties having 5 to 8 attendants," says Marie Dolce, a dress-designer/seamstress. "However, as I design and sew I set up 15- and 30-minute projects instead of blocking out 4 hours at a time at the start of the day for one major job. This brings variety to the day."

(5) "One of my favorite props to keep me on track is a clear, legal-sized Lucite clipboard that stands up on a base," says Ann McGee Cooper, business consultant, creativity expert, and author of *Time Management for Unmanageable People*. "I put my Post-it notes of to-dos on that stand and move it with me all day."[2]

(6) "I use 3 by 5 cards with one task written on each card," says Pam Kriston, time management and organizational consultant. "When I have phone calls to make I add phone numbers to my 3 by 5's. Then I carry all the cards around in a 9 × 12 folder that I always have with me."

**(7)** "For me, the solution is to look at to-do lists as opportunities-and-possibilities lists," sums up Marcia Yudkin, "and I advise that, whenever possible, you follow your natural motivational energy to do the tasks that appeal to your first."[3]

## How to Arrange Your To-Do List

Do a quick think-through of your work tasks for the day. Then divide your list into Morning, Lunch Break, and Afternoon. This gives you specific time frames in which to work through tasks. But leave spaces for switching the to-dos around since there will be times when it's imperative to change the sequence of the tasks. If you wish you can also color-code the Morning, Lunch, and Afternoon segments with the bright-colored stick-on dots available at stationery stores. This will help you check the segments at a glance.

### SAMPLE TO-DO-LIST FORMATS

Here are two guideline formats: (1) a filled-in sample list prepared by a nursing home administrator, and (2) a blank format for you to copy.

### SAMPLE TO-DO LIST

### To Do Today

#### *Morning*

1.  Staff Meeting

2.  Discuss personnel problems with Andy after meeting

3.  Finish writing monthly report

4.  Start putting figures together for next year's budget

#### *Lunch Break*

1.  Eat at desk and do paperwork

2.  Go for walk

3.  Make bank deposit while walking

*Afternoon*

1. Go through "In" basket, other mail and memos

2. Give assistant mail she can answer on her own

3. Check out kitchen and kitchen staff to be sure everything is in order for visit from state tomorrow

4. Return phone calls


## YOUR TO-DO LIST

### To Do Today

*Morning*

_____

_____

_____

_____

*Lunch Break*

_____

_____

_____

_____

*Afternoon*

_____

_____

_____

_____

## T I M E     B O O S T E R S

- Accept the reality that you won't always be able to check off all the tasks on your list at the end of the day. Getting part of a large task completed and moving the rest to the next day (or another time slot) is perfectly acceptable. "In the 80s the concept of managing a list was that everything *had* to be completed at the end of the day," says Dr. Mary Frame, "but what I see now is that women are learning how to deal with concepts and issues where they don't always achieve closure. That's a totally different way of looking at productivity and effectiveness."

- Get started by doing one small task or a little bit of a larger task. "This tends to motivate you to continue because it gives you the important feeling that your list is working for you," advises Dr. Joanna Good, a psychologist and therapist.

- Avoid letting list-making substitute for *doing*. As time-gaining as this tool is, taking too much time to prepare a list—without actually starting to work—leads directly to the Slow-Start Syndrome.

## CONTROL YOUR TIME WITH A DAILY PLANNING SHEET

A daily planning sheet is an extension of the calendar and to-do list. In setting it up, you

1. pinpoint your objectives and specific concerns for the day in greater detail,

2. estimate the time each task will take, and

3. set aside blocks of time to work on those tasks.

## Four Benefits of a Daily Planning Sheet

Once you review your calendar and to-do list you'll find it beneficial
to coordinate everything on a daily planning sheet because this tool
will

- give you a sense of control;

- help you assign a value and degree of importance to each task
  by showing in black and white what's urgent, what's important,
  and what looks pressing at the moment but may be insignifi-
  cant upon reflection;

- eliminate indecisiveness by telling you what to do first, what to
  do next, what to do last, and what you may not have to do at all
  if time doesn't permit it;

- encourage you to cut down on unnecessary internal and external interruptions.

Despite these benefits, however, Suzanne Frisse has found that
too many women think preparing a daily planning sheet is one
more time-stealer in their time-pressured lives.

"But 'winging it,' as opposed to noting projects and deadlines
on a plan, is much more apt to cause problems," she warns.

There are several ways to plan your day, depending on your
temperament and needs. Here are three options. Use the one that's
the right fit for you.

## Check Out Commercial Planners

Commercial planners, organizers, and other ready-to-use products
are now sold almost everywhere. "They're the single most important
development in the field of time management in the last two
decades," points out Alec Mackenzie.

"In the past the normal resources were to-do lists, diaries, and
prioritizing. Even though these are important and have their place,
using each one alone can be a piecemeal approach, and none of
these techniques working in isolation will suffice today. What's
required in today's competitive world is an integrated system that
includes all the techniques."

## Plan Your Day Electronically

Software time management programs with formats that let you view your calendar and daily tasks on your computer screen are available at computer stores. As they automatically list your appointments, prioritize your to-do list, and move information from one list to another, you can print them out and have everything in black and white. Some programs will even beep to remind you of when to do your what-to-do's.

## Create Your Own Planning Sheet

To prepare your own planning sheet and integrate your calendar notations, to-do lists, and priorities, divide your day's plans into three categories as shown in this basic format.

Make a copy of this blank format and fill in the spaces for one of your most time-pressured workdays. The sample filled-in format that follows this blank one will give you further guidelines for preparing your own planning sheet. Add as many lines under each category as you need, and when you don't accomplish a planned task on one day move it to the next.

### A Basic Format for the Three Categories of Your Day

1. **What *Has* to Be Done**                    **Deadlines/Due Dates**

   Projects that require immediate
   attention in the order of their
   importance.

   _____                    _____

   _____                    _____

   _____                    _____


   Essential Meetings                          Time Frame:

   _____                    _____

   _____                    _____

   _____                    _____

Appointments                          Time Frame:

_____                   _____

_____                   _____

_____                   _____


Important phone calls                 Schedule for:

_____                   _____

_____                   _____

_____                   _____


Absolutely necessary paperwork        Plan for:
and routine daily chores

_____                   _____

_____                   _____

_____                   _____


2.  **What *Should* Be Done**             **Upcoming Deadlines/Due**
                                          **Dates**

Down-the-road projects that
need to be done as soon as
possible

_____                   _____

_____                   _____

_____                   _____

Communications to fax or handle          Schedule for:
in letters or memos

_____          _____

_____          _____

_____          _____

**3.  What *Could* Be Done**                **Do "in-the-Middle" or
                                            "Catch-Up" Time**
                                            (15 minutes here and there)

Nondeadline projects

_____          _____

_____          _____

_____          _____

Extra routine daily tasks

_____          _____

_____          _____

_____          _____

Work-related reading material

_____          _____

_____          _____

_____          _____

## SAMPLE DAILY PLANNING SHEET FILLED IN BY A LIBRARY DIRECTOR

**1.**    **What *Has* to Be Done**             **Deadlines/Due Dates**

     a. Prepare automated catalog        Has to be ready tomorrow
        workshop to give at elementary
        school

---

     b. Continue working on proposal      June 1 deadline
        for Community Development
        Grant

---

     c. Get estimate for printing           Need figure for Tuesday
        pamphlets explaining library     night's Board meeting
        services to town residents

---

*Essential Meetings*

     a. Meeting with Board of Trustees'    Time: 10:00 A.M.
        Personnel Committee to go
        over salary recommendations

---

     b. Meeting with Friends of the      Time: 2:30 P.M.
        Library to discuss book sale

---

*Appointments*

     a. Lunch with literacy consultant     Time: 12:00 to 1:00 P.M.
        and other librarians to
        coordinate literacy program

---

     b. Interview applicant for library    Time: 4:00 P.M.
        assistant's job

---

c. Spend an hour at Literacy
International Party before
going home

Time: 5:00 P.M.

### Important phone calls

a. Call mayor about borough's
proposed budget cuts

Schedule 1:30 to 2:00 for all
phone calls

b. Call middle school principal
about class visits to library

Schedule 1:30 to 2:00 for all
phone calls

c. Call electrician about faulty
lighting in Children's Room

Schedule 1:30 to 2:00 for all
phone calls

### Absolutely necessary paperwork and routine daily chores
**Plan for:**

a. Sign checks

As soon as I get in

b. Work on monthly Director's
Report

8:30 before library opens

2. **What *Should* Be Done**

**Upcoming Deadlines/Due
Dates**

a. Statistical Report for Month

Must be done by end of
month

b. Talk to reference librarian
about her book order requests

Need to know by Friday

c. Finalize preschool programs
with children's librarian

A.S.A.P.

*Communications to fax or handle in letters or memos*

                                    *Schedule for:*

a.  Invite mayor and council          Feb. or March meeting
    president to board meeting

---

b.  Write borough attorney about      Must have written response
    legal protocol in Jackson matter  within a week

---

3.  **What *Could* Be Done**          **Do "in-the-Middle" or
                                      "Catch-Up" Time"**
                                      (15 minutes here and there)

*Nondeadline projects*

a.  Work on Service Plan for
    next year to submit to Board

---

b.  Explore possibility of a once-
    a-month participation with
    local TV station to make
    public aware of all we do

---

*Extra routine daily tasks*

a.  Spend half an hour at             Do at 3:00 today
    circulation desk to keep
    an eye on that

---

b.  Go over and approve all checks
    to be sent out for day and see
    that check #'s are put on the
    permanent record

---

c. Read computer printouts

---

| Work-related reading material—Read state's latest report on automation programs | Catch a few minutes for this before literacy party |

---

## TIME   BOOSTERS

- Keep your planning sheets as simple or as detailed as you want to make them. Do what works for you as they're only for your eyes.
- Break large tasks which could overwhelm you into brief daily segments that you can work on in bite-size pieces.
- Take into account your energy levels at different times during the day and arrange your day so you can do demanding tasks during your peak periods and less demanding ones during your below-par periods. For example, you may find it helpful to save routine paperwork for the midafternoon slump that hits many working women.
- Maintain a constant check on how well your plans are progressing so you'll be aware of when you should switch them. A high priority Monday morning's activities at 9:00 may not be what you need to do most on Monday afternoon at 3:00.
- Leave room for the unexpected, so you can cope with inevitable daily crises.
- "Think ahead to what you may need from other people," suggests Carol Painter Campi. "Then check with them before the time you need their input. If you know in advance that the person can't 'deliver' what you'll need, you can make other plans."
- Allow for occasional breaks and breathers. Marcia Yudkin points out that studies on human concentration show it rises and falls in 90-minute cycles. Every hour-and-a-half, take a break for at least 10 minutes so your capacity for work can be restored.[4]

# $\mathscr{S}$ET UP AN EVERYDAY FILE SORTER

Studies show that searching for and handling information is a problem that occupies up to 20% of people's time, so if your day starts with a morning paperwork hunt you lose time before you begin.[5] In fact, time management expert Jeff Davidson points out that if it takes you more than 45 seconds to find something on your desk, you're in trouble.

## QUICK STARTS

Tab each item as you put it in the file sorter.

Stick an index on the front of the sorter.

Put what's no longer active in your everyday file sorter into your regular files at the end of the day.

***Quick Check/Recheck*** The quickest way to start your day in a time-gaining, less stressful way is to subtract the Slow-Start Syndrome from your mornings and add the Six Tested Time Tools. Use your commuting and between-home-and-work time resourcefully for a fast rather than slow start. Get to your desk on time to increase your productivity for the day and to avoid losing time before you begin. A personal/work calendar you carry with you will eliminate the worry that you'll forget a commitment. A to-do list will provide you with a quick fix on what you need or would like to accomplish. A daily planning sheet will expand on your to-do list and help you estimate and set aside the segments of time you'll need to assign to each day's tasks. Finally, an everyday file sorter will set you up to begin your day with the information you'll need for that day in one easily available spot.

# Use Short- and Long-Range Planning to Keep Time from Slipping Away

*I need time for down-the-road plans.*

**—A toy/book shop owner**

As important as planning is to time management, it is often over-shadowed by the day-to-day concerns of the workplace. As Wendy Dixon, the shop owner quoted above, puts it, "The daily demands of running my store take precedence over long-term planning. Because I don't have enough time for all I need and want to do, doing my ads too quickly and buying my media less thoughtfully than I'd like are two work problems I face."

"This is not good," she continues. "I need to make time for the long-term plans that I want for my shop."

Whether you run your own business—or work for an outside employer—the need to make short- and long-range plans is critical for managing your time and competing in today's workplace. According to Felice Schwartz, founder and former president of Catalyst, a New York City research and advisory organization, workplace studies show women cost companies more than men due to pregnancy and family needs.[1] That's why it's important to show we're serious about short- and long-range plans.

In Point 2 we talked about jump-starting and planning your day. Now we'll provide a 7-Step Program for Weekly, Monthly, and Long-Term Planning that will give you real-life examples of proven ways to successfully handle planning on a broader scale.

You're no doubt familiar with the ideas that complement planning—*priorities, schedules, objectives,* and *goals*—and they still ring true. You *can't* manage time without these tools, so the tools—and the words—won't be out of date in the 21st century.

"The principles of time management and the basic advice on time management haven't changed in centuries," agrees Merrill E. Douglass, president of the Time Management Center in Marietta, Georgia and coauthor with Donna N. Douglass of *Time Management for Teams.* "You have only so much time and that's it."

What *has* changed is that people are realizing more than ever today that planning your time, in essence, equals planning your life.

In discussing time management vs. life management, Ralph Keyes, author of *Timelock: How Life Got So Hectic and What You Can Do About It,* wrote in *Parade Magazine:* "Only after determining what we want from life (as opposed to how much we can "get done") can we fundamentally change the way we use time. Think regularly about what you want from your life."[2]

## $\mathcal{H}$OW YOU BENEFIT FROM THE 7-STEP PROGRAM FOR WEEKLY, MONTHLY, AND LONG-TERM PLANNING

To obtain every benefit from the 7-Step Program you need to coordinate all your plans so your daily, weekly, monthly, and long-term planning sheets complement each other. When they are all compatible the six main benefits are:

✓ You *make* the time to plan for the "big picture" of what you want from your time, work, and life.

✓ You focus on the specific targets and goals that will help you achieve what you want.

✓ You break down into do-able portions what you need to accomplish in the weeks, months, and year ahead.

✓ You avoid time-wasting detours from main-road planning to less important side-road temptations.

✓ You match your priorities to your available time.

✓ You maximize your chances for the feeling of achievement meeting priorities brings.

## STEP 1: TRACK YOUR TIME IN A DAY-LOG

A log for every day of the week can be used in conjunction with the daily planning sheet provided in Point 2. Compare the two frequently to see how effectively your daily time management is working. This awareness is essential because *effectiveness* is the bottom linc in today's competitive workplace.

As a helpful warm-up exercise for working on your day-log, take this efficient/effective quiz reprinted by permission from the Priority Management and Atheneum Network.

Now that you have a handle on your effectiveness, get to work on your day-log. By logging *specifically* how much time you spend on each of your day's activities you'll discover where your time is going—or where it isn't going. This will give you a whole new view of how to arrange time effectively.

You'll see tasks that fritter away your time when you could be spending it better," says Barbara Brabec. "My work is so varied that earlier in my working life I had the problem of not really knowing what I did from one day to the next. My solution for seeing *exactly* how I was spending my hours was to take the time to record every hour in a daily log.

"I kept the log till I tallied up 2500 hours. Then when I took a good look at it I could see I was spending 20% of my time creating and maintaining mailing lists and another 20% at the printer, bank, and library. I realized that to reach my major goals I shouldn't be spending my time running around to printers and doing that sort of thing. I saw that to get control of my time I needed to delegate some of these tasks."

# ARE YOU EFFICIENT
# OR EFFECTIVE ?

☐ YES ☐ NO  When the mail arrives, do you look through it immediately to make sure
you aren't missing something that needs action?

☐ YES ☐ NO  When a fax crosses your desk, do you read it right away?

☐ YES ☐ NO  When someone asks for your help with something, do you pride yourself
on being able to respond immediately?

☐ YES ☐ NO  Do you judge how successful your day was by counting how many items
are crossed off your "to do" list without considering their relative importance?

☐ YES ☐ NO  Do you often get to the end of the day and find you haven't made "an
appointment with yourself" —a solid period of uninterrupted time?

☐ YES ☐ NO  Do you try to respond to phone messages immediately, even if it interrupts
something else?

☐ YES ☐ NO  Do you find that some days you don't even look at your "to do" list until
several hours into the work day?

## HOW DO YOU RATE ?

*Give yourself two points for each Yes answer and one point for each No.*

Stop reacting and start managing your priorities! You may put too much emphasis on responding quickly, rather than assessing which tasks are the most important. Don't mistake "urgent" for "important"!

Resist the temptation to react to interruptions, whether it's a fax, mail, phone message or co-worker with a question. If you aren't getting the important tasks done, you won't win any points for responding quickly to less important demands on your time.

Congratulations! You probably know how to identify and manage your priorities. This helps you focus your energies most productively. Remember to prioritize every task, so you can determine which ones should demand your attention first.

Almost every job requires us to react ... to a senior manager,

problems or even a crisis. It's up to you to discern what's "important" versus what's "urgent." By focusing your energy on important tasks, you control how you react in the workplace and enjoy higher productivity and job satisfaction.

Courtesy of The Priority Management and Atheneum Network *Choices,*
Issue 3, 1993[3]

## How to Prepare Your Day-Log

Copy the following blank format. Then fill it out each day for a week. Fill what you do for every half-hour of your day. List everything— including wasted time, goofing off, long or unnecessary phone calls, work duplication, whatever. The filled-out sample log that follows the blank one is a good example of how to prepare your day-log.

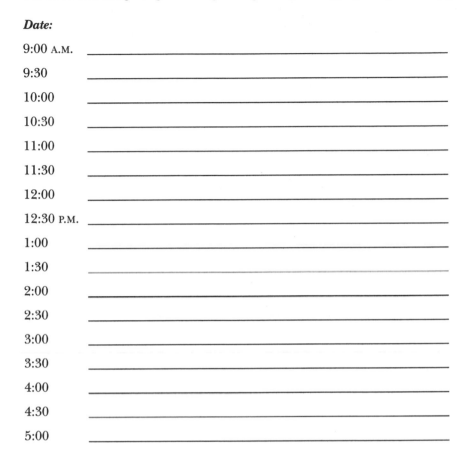

**Date:**

9:00 A.M. _____

9:30 _____

10:00 _____

10:30 _____

11:00 _____

11:30 _____

12:00 _____

12:30 P.M. _____

1:00 _____

1:30 _____

2:00 _____

2:30 _____

3:00 _____

3:30 _____

4:00 _____

4:30 _____

5:00 _____

## EXAMPLE OF DAY-LOG PREPARED BY AN ACTUARIAL ADMINISTRATOR

*Monday, February 9*

9:00 A.M.  Arrived at office, had coffee and got involved in discussing last night's TV special with Eileen and Jake

9:20  Organized my work station and put the file of forms and reports Joe left on my desk in a "Pending" file to look at and review A.S.A.P.

9:40  Called home to make sure I turned off my curling iron

| | |
|---|---|
| 9:50 | Did some of the filing piled on my desk |
| 10:05 | Checked facts for the annual administration of Pfeiffer Brokerage Consultants' plan |
| 10:30 | Worked on J. Morris's termination plan and started preparing forms for it |
| 11:00 | Coffee break and restroom |
| 11:15 | Staff meeting |
| 12:15 P.M. | Out to lunch |
| 1:15 | Continued with and completed forms on Morris termination plan. Sent forms to be typed |
| 1:40 | Phoned bank in response to a request |
| 1:50 | Called Dr. Jessup's office about changes in his plan |
| 2:05 | Began work on Jessup plan changes |
| 2:15 | Val called to chat and suggested going out to dinner tonight |
| 2:35 | Phoned several restaurants to see if they were open Monday nights. Made reservations at one and called Val to tell her we'd meet there |
| 2:55 | Continued work on Jessup plan changes |
| 3:15 | Restroom |
| 3:25 | Talked to Alice and others about shower for Rose |
| 3:45 | Responded to clients' phone calls—one very lengthy |
| 4:15 | Figured out changes in cost of benefits for Storm Associates' plan |
| 4:35 | Steve came by to discuss possible new client. Began researching initial information to present to this potential client |
| 4:55 | Wrapped up work for day by drafting two letters to be typed tomorrow |
| 5:15 | Left office |

Like Barbara, this working woman found several holes in her time that she could use to better advantage to manage her hours on the job.

## Q U I C K   S T A R T S

Look for holes in your time when you examine your log at the end of each day.

Circle in red each hole that could be eliminated to gain time.

Note the latter on an index card and use it to control time wasters.

Do this faithfully for a week.

Use your day-log as a foundation for a weekly plan.

# *S*TEP 2: CREATE A WEEKLY PLAN

You may find that making weekly plans works more effectively for you than daily planning sheets. Try different approaches until you discover what works best in keeping your time from slipping away.

"As a clergy [member], I do much better scheduling my week than I do scheduling my days," says Alexis Talbott, a United Methodist Church minister. "I now understand a warning I received from a wise professor who said 'Your days as a clergy [member] are best described as one interruption after another.'

"How right he was," she adds, "because there's no such thing as a precise daily schedule for me. Among other things my day's work includes critical and emergency phone calls from parishioners, deaths (and getting back to a schedule after a funeral), late night phone calls, unannounced drop-ins, too many home visits in one day, and staying too long at each visit. I also confront the problem of putting the immediate ahead of the important—say, attending to Sunday school matters instead of working on Sunday's sermon.

"Because this is my problem, my solution—and an absolute necessity—is weekly planning. I also record whatever I accomplish during each week. This makes me feel I haven't been simply spinning my wheels—even though I'd like to do more."

## SAMPLE WEEKLY PLANS

The first example is from Alexis Talbott.

*Monday*

| | |
|---|---|
| 10:00–12:00 | Office hours. <br> Return phone calls. <br> Go through mail. <br> Do light filing. |
| Noon | Have lunch meeting or take an hour to relax, run errands, read a chapter in a book or nap briefly. |
| 1:00 to 3:00 <br> or 4:00 | Office hours. <br> Work on sermon/Bible study. <br> If an evening meeting is scheduled from 7:00 P.M. to 9:30 leave office between 4:00 and 5:00. |
| *Tuesday* | Home and hospital visits. |
| *Wednesday* | Same as Monday during the day. <br> 7:00 P.M. evening Bible study group. |
| *Thursday* | Day off. If someone is in the hospital make hospital calls. If a district meeting is planned go to the meeting. |
| *Friday* | Flexible, catch-up day. Do lots of filing. |
| *Weekend* | Church work and church services. |

The second sample applies to a more traditional workweek and schedule. In this one, Monday is filled out as an example of how to plan each day. It's reprinted by permission from Alec Mackenzie's Time Tactics System, with the following directions from Mackenzie:

1. List your most important tasks (your top priorities) for the day under Goals and prioritize according to your own and your organization's objectives.

2. List scheduled appointments, meetings, deadlines, calls, and callbacks under Appointments. Draw arrows to designate time required. For example, the annual physical on Monday is projected to take from 10:00 to 12:00.

3. Under *To Do,* write items to be discussed in scheduled phone calls or visits; agendas for meetings; special directions for getting to an appointment; and other tasks to be done during the day.

"By seeing your week at a glance you can schedule your activities evenly across the week in accordance with the time actually available," advises Mackenzie. "This avoids overloading any given day. When plans aren't completed in your current weekly plan, transfer them to your next week's plan.[4]

## FILL OUT YOUR OWN WEEKLY PLANNING SHEET

This is a small-scale format for working out the second sample. Allow yourself more space when you recreate it. Also, when copying it and filling it out refer to your daily planning sheets and day-logs.

**Week of** _____

| | *Mon.* | *Tues.* | *Wed.* | *Thurs.* | *Fri.* |
|---|---|---|---|---|---|
| **GOALS:** | ____ | ____ | ____ | ____ | ____ |
| | ____ | ____ | ____ | ____ | ____ |
| | ____ | ____ | ____ | ____ | ____ |
| 9:00 A.M. | ____ | ____ | ____ | ____ | ____ |
| 9:30 | ____ | ____ | ____ | ____ | ____ |
| 10:00 | ____ | ____ | ____ | ____ | ____ |
| 10:30 | ____ | ____ | ____ | ____ | ____ |
| 11:00 | ____ | ____ | ____ | ____ | ____ |
| 11:30 | ____ | ____ | ____ | ____ | ____ |
| 12:00 | ____ | ____ | ____ | ____ | ____ |
| 1:00 P.M. | ____ | ____ | ____ | ____ | ____ |
| 1:30 | ____ | ____ | ____ | ____ | ____ |
| 2:00 | ____ | ____ | ____ | ____ | ____ |
| 2:30 | ____ | ____ | ____ | ____ | ____ |
| 3:00 | ____ | ____ | ____ | ____ | ____ |
| 3:30 | ____ | ____ | ____ | ____ | ____ |
| 4:00 | ____ | ____ | ____ | ____ | ____ |
| 4:30 | ____ | ____ | ____ | ____ | ____ |
| 5:00 | ____ | ____ | ____ | ____ | ____ |

## Example of a Weekly Plan

# January   Week 2

| Monday 6 | Tuesday 7 | Wednesday 8 |
|---|---|---|
| **Goals** | **Goals** | **Goals** |
| 1. *Agenda Staff Meeting* | | |
| 2. *Monthly Marketing Letter* | | |
| 3. *Performance Appraisals* | | |
| **Appointments** | **Appointments** | **Appointments** |
| 8:00 am *Quiet Hour* | 8:00 am | 8:00 am |
| *(Agenda staff mtg.)* ↓ | | |
| 9:00 | 9:00 | 9:00 |
| 10:00 *Annual Physical* ① | 10:00 | 10:00 |
| 11:00 | 11:00 | 11:00 |
| 12:00 pm *Lunch – Boss* | 12:00 pm | 12:00 pm |
| *(appraisals)* | | |
| 1:00   *Return calls* | 1:00 | 1:00 |
| 2:00 | 2:00 | 2:00 |
| 3:00 *Discuss appraisals* –PC | 3:00 | 3:00 |
|                              –JB | | |
| 4:00                         –RS | 4:00 | 4:00 |
|                              –TW | | |
| 5:00 | 5:00 | 5:00 |
| 6:00 | 6:00 | 6:00 |
| 7:00 | 7:00 | 7:00 |
| **To do** | **To do** | **To do** |
| *call –Joe Burnet* | | |
| *Bill Way* | | |
| *dictate –Smith Co.* | | |
| *J.K. License* | | |
| ① *Dr. Jones 1st Floor* | | |
| *Medical Center, Jersey Blvd.* | | |
| *796-5000* | | |

Courtesy of Alec Mackenzie's Time Tactics

## T I M E   B O O S T E R S

- Pencil in your goals, appointments, and to-do's so you can switch them as necessary.

- Write the phone numbers next to people you must contact so you won't waste time looking up numbers.

- Review and evaluate how your plan worked at the end of each week. This will show you where improvements are needed.

# STEP 3: BUILD UP A MONTHLY PLAN

Just as Alexis Talbott discovered a weekly plan was her mainstay, other women find a monthly plan—as an extension of daily and weekly plans—is the best solution for their time management problems.

"Because I'm overly optimistic about what I can accomplish in a day or week, my problem is with completing those daily and weekly priorities according to my time estimates," says Mary Flood, a workshop leader and publisher of financial information. "What works for me is to think of where I am right now, and then revise and build my planning on what is most important to do in the next month and year."

To build your monthly planning on what you want to accomplish in the coming month evaluate, revise, and consolidate the in-process daily and weekly tasks you won't be able to complete in shorter time segments and move them to a monthly plan. Add anything new you need to include, such as business or personal trips.

### How to Set Up Your Monthly Planning Sheet

Make a copy of the following blank monthly planning sheet. Then, as a guide for filling in your own, use the sample of the planning sheet filled in by the actuarial administrator.

## BLANK FORMAT FOR MONTHLY PLANNING SHEET
### Month of _____

| Monthly Plans (Goals and Subgoals) | Target Date to Shoot for | Actual Deadline Date or Self-Set Goal for Completion of Entire Project |
|---|---|---|
| WHAT HAS TO BE DONE | | |
| _____ | _____ | _____ |
| _____ | _____ | _____ |
| _____ | _____ | _____ |
| WHAT SHOULD BE DONE | | |
| _____ | _____ | _____ |
| _____ | _____ | _____ |
| _____ | _____ | _____ |
| WHAT COULD BE DONE | | |
| _____ | _____ | _____ |
| _____ | _____ | _____ |
| _____ | _____ | _____ |

## SAMPLE FILLED-IN MONTHLY PLANNING SHEET
### Month of July

| Monthly Plans (Goals and Subgoals) | Target Date to Shoot for | Actual Deadline Date or Self-Set Goal for Completion of Entire Project |
|---|---|---|
| WHAT HAS TO BE DONE | | |
| Dr. Walters' govt. forms | July 15 | July 31 |
| Filing of Kane Co.'s termination with IRS | July 31 | Aug. 31 |
| Draft new plan for Swann Co. | July 5 | July 24 |

| Monthly Plans (Goals and Subgoals) | Target Date to Shoot for | Actual Deadline Date or Self-Set Goal for Completion of Entire Project |
|---|---|---|
| WHAT SHOULD BE DONE | | |
| Annual valuation for R & R Electric Co. | July 24 | Aug. 15 |
| Prepare exhibit for meeting with potential client | July 7 | July 21 |
| Follow up on dates for clients with anniversary year ending Aug. 31 | July 15 | July 31 |
| WHAT COULD BE DONE | | |
| Review monthly billing reports | July 31 | Sept. 30 |
| Catch up on filing | July 31 | Arbitrary |
| Reorganize desk | July 31 | Arbitrary |

## T I M E   B O O S T E R S

- Keep department (and company) goals in mind when you formulate your goals. Unless you work for yourself, goals must be compatible.
- Avoid getting sidetracked by unnecessary Could-Do tasks that don't contribute to your monthly goals.

## STEP 4: PROFIT FROM A LONG-TERM YEARLY PLAN

The monthly plans that you prepare will help you look down the road to see what you will need to work on for a long-term yearly plan.

In conducting seminars I find that some women work without yearly plans because they feel it's difficult to look ahead for twelve months. But once you define your long-term goals—and have them down in *writing*—you can integrate them, bit by bit, into daily, weekly, and monthly plans. You can make extra time for them by working on them in spurts—occasional evenings, or half-a-day on a weekend. Or now-and-then vacation days.

The following samples will help you prepare your long-term yearly plan.

## Sample Long-Term Planning Sheet

Copy this blank form. Then, as a guideline for filling in your form, use the filled-in sample done by the library director whose daily planning sheet was in Point 2.

### OBJECTIVES

*January*

_____

_____

_____

_____

_____

*February*

_____

_____

_____

_____

_____

**March**

_____

_____

_____

_____

_____

**April**

_____

_____

_____

_____

_____

**May**

_____

_____

_____

_____

_____

**June**

_____

_____

_____

_____

_____

## July

_____

_____

_____

_____

_____

## August

_____

_____

_____

_____

_____

## September

_____

_____

_____

_____

_____

## October

_____

_____

_____

_____

_____

## November

_____

_____

_____

_____

_____

**December**

_____

_____

_____

_____

_____

## FILLED-IN SAMPLE OF LONG-TERM PLANNING SHEET
### *Objectives*

**January**

Begin collection development project that will emphasize purchase of high demand, high interest materials with quick circulation turnover

Initiate the electronic request system to request books and other library materials by patrons through the On-Line Patron Access Computer

Plan library displays for six months

Prepare for Mayor and Council Meeting on this year's budget Review and weed Adult Reference

**February**

Personnel Evaluation

Dedication Ceremony for new auditorium

Library Services pamphlet mailed to local residents

Mailing to community groups announcing opening of renovated auditorium

Registration for Preschool Story Time

Review and weed Adult Nonfiction

### March

Program for Council and Board on library services emphasizing Automated Catalog use

Preschool Story Time for ages 3 and 4. Wednesdays 10:00 A.M. and 1:30 P.M. through mid-June

Reading Is Fundamental program Grades K to 6. Tuesdays 3:30 to 5:30 P.M.

Literacy Workshops begin to be held every Tuesday from 7:00 to 9:00 P.M. through November

Community groups begin using renovated auditorium

Review and weed Children's Reference

### April

Elementary class visits to library Tuesday mornings 9:30 to 10:30 through June

Preschool Story Time—same as previous month

Reading Is Fundamental program—same as previous month

Literacy Workshops—same as previous month

Program for Chamber of Commerce on library services emphasizing Automated Catalog use

Review and weed Children's Nonfiction

### May

Open House

Elementary class visits—same as previous month

Preschool Story Time—same as previous month

Reading Is Fundamental program—same as previous month

Literacy Workshops—same as previous month

Literacy International Party

Review and weed Children's Fiction

## *June*

Senior Citizen's Day

Visits to local schools by children's librarian

Elementary class visits—same as previous month

Preschool Story Time—same as previous month

Reading Is Fundamental program—same as previous month

Literacy Workshops—same as previous month

Review and weed Children's and Adult's Paperbacks

## *July*

Children's Summer Reading Program Grades K to 6

Plan library displays for six months

Follow-up February mailing of Library Services pamphlet to local residents with letter re-emphasizing our services

Review and weed Adult Reference

## *August*

Children's Summer Reading Program

Write narration for Local History Slide show

Marketing of and publicity on library materials, programs, and activities

Review and weed Adult Nonfiction

## *September*

Local History Slide show ready for presentation

Local History Video ready for sale

Workshops on Automated Catalog for adults

Literacy Workshops—same as previous months

Attend teachers' meetings at local schools

*September (cont'd)*

Registration for Preschool Story Time

Prepare next year's budget

Review and weed Children's Reference

*October*

Preschool Program Ages 3–4. Wednesdays 10:00 A.M. and 1:30 P.M.

Reading Is Fundamental program Grades K–6. Tuesdays 3:30 P.M.–5:30 P.M.

Literacy Workshops—same as previous months

Automated Catalog workshop for local teachers

Friends of the Library Book Sale

Children's Halloween Program

Present next year's budget to Library Board of Trustees for approval

Review and weed Children's Nonfiction

*November*

Automated Catalog workshop for Grades 5 and 6

Local History Video show for children Grades 3 and 4

Literacy Workshops—same as previous months

Submit next year's budget to Mayor and Council

Review and weed Children's Fiction

*December*

Friends of the Library Hospitality Week

Holiday Cooking Contest

Review and weed Children's and Adult's Paperbacks

*Courtesy of Westwood Public Library*

## TIME   BOOSTERS

- Avoid getting so caught up in treadmill activities—day by day, week by week, and month by month—that you lose sight of your big-picture planning.

- At the end of each month evaluate what you have done to move your long-term planning along. It will help you keep pace with your goals if you set up twelve index cards—one for each month—and at the end of each month's evaluation, write down (1) what you did toward accomplishing your long-term goals, (2) when you worked on this, and (3) how much time you invested in it.

# STEP 5: EXPECT TO ADAPT YOUR AGENDA TO TEAMWORK AGENDAS

Today is the era of teamwork and merging of job-related tasks, so regardless of how you plan your own time there will be situations in which you'll have to rearrange your schedule to fit other people's agendas.

In an interview in *"Boardroom Reports,"* Alan Lakein, generally considered the father of the A, B, and C priority system and author of the 1973 classic *How to Get Control of Your Time and Your Life* was asked for his advice on time management today.

His answer?

"Back in 1973 I emphasized the importance of setting your own individual priorities . . . but if I were writing the book for today's more complex world, I would pay more attention to the importance of teamwork. Today businesses—and families—realize that success depends on groups working together."[5]

Grace Mastalli, an attorney who serves as a Deputy Assistant Attorney General in the Office of Policy Development in the U. S. Department of Justice experiences this every day.

"I've often described my job as being somewhat akin to being on a television game show around the clock with questions being thrown at you every time a bell rings," explains Grace. "I'm frequently involved in crisis management and am daily at the beck and call of a large number of people. I rarely leave the building without a portable cellular phone in my handbag, and the Department of Justice's Command Center must know how to reach me 24 hours per day.

"I set priorities and make to-do lists. But both are subject to constant revision because it's more likely than not that my priorities will be changed by forces outside my control, no matter what I may have planned at any given time.

"Meetings which I must attend are scheduled and cancelled with little or no notice, often late at night or on weekends, though sometimes missing one is unavoidable. For example, after I worked late into the night on a crime bill the Command Center reached me the next morning at 7:30 while I was in the shower to tell me about a just-scheduled urgent meeting with the Attorney General and others beginning at 8:00 A.M.

"I live at least 40 minutes away from work during rush hour, and I needed time to dry my hair, dress, and arrange for my mother to watch my son till his sitter came at 8:30. Consequently I arrived in the Attorney General's conference room just as the meeting was breaking up, so despite the plans I'd made, I had to spend much of the day debriefing those who had participated in the meeting in order to catch up and get my part of the job done properly."

"But I've thrived in this environment of unpredictability for 15 years," adds Grace, whose multiple roles along with her job, include being the single-mother head of an active household made up of her 21-month-old son, 85-year-old mother, two aging dogs, and two geriatric cats.

## T I M E     B O O S T E R S

- Discuss your plans and priorities with the group with whom you work and learn what other people's plans and priorities are. This facilitates coordinating activities.

- Anticipate needs to match your time and temperament to group-project priorities to make them compatible.

- Roll with the punches when you have to make modifications in your plans to coordinate and balance them with the overall plans of groups working together. It's the end results that count.

## *S*TEP 6: LEARN TO SAY "NO" TO TIME BANDITS

Although you will always be on call for other people's agendas it's vital—as mentioned in Point 1—to know when it's right to say "No" (*especially* to excessive demands that cut into the time you need for your short and long-term plans).

As women, we lean toward saying "Yes" because of our (1) inclination to help others, (2) fear of displeasing others, and (3) feeling of false obligations. But too often this adds still another time problem to our overcommitted lives and gets us caught up doing too many jobs and going in too many directions at once.

"I'm an extrovert, inclined to be very impulsive," admits Gail Stewart Hand, a newspaper editor and writer of a "Time Crunch" column, "and since I love being with people I tend to want to do far more than is humanly possible.

"But when I agree to do too much I often get swamped and resentful. So how good is that?"

"Not good!" declares management consultant John Campi who believes too many people say "Yes" to everything.

"Just as one scenario," he explains, "someone from your office says 'Do you have a minute for me to stop by?' Instead of saying you're working you tell that person 'Yes,' only to find when the person arrives that you're trapped with someone who's taking a break and has nothing to do at the moment."

This is but one example of a "Yes" that should have been "No." Other examples are agreeing to (1) take on extra assignments, responsibilities, and obligations; (2) chair or join new committees; and (3) attend unexpected and unscheduled meetings.

Naturally there are situations when you have to say "Yes" to some requests because, as Grace Mastalli puts it, "There are no two ways about it. Saying 'No' and missing critical meetings does hurt one's career advancement and frustrates ambition. No amount of time management will ever change that.

"It was only after I was fairly well-established in my career that I began saying 'No' even occasionally to extra assignments," she says. "Now I do my best to carry out all my responsibilities, but I also know how to say 'No, I can't do it in that time frame' or 'Someone else has to do it if the deadline cannot be changed.'"

The important thing in your job, timewise and careerwise, is making smart decisions between your "Yes" and "No" choices. Here are Quick Starts for saying "No" when you have that choice.

### Q U I C K   S T A R T S

 Stall and count to 10 before replying if you must give an instant "Yes" or "No."

 Consider the cost in time of saying "Yes" instead of "No."

 Forget about saying "I'll let you know" when what you really mean is "No." You only postpone the inevitable and lose time fretting about it.

Point out to your boss how handling a new task he or she asks you to do will interfere with the time you can spend on the jobs already assigned.

 Figure out ahead of time how to say "No" to a variety of situations. Then write your "No" responses on a large index card and keep the card by your telephone. Refer to the card when you need to say "No" in a firm, well-poised, and positive manner.

 *Believe* in your right to say "No" to unnecessary requests that interfere with your work objectives.

## $\mathscr{S}$TEP 7: STAY ON TOP OF YOUR PLANS WITH A TIME JOURNAL

Keeping a journal is one more means of seeing what you do, what you don't do, and how much time you let slip away through time wasters, diversions and busy work. Once you form the habit of maintaining a journal regularly, three of the greatest benefits are:

- it serves as a reality check by indicating in black and white exactly how you're progressing with your weekly, monthly, and long-term planning.

- it gives you insight on how to plan your time better.

- it makes you feel good about the things you do accomplish.

Many women tell me they make their entries in their journals the last thing on Sunday nights. This is the time I do it, too, in inexpensive shorthand pads that I keep from year to year. Here is a one-week's entry from my journal that may give you thoughts for writing yours. In my case I've recorded work-at-home chores. If you work outside of your home you'll obviously record at-work activities.

### WEEK OF NOVEMBER 29

Had a good week getting myself out of bed to work from 5:00 to 7:00 A.M. on upcoming deadline on corporate assignment for workbooks and tapes. Continued working on that project during rest of morning and afternoon writing schedule throughout the week. Did two telephone interviews gathering information for the workbooks. Spent one evening coming up with concepts for magazine articles in preparation for two "idea" meetings with editors. Spent one evening at a library trustees' meeting and another at choral group rehearsal for upcoming holiday concert. Practiced music we need to memorize after lunch and before dinner all week as I could fit this in. Took one longer-than-usual lunch break to buy evergreen roping and velvet bows for decorating porch railing. Also bought plants for business gifts while at garden center. Although I accomplished a lot on the corporate project this was a Did-Not-Do week in many respects, too. Did not get to any correspondence. Did not start writing Christmas cards to business contacts as planned. Did not get banking done and checks written for end-of-month bookkeeping.

Did not get to take my 3-mile morning walk every day because of corporate writing deadline. Needed that time to work on formatting text in the workbooks. Goofed off and took a one-hour nap on Wednesday when I should have been working. Maybe I needed the sleep after getting up so early, but I end up frustrated and mad at myself when I give in to naps.

## T I M E   B O O S T E R S

- Think about your entries and what you will write throughout the week. This will motivate you to keep moving and to allot the time for what you want to accomplish.
- Write about your feelings as well as your activities, progress, and lack of progress.
- Keep the journal simple so you won't regard it as a chore.
- Avoid censoring what you write. Your journal is only for your eyes.

***Quick Check/Recheck*** Never lose sight of the benefits of the short- and long-term planning that focuses on specific goals and prevents time from slipping away from you before you even know it. Refer to the 7-Step Program and your planning sheets, day-logs and time journals on a regular basis and constantly reinforce your time management with "This is what I want to do," "These are the steps I'll take to achieve it," and "This is how I'll follow through." As you do this you'll find that planning your time equals planning your life.

# Get More Done in Less Time with the 6–D System

*I want to do more in eight hours and finish my work on time but . . .*
—**A home health-care case manager**

**D**o you accomplish less than you'd like to because you're stuck in outmoded procedures you have followed for years without reassessing your modus operandi and changing negative worn-out habits? Take this 6–D System Self-Test to see if you're getting all you can out of the time you have. I've seen the 6–D's work miracles for many working women.

## SELF-TEST:
### Are You Getting All You Can out of the Time You Have?

|  | Yes | No |
|---|---|---|
| 1. Do you always try to meet deadlines but hardly ever finish on time? | ____ | ____ |
| 2. Do you think you should do everything yourself because you feel you can do it better than anyone else? | ____ | ____ |
| 3. Are you constantly wimpy about making decisions? | ____ | ____ |
| 4. Do you stop what you're doing *whenever* people want to talk to you? | ____ | ____ |
| 5. Do you feel you must wait for the *right* time to start a major job and then end up being so short of time you have to work long hours to do only so-so work? | ____ | ____ |
| 6. Do you gulp your lunch, then run around in circles rushing through a batch of errands rather than turning your lunch break into a more relaxing time-gaining or time-pleasing time? | ____ | ____ |

**Scoring:** If you answered "Yes" to most questions, it's time to eliminate worn-out habits and let the 6–D System help you

1. *D*eal with deadlines
2. *D*elegate work
3. *D*ecide what actions to take
4. *D*ecrease interruptions
5. *D*iminish procrastination
6. *D*o lunch in time-gaining, time-pleasing ways

# D–1: $\mathcal{D}$EAL WITH DEADLINES WITHOUT STRESS

One reason we have deadline problems and get stressed out by them is because we don't always understand exactly what's expected of us when deadlines are assigned. When that happens you can waste huge chunks of time if you're afraid asking questions will make people think you're stupid.

"That's the problem I face," admits Doris Barnes, a paralegal in a suburban law firm. "I'm responsible to two of the partners, and often their double instructions are so offhand and confusing, I end up losing a lot of time trying my best to understand what I'm supposed to do."

What Doris needs to do—and what you need to do if you see yourself in this picture—is to save time instead of lose it by (1) clarifying *immediately* what's expected of you, and (2) getting complete and specific information from the person (or persons) assigning the deadline. In that way you can begin moving toward deadlines without delaying your start while you figure out what to do.

## What Successful Women Say About Deadlines

Here are other ways women move toward deadlines without losing time.

"I find the best solution for avoiding a deadline countdown is to use the salami approach," says Donna Goldfein. "Think of a job as a large salami, encased in plastic and presented without a knife. Until a knife is used to carefully peel away that plastic and make paperthin slices of the huge salami it remains untouchable. However, carving it piece by piece provides a comfortable control of working through the salami. The same is true of working through a project to its completion."

"I use 3 × 5 cards arranged in monthly order from the first to the last day of the month to remind me of my deadlines," explains Sandra Sharp. "As an extra boost, I also keep manila folders with yellow stick-on labels in my pending tray. For example, let's say corrections on one of my reports are being typed by someone in the typing pool. I put my original report that I first sent to be typed with a copy of those typed pages in my folder. Than I mark on the stick-on label what corrections are currently being typed. This saves me time because the label tells me exactly where I'm at in my deadlines."

"I make a written plan that starts at the point where I must be finished, and then work backwards to the beginning," adds Barbara Brabec. "As I work I keep tabs on whether I'm still on schedule or running behind. When I find myself running behind I begin looking for ways to find the extra time I'll need to finish on time.

"For example, while I work on my main deadline job I keep file folders of work that will have to wait till I complete my deadline job. I mark those files 'High priority' and 'Low Priority' jobs. I also set up a basket labeled 'Handle Anytime.' Periodically I weed out that basket."

## T I M E   B O O S T E R S

- Request sufficient time to do the job and factor in a little extra for good measure.

- Establish a starting time that will enable you to complete the job on time and *begin* at that time.

- Ask yourself as you proceed "What is the most important area to concentrate on now?" Then mark that portion of the job on your planning sheet, to-do list, and calendar.

- Be realistic about how much you'll be able to accomplish in each work session and know the difference between the ideal and the possible.

- Monitor your time as you work and check your progress against the deadline each day.

- Keep in touch with the person who's waiting for your deadline job. Jeff Davidson advises that, without creating any extra pressure for yourself, you can ask the person waiting for the job to prod you periodically. This is advantageous in letting you know you're not the only one seeking completion of a deadline.

- When you finish a portion of the deadline job give yourself a reward—a special night out, a sleep-late Saturday or something else that celebrates a partial finish line.

### What to Do When You Can't Make a Deadline

Though we need deadlines to spur us on, there are occasions when it's genuinely impossible to finish a job on time because (1) other Must-Do's appear on the scene, or (2) unanticipated events throw you an unwelcome curve. Ask for a necessary extension when you must and have a logical reason for your need for more time. Then forgive yourself for being late and get on with the job.

"I used to flog myself mentally every time I missed a deadline," says Barbara Brabec. "But no more. It's sensible to avoid needless stress by forgiving yourself."[1]

## D–2: *D*ELEGATE WORK TO STRETCH YOUR TIME

As noted in Point 1, most women have greater problems than men delegating work, and even when they let go of tasks they're still more likely than a man to feel they should gather background information their helpers could get on their own.

But no one can cover all bases in our complex working world, so managing your time effectively means entrusting *some* of your workload to coworkers, assistants, subordinates, business services, and technology.

"My assistant makes decisions about with whom I will meet, where we will meet, and when we will meet," reports Helen Pastorino, owner of a large real estate company. "She sets up two major meetings and two minor meetings in a day, and at the beginning of the day she hands me my daily agenda and any support materials I'll need and walks me through the meetings.

"However, when you delegate this kind of responsibility to an assistant you have to be able to act with minimal preparation time yourself."

You needn't be a top executive to ask people to give you a hand, so adapt these Time Boosters to your situation.

## TIME   BOOSTERS

- Give up the "It's easier to do it myself" syndrome and the worn-out idea you can do everything—and probably do it better than anyone else.

- If you have an assistant, rely on your assistant as much as you can.

- Arrange to exchange favors with coworkers for such routine tasks as reading or clipping articles, answering clients' or customers' questions, or doing whatever other jobs are involved in your work.

- Let computers, answering machines, voice mail and other techno-logical "delegatees" take over tasks you may be doing in nonbenefi-cial ways. If you don't know how to use all available equipment at your place of work, learn immediately. Though learning takes time in the beginning it saves time in the end.

- Consider farming out time-consuming chores—say mailings and stuff-ing envelopes—to nearby business services, if you have the authority to do it. If you don't have the authority, suggest it to your boss.

- Train other people to do the jobs you could delegate. To do this, think through exactly how you want things done and spell out your expectations clearly and specifically.

- Take into account other people's abilities and the pace at which they work and match your expectations to each.

- Once you show people how things should be done so they can go for-ward without unnecessary questions let go of the feeling it's your job to provide them with extra information they can get on their own.

- As you let go, allow them to do things *their* way as long as the end results will be what they should be.

- While staying out of their way, however, be available when needed for clarifying directions, checking work, and showing support and appre-ciation.

- Similarly, review the progress people are making. Says consultant Stephanie Winston, founder of The Organizing Principle and author of *Getting Organized* and *The Organized Executive*, "Whenever you assign a task to someone or whenever you want someone to get back to you put the date on your calendar. When the day comes you can call and say "What happened to thus and so?"

- Keep a record of jobs you delegate (and the facts relating to them) so you'll never be set back by such things as a delegatee's loss of important material, illness, absenteeism, or departure from the company.

- Trust other people's abilities to do a job. "The whole concept of delegation is very similar to a parent and child," explains consultant John Campi. "When a 17-year-old says, 'I want to go out on Friday night' there has to be a separation where the parent says, 'Okay.' I trust you know how to drive. I trust you understand right from wrong.' The same thing is true of delegating work."

---

## What Could You Delegate?

Take a good look at your current work week. Then copy the following blank format for the Delegation Chart and list what you can conceivably delegate. The filled-out sample chart that follows is an example of how to prepare yours.

### FORMAT TO COPY AND FILL OUT

| *Jobs I Could Delegate* | *To Whom I Could Delegate Them* | *When I Could Delegate Jobs* |
|---|---|---|
| _____ | _____ | _____ |
| _____ | _____ | _____ |
| _____ | _____ | _____ |
| _____ | _____ | _____ |

**EXAMPLE OF FILLED-IN DELEGATION CHART**

| *Jobs I Could Delegate* | *To Whom I Could Delegate Them* | *When I Could Delegate Jobs* |
|---|---|---|
| Drafting Johnson Co. Summary Plan Description | Fred | Immediately |
| Calculation of Prince Co. Contribution | Jake | After reviewing data |
| Preparation of Form 5500 for A & D Co. | Bert | After I complete annual valuation |
| Input of employee data on computer for Phil's Packaging Co. | Carol | After reviewing data |

# D–3: DOUBLE YOUR DECISION-MAKING SKILLS

In my consultations with working women the decision-making problems I hear most often are:

- Should I change jobs or stay where I am?

- Should I tell my employer I'll need maternity leave now—or should I postpone it till next month?

- Should I continue to work full-time or should I try for a part-time arrangement after the baby is born?

- Should I hire one of the applicants I've already interviewed or hold off and do more interviews?

- Should I delay faxing reports to a client who wants them immediately until my boss can approve them or should I fax them on my own while the boss is away?

- Should I ask about this year's bonus or sit tight and see what happens?

- Should I explain to our new client that she probably can't have what she wants as soon as she'd like it—or just play "Wait and see?"

- Should I say "Yes" to the invitation to take part in the seminar?

- Should I inform an employee I have to fire her first thing tomorrow morning or should I let it go till afternoon?

The three most common underlying reasons for these and other decision-making problems are:

✔ fear of making a wrong decision

✔ anxiety about the risks and consequences

✔ concern we'll hurt a person or persons affected by our decision

Regardless of our reasons, too many of us waste too much time with a round of "Should I's" or "Shouldn't I's" as we face daily problems in our jobs. But we need to develop this vital skill to save time and get ahead. In fact, Priority Management Systems has found that decision making comes in second among the most important skills needed to succeed in business.[2]

## DECISION-MAKING WORKSHEET

Answer the following questions when facing a workplace decision to help you save time and improve your decision-making skills.

1. Why do I need to make this decision?

\_\_\_\_\_

\_\_\_\_\_

\_\_\_\_\_

2. What will be the most beneficial thing that can happen from making this decision?

\_\_\_\_\_

\_\_\_\_\_

\_\_\_\_\_

3.  What would be the worst thing that could happen?

    _____

    _____

    _____

4.  What facts and information do I need to make this decision?

    _____

    _____

    _____

5.  Where can I get this information?

    _____

    _____

    _____

6.  What are the possible options and alternatives to making this decision?

    _____

    _____

    _____

7.  What is the right timetable for making this decision and acting on it?

    _____

    _____

    _____

## QUICK STARTS

 Have confidence in your own judgment to make a good decision (as opposed to letting others make your decisions for you).

Stick to your decisions once you make them (unless you're proven wrong!) so you don't waste time dilly-dallying about whether it would have been better to take another direction.

Speak up directly and say what you have to say when a decision involves another person. Rather than stewing about it and spending forever, try getting it off your chest quickly. Elizabeth Randall recalls that in her early days of practicing law she had to fire a person. Instead of being direct about it she beat around the bush and took so long to say it in a veiled and cautious way the employee didn't even know she'd been fired!

# D-4: DECREASE TIME-BUSTING INTERRUPTIONS

Handling interruptions is an ongoing problem for women whose days are fragmented with small and large tasks and who feel they should always be accessible.

"My problem is being both a worker and a boss, so staff members who really need time with me come to me constantly," says Gail Stewart Hand. "I feel obligated to give them time, and it's helpful and fun to share ideas. But it also takes a toll on my time and distracts me from the tasks at hand."

You can't eliminate all interruptions, since you're paid to handle some of them (such as requests from your boss or customers' questions). Moreover, there are no magic solutions for avoiding every distraction, whether they are:

- *external in-office interruptions*—people come to you or call you to ask for information, discuss a problem, or simply pass the time of day

- *external nonoffice interruptions*—the school nurse calls with a message that your child fell on the playground or your mother phones and asks "When are you coming over?" since she hasn't seen you for a week

- *internal interruptions*—you stop what you're doing on your own to handle other matters that suddenly cross your mind or your desk

"Even though people want a quick fix that doesn't require much effort, there's no one thing that's going to take care of all interruptions," emphasizes Merrill Douglass. "Reducing them from your work day is easier said than done."

According to Douglass, the interruption problem can have a variety of causes. A few examples:

- people may interrupt you for further instructions if you don't delegate explicitly

- they may stop by for answers to questions if you don't train them well

- they may pop in at inconvenient times because they have no regular time to have access to you

- they may interrupt when they're looking for approval or recognition

One of Douglass's first guidelines for juggling and decreasing interruptions is to keep a careful record of your actual interruptions. Note when an interruption happens, why it happens, what it's about, and how long it lasts.

"Few people do that so that's one reason why they can't minimize interruptions." he says. "But when you keep a record you discover there are patterns.

"For example, there's the Frequent Interrupter Pattern. When you study that pattern you find there are certain people who interrupt you far more than all the rest of the people with whom you work."

Whatever the cause or pattern, interruptions spell lost time so here are some practical answers on how to juggle and decrease them.

## Q U I C K    S T A R T S

 Avoid internal interruptions by disciplining yourself to stick to the task at hand without hopping up to check out something else or picking up the phone to return a call-back you've promised.

 Train people who work for you to do things the way you want them done so they won't interrupt you with questions and requests for information about what you want.

 Keep your accessibility under control by making it clear there are regular times when you're available as well as times when you're not available. It's helpful to ask people to save up all the things they want to mention (unless something is so urgent it won't wait) and—instead of interrupting you several times a day — come to you when you can handle several at one time.

 Put a sign on your door (or in the hall outside of your office) saying "Except for emergencies not available until 3:00 P.M." (or whatever time you choose to be available). One word of warning, however! Let your coworkers know *your* definition of emergencies. *Their* definition could be different.

 Tell people directly when it *isn't* a good time for you to talk. "Two valuable phrases are 'Not now, please' and 'I can't do it now,'" says Grace Mastalli.

Stand up and start shuffling papers around. Try putting papers on your empty office chair to keep unwanted visitors from sitting down.

Anticipate the inevitable outside nonoffice interruptions and crises — children getting ill unexpectedly, a classroom function that's a "Must attend," or a spouse who breaks an elbow while coaching a school tennis team. These interruptions are bound to happen so think about how you'll handle them *before* they arise. In that way you can respond to and juggle things around when they do occur. (See Point 5 for full information on how to think through and make contingency plans for crises and the unexpected.)

 Follow Douglass's advice: keep a record of your interruptions and analyze when and why they happen.

 As you record and analyze, note interruption patterns and people who interrupt you most. Then determine which of their constant interruptions can be eliminated and which can be diverted to someone else.

 Get back to what you were doing as soon as possible after an interruption to minimize being behind at the end of the day.

## D-5: *D*IMINISH THE PROCRASTINATION TEMPTATION

The tendency to fall behind because of procrastination results in stress and anxiety and a great waste of time.

There are many reasons for procrastination. The main ones are: (1) perfectionism, (2) dislike of a project, (3) scheduling a task when you're exhausted, (4) aversion to the individual who delegates the job, (5) fear of failure, (6) half-hearted goals, and (7) hidden reasons.

In explaining the latter Marcia Yudkin describes one woman who put off cleaning up her desk and tackling the mound of piles that accumulated for two years.

Her hidden reason for procrastination?

"She realized that going through the piles and cleaning off her desk would force her to confront opportunities she'd let drop with the passing of the time," explains Marcia. "She didn't want to face that."

## Motivating Yourself Defeats Procrastination

Marcia suggests motivating yourself when procrastination sets in by answering the following questions. Fill in the lines below each question.

1. What purpose does your procrastination serve?

_____

_____

_____

_____

2. What could you like about the put-off job once you got started on it?

_____

_____

_____

_____

3. What wouldn't you like about it?

_____

_____

_____

_____

4. What would be the consequences if you continue procrastinating?

_____

_____

_____

_____

5. What have you done in the past to overcome procrastination that might work for you now?

_____

_____

_____

_____

## Overcome Procrastination with a Balance Sheet

In his book *Getting Things Done* Edwin C. Bliss advocates a Balance-Sheet Method for overcoming procrastination.[3]

"On the left side of a sheet write a list of all the reasons why you are procrastinating on a particular task," advises Bliss. "On the right side list all the benefits that will accrue if you go ahead and get the job done.

"The effect is striking," he emphasizes. "On the left side you will usually have only one or two pathetic excuses, such as 'It might involve an awkward confrontation.' On the other side you will find a long list of benefits, the first of which usually will be the feeling of relief that will come with getting a necessary task behind you."

### QUICK STARTS

 Resolve not to try to do too much all at once. Instead set aside half an hour a day or several times a week to do a task you've been putting off.

 Stop being overly anxious about how perfect the jobs will be. (This *can't* be stressed enough.)

 Talk to supportive colleagues when you can't get started—or keep moving—on a job. "Sometimes when I have a job to do and am having a hard time progressing with it myself," says Joanna Good, "I discuss it with colleagues and together we may say, 'Okay, there's half an hour to get this done. Let's sit down and do it.' This talking about it can be very helpful."

Avoid scheduling tasks you're tempted to put off for a time in your day when you're usually exhausted.

 Finally, if one of your greatest procrastination problems is getting started in the morning, review Point 2 for specifics on overcoming the Slow-Start Syndrome.

# D-6: *D*O LUNCH IN TIME-GAINING, TIME-PLEASING WAYS

"Men do lunch, women do errands," wrote Kathryn Cave in *The Orange County Register.*

"Any weekday at lunchtime, the drill is the same," she reported. "You'll see women in blazers and pumps clickety-clacking across the tile floor at the supermarket, filling their carts with shampoo, laundry soap, or toilet paper. Across town in the mall food court, you'll see tables of men in white shirts, ties flung over the right shoulder, enjoying a meal."

The use of time at the lunch break is so gender-oriented that in research done at the University of California at Irvine, 51% of the women surveyed said they shopped or ran errands at lunch, while only 39% of men claimed to do the same.[4]

"It's the pressure of time," explains a quality control specialist. "Time to do everything I have to do is difficult to find."

"When else can I find time to get to the bank, the dry cleaner—or whatever?" adds a receptionist.[5]

Women are also more apt than men to pack their lunches and "eat in." In fact, according to a survey from the National Restaurant Association and the Roper Organization, 82% of the executive secretaries surveyed reported that they do not normally leave their place of business to eat lunch. Nearly half dine in their office, and a third eat their lunch from home in a company cafeteria, lunchroom, or conference room.[6]

Wherever you choose to have your lunch there's still no need to fall into a rut in which you gulp a sandwich, and then run around to rush through errands in an hour's time. Granted, the errands won't go away and it's timewise to try to do some. But along with making lunchtime a time-gainer for things you need to do, you deserve to make it a time-pleaser for things you want to do that too often go by the board because you don't have the time. Here are time boosters for spending lunch breaks in time-gaining, time-pleasing ways.

## TIME    BOOSTERS

- Use discretion in committing yourself to too many "Let's do lunches" with business colleagues or friends. Though these can be pleasant and sometimes productive, some can also be wasted time you could use for more rewarding activities.

- Determine the difference between wasted-time lunches and networking lunches. The latter are important aspects of your life as a working woman, so use some lunchtimes (like once a month in a restaurant and once a week in your company lunchroom) to cultivate a network of contacts and associates with whom to give and take job talk.

- Catch up on your morning work— or get a head start on your afternoon tasks —by eating at your desk. "My choice is heating soup in the microwave and continuing to work," reports college professor Dr. Eileen Gardner.

- Get away from the hubbub of your workplace by retreating to a church, park, or library and sitting quietly by yourself for a while.

- Invest the hour in a hobby or interest for which you never have time. If you work in a city and love museums, go to one. If you work in the suburbs or country and like antiques and crafts, visit antique and craft shops.

- Spend time reading if you're constantly short on time for that. One secretary goes to the office parking lot and reads in her car while she has her lunch.

- Walk or exercise.

- Avoid trying to do *too many* food-shopping, clothes-shopping, gift-buying, and banking errands. But *do* do some so they won't pile up and take blocks of time on your weekend.

- Save future standing-in-line time for cards you want to send by buying birthday, anniversary, get well, and sympathy cards in bulk so you'll always have them when you need them.

- Make the keep-in-touch phone calls to friends that you've been wanting to make.

---

***Quick Check/Recheck*** The more you incorporate the 6–D System into your work life the more successful you will be at doing more—more comfortably—in less time. You'll deal with deadlines more effectively by (1) getting specific information on what's expected, (2) breaking up the total project into smaller segments, (3) starting with the first segment in time to meet your deadline, and (4) monitoring your time and progress through the other segments as you proceed. You'll give up the "It's easier to do it myself" syndrome and the worn-out idea you can do everything by delegating some of your workload to coworkers, assistants, subordinates, business services, and technology. You'll avoid wasting too much time on "Should I's" or "Shouldn't I's" and improve your decision-making skills by having confidence in your own judgment to make good decisions. You'll accept the fact that you can't eliminate all interruptions but you'll know how to handle and decrease external in-office interruptions, external nonoffice interruptions, and internal interruptions. You'll identify the reasons for procrastination problems and pick up real ways to gain control over them by listing all the reasons you procrastinate on a particular task on the left side of a sheet of paper and all the benefits that will accrue if you go ahead and get the job done on the right side. Finally, you'll swap in-a-rut lunchtime breaks for the benefits of more time-gaining, time-pleasing pursuits that often go by the board because you haven't found time for them.

# Whittle Your Daily Work Down to Size with the 6–P Techniques

*If only I could do everything that comes to my desk every day—but the piles of requests and demands on my time multiply and reproduce.*

**—An assistant researcher**

"I see each day as a puzzle," says time consultant Merrill Douglass, "so fitting all the pieces together becomes a daily challenge."

That description probably fits your day, too—*especially* on those days when you feel completely overwhelmed by the pile of work that's a normal function of your job. You're likely to experience this feeling more than men, too, since many tasks are heaped on women because of our reputation for being good at details.

But there are ways to put together the pieces of your daily puzzle, and they all begin with knowing where you stand on the following 6–P Test.

## SELF-TEST:
### *How Well Do You Manage Your Daily Workload?*

Mark A for "Usually," B for "Sometimes," C for "Never"

—— 1.  I work in such a perpetual mess, while trying to beat the clock, that I can't lay my hands on what I need without playing hide and seek.

____ 2.  I'm surrounded by mountains of paperwork.

____ 3.  I waste hours of time at meetings.

____ 4.  I get thrown off my schedule by crises and the unexpected.

____ 5.  I feel I don't have a minute to get little things out of the way.

____ 6.  I end each working day in frustration.

**Scoring:**

*Mostly C Answers:* You're better than many working women at keeping the pieces of your day together.

*Primarily B Answers:* You put some pieces of the day's puzzle together but you need to use more of the 6–P Techniques to minimize feeling over-whelmed.

*Chiefly A Answers:* You're receiving *none* of the benefits the 6–P Techniques provide.

You'll begin to see instant time-saving results when you learn how to use the 6–P's to:

1.  *P*lan your work space to conserve time
2.  *P*ut paperwork in its place
3.  *P*ass up waste-of-time meetings
4.  *P*repare for crises and surprises
5.  *P*rogram in-the-middle time
6.  *P*ack it in at the end of the day

# P–1: $\mathscr{P}$LAN YOUR WORK SPACE TO CONSERVE TIME

Few things contribute to feeling overwhelmed as much as a poorly planned work space in which the arrangements of your desk top and drawers, filing system, and tools and supplies are a hodgepodge of disarray. You can gain time by rearranging your work area in these three ways.

## (1) Match Your Desktop and Drawers to Your Work Style

In consulting with women in their workplaces I find— since we all work differently—that a desk that's considered a disaster zone for a woman in the corner office may well be necessary "orderly disorder" for a woman down the hall. The key is to match your work style to the way you maintain your desk, even if your drawers and desk top don't seem organized and neat in the eyes of others.

"It's essential to recognize one's style and habits and figure out how to work with your own strengths and weaknesses," agrees Grace Mastalli. "I'm naturally intuitive and nonlinear—some would say that means disorganized. But my desk and documents are in good enough shape for me if I can find what I'm looking for in less than 10 minutes. I clean my desk and reorganize only when I have failed to meet the under 10 minutes requirement."

Can you meet the under-10-minutes requirement? Better yet, how about under 5? The following Quick Starts will help you improve your desk management, regardless of your work style.

## Q U I C K   S T A R T S

Avoid having too many things screaming for attention all at once by keeping what you're *not* working on off the middle of your desktop.

Keep your workbaskets and trays to one side of your desk (if you don't have another spot for them entirely) and stay on top of their contents by regularly clearing out 20% of what's in them. "The reality is that more stuff will come along and fill that space," says Jeff Davidson.

Make sure your computer equipment, calendar, notepad, pencils, pens, and everyday file sorter are always available.

Have your phone and fax on the right side (for you) of the desk.

## (2) Get Your Files in Useful Order

It takes time to turn a filing system into something so manageable you know exactly where every paper should go as it crosses your desk. But this is a proven solution for saving time in the long run because, as Jeff Davidson stresses, "You cannot manage a horizontal pile. No one can efficiently negotiate this spatial arrangement; horizontal piles cannot be a final resting place for the items in them."

Here are eight Quick Starts for putting your files in order.

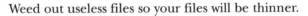

### Q U I C K     S T A R T S

Weed out useless files so your files will be thinner.

Avoid filing unnecessary items.

Ask "If I want this paper again and don't have it is there some other place where this same information is available?"

Organize your material *vertically* either in a filing cabinet with all labeled tabs facing upward or in a vertical divider with tabs facing outward.

Alphabetize and cross reference your files. Alex Mackenzie suggests color-coding and labeling files for common categories. For instance, files can be labeled "Urgent," "Dictate," "Call," "To Do," "To File," and "From a VIP."

Create a simple master-file index on which you list what files and information are in your file cabinets, drawers, baskets, and trays.

 Revise this index as you need to.

Always keep your files up to date.

## (3) Put Supplies Where You Can Find Them Fast

You'd think it would be a given that smart working women would keep their supplies in convenient, accessible spots—unless you've encountered, as I often have, people who waste your time and theirs by coming to you for things they can't find in their own work place.

I'll never forget the time a reader for a literary agent (who worked at home in her basement) phoned me during *my* working hours to ask me to check *my* dictionary for the spelling of a word because *her* dictionary was in a bookcase in her attic! She wasted her time and my time on a task she could have avoided by having her own working tools in an accessible spot.

### Q U I C K   S T A R T S

 Set up specific places for your working tools and supplies and work by the motto "A place for everything and everything in its place." As hackneyed as this sounds, it saves and gains time.

 Keep all your tools and supplies in top shape. Pens that no longer write or pencils that need to be sharpened only succeed in wasting minutes when you have to grab three or four pencils or pens before you can write down a telephone message.

 Place tools and supplies you don't use daily in large wicker baskets or stacking file baskets so you can retrieve them quickly when you do need them.

 Form the habit of putting things away as soon as you finish with them.

# P–2: $\mathcal{P}$UT PAPERWORK IN ITS PLACE

"Drowning in paperwork is the problem that makes most people cry 'Help,'" says Stephanie Winston. "They put papers to the side of their desks saying 'I'll deal with that tomorrow.' But tomorrow never quite comes so they build up giant accumulations."

Those huge stacks of paperwork are one of the major causes for feeling overwhelmed, so I'm a believer in Edwin G. Bliss's advice: "Do it, delegate it, or ditch it when you get a piece of paper."[1]

Admittedly no one technique solves *every* paperwork problem. But putting paperwork in its place in a way that works for you will help you solve many problems—and keep you from being a Scarlett O'Hara and thinking about paperwork tomorrow.

## Six Ways to Tackle Paperwork So It Won't Eat Up Your Time

**(1) Don't Waste Time Pouring Over the Daily Mail.** Instead, make fast work of sorting mail at whatever time of day you do routine paperwork. (Your downtime is often a good time.) Alexis Talbott finds it works well for her to check mail (maybe three times a week) only when she can sort and do something with it immediately.

**(2) Throw Out Junk Mail and Useless Papers as Soon as They Arrive.** Time consultants call this the "art of wastebasketry," and Barbara Hemphill advises women to ask themselves what's the worst possible thing that would happen if they didn't save a particular piece of paper.

"Then ask if you're willing to live with those consequences," she says. "For example, one person might say 'I know this information is in the personnel office so I'd have to go and get it from there.' Another might say 'I can't stand to deal with that office. Therefore, I'm going to save this paper.'"

**(3) Whenever Possible, Make Decisions About Paperwork at a First Reading.** Elaine Gardner, an attorney and advocate for the deaf, recommends answering letters as soon as they come in as a way to cut down on piled up paperwork. When you (1) read a letter, (2) think about how you'll answer it, and (3) put it "on hold" till you have more time, you set yourself up to waste time. More often than not when "more time" comes you'll have to take time to reread the letter and rethink your response.

In situations when you can't respond after a first reading, at least write down your ideas for responding in the margin of the letter. In that way you won't be starting from scratch when you get back to it.

**(4) Save Time and Paper with Short, Informal Responses.** Rather than automatically drafting a separate formal letter, hand-write your answer directly on the letters and memos you receive—and keep your messages short. "I'm a great believer in dispensing with formalities," says Wendy Dixon. "I handwrite what I need to say when and where it's convenient to respond. I'm not chained to a keyboard."

**(5) Develop a Simple System for Getting Papers Off Your Desk Till You Can Handle Them.** When you can't respond immediately, you need a consistent method for setting aside paperwork so it won't clutter up your desk. A simple system many women find works well is to put:

- what you're going to respond to in your "To Do" file

- what you don't plan to respond to—but still need to save—in your "To File" file

- what you want to read later in your "To Review" file.

Keep the latter in your briefcase or carry-along bag so you'll have it with you at all times. Jeff Davidson suggests that, as you read, you tear important pages out of magazines, newsletters, and reports. Later you can integrate these pages into your filing system and toss the rest. Copy key pages from books when you get to a copy machine.

**(6) If Necessary, Devise a Special System That Will Fit Your Special Needs.** Though the "To Do," "To File," and "To Review" system described above works for most working women, there are always the proverbial exceptions. Take Grace Mastalli with her work in the U. S. Department of Justice. If you have a similar special-needs job, adapt some of her tips:

"I receive so much paper I have a sorting system of incoming boxes for 'Urgent Attention,' 'Immediate Action,' 'Routine Action,'

'Legislative Tracking,' and 'Background Reading Materials,'" explains Grace. "I also have 'Routine Outgoing' and 'Routine Incoming' boxes and a 'Special Subject Matter' system for stacks of such things as Senate Crime Bill Amendments and Drug Policy Strategy drafts. Classified documents require special handling and security precautions.

"As I make these categorizations I have to depend heavily upon a strong memory for both where a document is and what it says. Otherwise documents would be buried forever in the absolute blizzard of papers that pass through my office. The volume is so staggering that just being able to sort all the incoming priority items and make urgent assignments on a daily basis is a major accomplishment.

"For instance, one day on two different fax machines I received 200 faxes of crime-bill-related Senate amendments averaging 5 pages each for immediate policy review, coordination and clearance. For that handling of paperwork my secretary and I set up a temporary file system just for those materials in a standing file on my office coffee table."

## TIME   BOOSTERS

- If you have a secretary or assistant, have the person (1) screen all paperwork before it comes to you, (2) handle what he or she can take care of, (3) reroute what someone else can handle, (4) put appropriate papers in a follow-up file for your future consideration, and (5) expedite emergency items.

- Ask to have your name dropped from mailing lists of advertisers, agencies, and organizations that offer products or materials for which you have no use or interest.

- "Start organizing your paperwork gradually and begin with today's mail," advises Stephanie Winston. "Don't look at your desk and try to reorganize the backlog until you get the feel of how to do it on a day-to-day basis. Then each day—say, for half an hour—work on a single stack of accumulation. Tackle adjoining stacks bit by bit and proceed from there."

- "Once every three months reexamine everything in your office and practice creative trashing," sums up Jeff Davidson. "Be ruthless. Make every paper that comes into your office justify its existence."

# P–3: *P*ASS UP WASTE-OF-TIME MEETINGS

The person who labeled meetings as occasions "where minutes are kept while hours go down the drain" had a strong sense of time management priorities because so many drawn-out meetings waste inordinate amounts of time.

## When You're Asked to Attend Meetings

Your ability to pass up meetings is obviously dependent on whether or not your boss or someone else is the person who requests your attendance. "But, in any case, unless you establish the fact that you put a value on your time and want to avoid unnecessary meetings, no one will respect your nonattendance," says John Campi.

Note the following two scenarios:

### Your Superior Asks You to Attend

| | |
|---|---|
| **Your Superior:** | We're going to have a meeting in the conference room, and I want you to be there in 5 or 10 minutes. |
| **You:** | What will the focus be? What will you need from me? |
| **Your Superior:** | A couple of staff problems have come to a head, so I need to rethink some job assignments and possibly reshuffle Joe and Jean's jobs. |
| **You:** | If it's absolutely necessary, I'll certainly be there, but considering the other priorities I'm working on for you it might be more beneficial to you for me to continue with those priorities. Or, if you feel I *must* be on board, maybe I should attend for just the portion that would relate to any contribution I could make and stay only for as long as I'm needed. |

### A Colleague Asks You to Attend

| | |
|---|---|
| **Your Colleague:** | I'm getting the team heads together for the weekly brainstorming meeting promptly at 1:00 today. |
| **You:** | What's the agenda this week? At the last three meetings nothing really happened. |
| **Your Colleague:** | Well, there's no real agenda for today. |

| You: | Then what are we going to accomplish? |
| Your Colleague: | Well, we don't really know. We'll just talk and wait and see. |
| You: | In that case I can't go. Send me the minutes and when you want to meet again send me an agenda. If it's a meeting I can contribute to or learn something from, I'll come. |

## How to Plan *Non*-Waste-of-Time Meetings

In an article in *Working Woman,* "A Short Snappy Guide to Meaningful Meetings," Kirsten Schabacker passes on advice from Robert Townsend, author of *Up the Organization.* When it's your job to plan meetings you'll find it beneficial to follow his advice and limit your meetings to groups of people who have:

1. enough knowledge to make a contribution,

2. the power to make decisions,

3. responsibility for implementing decisions,

4. the authority to represent those affected by the decisions.[2]

## TIME     BOOSTERS

- Ask yourself before scheduling any meeting whether calling a group together is the best way to accomplish your goals.

- Consider, as an alternative, whether you could save time and keep communication lines open through memos, phone calls, updates and reports, and then make decisions without a meeting.

- Avoid time-consuming interruptions between meetings by having your colleagues hold routine questions and comments for the next scheduled meeting.

- Call meetings right before lunch or at 4:00 P.M. or 4:30 P.M. so no one will want to drag them out.

- Stick to the three or four important points on your agenda and don't get sidetracked.

- Begin and end on time.

# P–4: $\mathcal{P}$REPARE FOR CRISES AND SURPRISES

Crises and unexpected problems have no respect for time! In fact, in "The Best Ideas in Time Management" the editors of *communication briefings* point out that you should realistically expect to be able to control only about 50% of your day.[3]

Undoubtedly you've felt that way—more times than you can count—when you confront unanticipated events:

- your assistant comes raging into your office and says she's going to quit

- your printer breaks down in the middle of a presentation you're to give in an hour

- your teenager has a fender-bender and phones you at the office to ask what she should do

- your father-in-law has a heart attack—and your husband is out of town

You can't avoid such crises and the way they fracture your time, but you can make contingency plans for the unexpected. You'll save time when you do this, too, because you can solve problems faster when you have back-up arrangements.

"Working women— especially, working mothers—are probably far more likely than men to have contingency plans that are not only useful but probably mandatory in many cases," says Merrill Douglass. "Certainly you don't have to have contingency plans for everything. But you should have them for critical situations where you'll need to be able to act quickly without losing time having to weigh your options.

"To prepare for crises and the unexpected, think ahead and plan for 'What do I do if _____?'" advises Douglass. "Then mentally practice what you'd do so you can respond with a well-thought-out plan when the crisis occurs.

"For instance, suppose you're scheduled to show a video at a seminar. What do you do if the electricity goes out? This happens. Have a plan for it!"

Over and above office crises there are other unexpected situations working women encounter that put a monkey wrench into the best-laid time management plans.

## Handling Day-Care and School Problems

You shouldn't always be the one who has to ask for time off for the unexpected, but the chances are great you'll occasionally face a situation in which:

- the day-care center or school is closed
- your child becomes suddenly ill in the morning and can't go to the center or school
- your child gets sick while in school and has to be picked up
- you have to attend a school function or conference

Generally you know in advance when the school or center will be closed for vacations or other official reasons, so you're able to plan ahead for that. But what can you do when it's unanticipated—a snow day or a heating problem?

The ideal solution is to *always* have alternative child-care arrangements so you can set up contingency plans at a moment's notice. Here are some plans that work. At least one should work for you.

## T I M E   B O O S T E R S

- Call on willing family members who are available on short notice.
- Have a list of available baby-sitters whose references you've checked.
- Keep another list of women from your church or temple who care for members' children.
- Prearrange with friends or neighbors to come to your rescue at the last minute.

- Enlist the help of your husband or mate. This is a growing (and long overdue) back-up trend. A poll conducted by Ethel Klein of EDK Associates found that 50% of the younger women polled said they'd ask their husbands to take a day off, and 50% of the thirtysomething men said they'd offer to stay home.[4] In one household where this works out well, the wife, an employee benefits specialist, stays home in the morning when emergencies strike while the husband, an office manager, goes off to his job. At noon the couple reverses roles and the husband comes home while the wife goes to work. In another household, a publicist and marketing specialist who owns her own business splits the time at home with her husband if one of their children gets the chicken pox and can't go to the day-care center. "On those occasions we both do our work at home, nurse our sick child together, and sometimes, sneak a peak at 'Oprah' while our child naps," she says.

## Overcoming the Nanny's Absence

What can you do in the morning if a nanny or sitter calls in sick—or isn't able to come to work for any other reason?

When you lose your nanny for a day (or days), your first solution should be to try to use the same procedures suggested for day-care and school matters. Another is to see if you can arrange one-day or short-term child care in your company's day-care center if your place of business has one.

Still another possibility is to take your child to work with you. According to Dana Friedman, copresident of the Families and Work Institute, bringing children to the workplace is happening to a much greater degree than we realize and is happening at every income level.[5]

Admittedly, this can be distracting, and companies don't particularly like it. But since bringing children to the workplace is now a reality, many employers turn their heads the other way.

## Six Ways to Handle "Can You Stay Late?"

It's 5:00 P.M.—and do you know where your children are?

If your child-care arrangements are like those of other working mothers, your children are probably:

- at the day-care center or after-school program waiting for you to pick them up

- safe in the hands of a nanny or sitter till you get home to take over

- at a relative's, neighbor's, or baby-sitter's home until you arrive for them

- home alone if they're old enough

All of this is good child-care planning *if* it works as planned. But what if your baby-sitter leaves at 6:00 P.M. and your boss has asked you to stay late to work on a deadline report, attend an unplanned meeting, or take a client to dinner? Here are six Time Boosters for situations like that.

## T I M E   B O O S T E R S

- If you'll be working in your office, take time out to pick up your child at the day-care or after-school school program and bring him or her to the office for an hour or two. Younger children can color, draw pictures, or watch TV if that's available. Older children can read or do their homework.

- See if the relative, neighbor, or sitter at whose home children stay till you get home can keep them a while longer.

- Have a support group of people you can call to pick up your children from wherever they are and take over at home till you or another adult gets there.

- Keep a dinner in the freezer that anyone taking over for you can heat up quickly. A hearty soup or casserole (plus French bread you've frozen) makes a good emergency dinner; so do individual frozen dinners you purchase from the supermarket or prepare yourself from entrees and vegetables left over from home-cooked meals.

- If there's simply no way you can stay, have a polished, practiced script in mind for when you're asked to stay late. Say something like: "As much as I want to I can't stay tonight. But if it will help I can take the work home. I'll be just a telephone call away, and I'll have the work done by morning."

- Realize that sometimes you simply have to refuse some unexpected requests whether they're for after-work or other nonwork hours. Grace Mastalli recalls how she has refused to go in to work for 6:00 P.M. meetings on Saturdays that are called at 4:00 P.M. "But the trade-off is I spend a week catching up on what happened at the meeting in my absence," she says.

---

## Be Prepared for Unexpected Business Trips

It's hard enough for working women to go on business trips, when along with getting things in order at work, they must also plan for their absence at home. But it can be even harder when you learn on a Friday afternoon that you must leave on Monday for an unscheduled trip.

However, you can make arrangements to do this with these nine Quick Starts.

### QUICK STARTS

Have a carry-on suitcase packed and a wardrobe planned and ready at all times. This will save time and tension in your rush to get off on a trip. Once when I learned on a Friday morning I had to leave for London that night, I was able to work in New York City all day, take a bus home at 5:00 P.M., pick up my ready-to-go suitcase, write necessary "Things To Do" for my family, and get to the airport and on the plane without an anxiety attack. But none of this could have happened without a ready-to-go suitcase and wardrobe.

Keep a cosmetic bag with small sizes of your toiletries and cosmetics and a hair dryer and hair-care supplies in the case, along with an extra pair of comfortable shoes, panty hose, underwear, sleepwear, travel iron, and paperback book.

In the far end of your closet hang a good winter or summer non-wrinkle suit fresh from the cleaners that's always ready to go into your packed suitcase. You can change the look of the suit daily with scarves, easy-to-pack nonwrinkle tops and pants, and a wool or cotton sweater, depending on the season.

 Choose one neutral color for all your business travel, including your shoes and purse.

 Use the large purse you carry to work every day for many of the things you'll need on the trip—jewelry, tissues, medications, tickets, glasses, and whatever you'll require from your everyday carry-along bag.

 Draw up a list of people or relatives who can take over for you at home while you're gone. Similarly, have people at work who can pinch hit for you to keep you from losing too much time catching up when you return from the trip.

 Maintain a master list of your household routine that you can post in your kitchen in case someone other than your family will take over while you're away.

 Have a week's supply of "Only for Emergencies" staples and dinners stashed away in your freezer and cupboard.

Keep enough reserved cash in a strong box at home to cover family needs while you're away (and to give you cash for your wallet) if you're called away so unexpectedly you can't get to the bank or automatic teller.

## SELF-TEST:
### *How Good Are You at Controlling Crises and Surprises?*

Take the following quiz and circle the "T's" (True) and "F's" (False) to measure how well you prepare for and manage crises and unexpected events. Be honest with yourself as you check your answers.

1. You're in the habit of making contingency and back-up plans for the professional and personal crises you think you might encounter.    **T**    **F**

2. You do preventative maintenance on your work tools; e.g., when your personal computer begins acting up you take care of it.    **T**    **F**

3. You always carry addresses, phone numbers, and appointments with you so you can make calls on the spot to replan, reschedule, or cancel arrangements.    **T**    **F**

4. When a crisis or unexpected event happens you take time, after the fact, to analyze what caused it.    **T**    **F**

5. You evaluate whether the unexpected came about because of something you did.    **T**    **F**

6. Similarly, you consider whether it occurred because of something you didn't do.    **T**    **F**

7. If the same crises keep recurring, you determine what you can do to prevent the recurrences.    **T**    **F**

8. You review what you did in the past to resolve similar crises.    **T**    **F**

9. You remain calm and logical and avoid blaming others when the unexpected occurs.    **T**    **F**

10. You leave breathing space on your daily calendar for the inevitable crisis.    **T**    **F**

**TOTALS**    __ __

**Scoring:**

8–10 True:    Your management of crises and surprises is good.

5–7  True:    You're partially there but you still lose time that you could save by think-ahead planning.

1–4  True:    You definitely need to improve your skills for putting contingency plans in place.

# P–5: PROGRAM IN-THE-MIDDLE TIME

While we all want to take full advantage of our 1,440 minutes each day, we don't have to make *every* minute count during 24 hours! In fact, you'll push yourself over the edge if you try!

There are times to "do" and times to just "be"—to stare into space, to sit in the sun, to savor a breeze on your face. Even Grace Mastalli (whose schedule often makes me feel that I do nothing at all) says, "I schedule and protect time in which to do nothing, even if it's only 10:00 to 11:00 P.M. daily."

But along with protecting do-nothing time to alleviate stress, it's timewise to make practical use of some of the in-the-middle time everyone has every day to do minitasks. In her "Creative Ways News" Marcia Yudkin refers to this time as "upside-down time" in which to get things done in short periods of time.

"Use odd chunks of time," she writes. "Instead of getting angry or impatient, have a variety of tasks you can do in the stray moments that unexpectedly appear in your schedule. When stuck in traffic, how about brainstorming ideas or listening to music that will restore your ability to get things done the rest of the day?"[6]

Many successful women recognize the time-gaining potential of these in-between moments.

"I wouldn't dream of going anywhere without my folder of cards to be handwritten and catalogs, articles, or books to be perused and highlighted," says Suzanne Frisse. "I also carry bills to be paid, miscellaneous items to check, goals to be looked at, and a cassette tape to listen to if needed."

"I have a list of filler jobs I can do in 10 to 30 minutes, and I always keep that list handy for those 10 or 30 minutes I have between more highly concentrated jobs," says Barbara Brabec.

Instead of completing small tasks, you can also use these time breaks for creative thinking.

"Some of my most creative problem solving has occurred during nonwork time when I could give my brain the chance to work while I relaxed," says Grace Mastalli. "In my car—or after most of the staff has left for the day—I focus on important things which require deliberate thought."

## T I M E   B O O S T E R S

- Organize your carry-along bag (or briefcase or tote) with sections for (1) magazine, newspaper, and work-related articles you've clipped to review and read; (2) catalogues to quick read; (3) notes, memos, postcards, and letters to write; (4) birthday and greeting cards to send; (5) lists and plans to make; (6) bills to pay and checks to get out (you can easily take care of one or two in your in-the-middle time).

- You can also arrange coupons you've clipped by their expiration date, and if you earmark an envelope for your business receipts you can organize them and keep up with your expense account.

- If you have insufficient reading-for-pleasure time carry a book. A paperback takes little room and is always available for 10-minute breaks.

- Consider all the following interludes in your day as "in-the-middle" time and make good use of them—going to and from work on public transportation; in the car when you're stuck in traffic; in restaurants when waiting for lunch; in reception rooms where you go for appointments; standing in lines; riding in cabs; sitting in train stations and airports; and watching TV.

## Doing Two Small Tasks at the Same Time

Along with in-the-middle time, doing two small tasks at once can put time in your time bank. This is a stock-in-trade for me and a time-saver that works well. However, you must be able to recognize the difference between *little* tasks that require minimal thought and *big* tasks you're better off doing one at a time.

"Occasionally you can do two things at once as long as they're both trivial," warns Merrill Douglass. "But you can't do two significant things at one time. I've seen too many people who think that the faster they run and the more things they get their thumbs in the more they're accomplishing. I don't agree with that. But I do agree that there are small tasks you can do this way."

Here are three easily managed two-things-at-once time-gainers.

## TIME   BOOSTERS

- Listen to a motivational or educational tape while walking, riding, or driving to work.
- Do simple sitting exercises while handling routine desk work.
- Use on-hold phone time to fill out forms, make lists, sort mail, file, or do low-attention paperwork.

# P–6: PACK IT IN AT THE END OF THE DAY

Since your working life isn't your *only* life know when you've done enough for one day and let the workday go. Says Suzanne Frisse, "I will often say 'I did the best I could. Now this day has become my past. Learn from it and move on.'"

An important part of "packing in the day" is winding down with transition time. This is especially beneficial if you're going home to children, since sudden switches from one role to another can be particularly stressful.

Depending on how you travel to work—car, bus, train, or foot— use the time between work and home to (1) think and relax, (2) do small tasks and errands, or (3) wind down and do nothing at all.

## What Successful Women Say About Transition Time

"If all goes well when I leave work I arrive at my children's school at 3:00 P.M. and have a 15-minute wait before the children are out," says Sandra Sharp. "I spend this transition time in the car pulling things out of my bag and doing such tasks as letter writing, coupon cutting, and grocery-list making. I *like* that I'm not talking to anyone—just organizing myself and my thoughts."

"I turn on classical music and try to imagine I'm switching from Channel 4 to Channel 11 as I drive home," says Gail Stewart Hand. "I make it a point to do very slow breathing and maintain a calm. When I start obsessing about anything relating to work I try to put those worries aside and wait till I get home to jot them down on Post-its. Once I'm home I go through most of the mail before the children come in to tell me about their day. It's really helpful to try to manage this little bit of time alone before I go into my other life. Those 10 minutes make me more calm and relaxed."

The following Quick Starts will help you pack in the day and prepare for the next day.

### QUICK STARTS

 Clean up your office as much as possible before leaving so you're not overwhelmed by the mess in the morning.

 "Think 'What did I do today?' 'What didn't I do?' and 'Why didn't I get it done?' advises John Campi. "Then give some thought to the next day and formalize your plans for that."

 Prepare a quick and abbreviated agenda and put your plans on a single piece of paper as a starter for your Daily Planning Sheet. "When you do that you can leave the office comfortably and arrive the next day focused on completing your planned schedule," says Donna Goldfein. "This single-piece-of-paper agenda should include phone calls with names and numbers and the time to call, follow-up memos, meetings, and appointments."

Get out all papers you'll need for the following day. That will give you a head start.

Reflect on the positive outcome of the day. Accept the fact that you can't always be caught up and look at what you've accomplished instead of dwelling on what you didn't get done.

**Quick Check/Recheck** You now have the 6–P resources to put your days together and minimize the negative feeling of being overwhelmed by the tasks facing you: planning your work space to save time; putting paperwork in its place; passing up waste-of-time meetings; preparing for crises and surprises; programming in-the-middle time; packing it in at the end of the day. When you manage your time in this way you'll benefit from the positive feeling of working your way through the day without being caught in a time squeeze in which everything and everyone seems to be screaming for your attention at once.

POINT SIX

# Beat the Clock with Four Alternatives to a 9 to 5 Job

*I like gaining time and having a choice.*
**—A customer service representative**

- A federal employee who needs time at home to care for her elderly mother arrives at her office at 6:45 A.M. and leaves at 3:15.

- A caseworker in a rehabilitation center works at the center three days a week and attends school the other two.

- A saleswoman for a mutual funds firm stays home with her infant during the day and sets up appointments for evening calls. When her husband comes home at 7:00 P.M. she goes out on the calls.

- A newscaster broadcasts at 8:10 A.M. from a hooked-up studio near her laundry room after first nursing her baby.

- A nurse works at night 24 hours a week to have daytime hours at home.

- A computer programmer with year-old twins keeps her pretwin job by compressing her 40-hour week into four 10-hour days.

These six are just a few of the working women across the country who find that, instead of a traditional 9:00 to 5:00 schedule five days a week 50 weeks a year, alternative schedules offer time benefits. In fact, people who choose alternatives are far more apt to be women than men.[1]

The four main alternative work arrangements are part-time work, flextime, temporary work, and job sharing. There's a growing trend toward each of these alternatives. There are three primary reasons for this:

- technological advances are creating new ways to work

- the increasing number of working parents is making it necessary for employers to adapt their scheduling to the changing needs of the work force

- employers who want to downsize their (1) work force, (2) operating expenses, and (3) office space are finding it beneficial to hire a "contingency work force." (Though all alternatives and options are not classified as "contingency work" this term broadly defines a force of part-time, temporary and independent contractors.[2] (See Point 7)

## What You Gain with Alternatives

There are many advantages, especially for women, in setting up an alternative work schedule.

"The *big* benefit is that options and alternatives give women a choice on when and how they work," says Linda Marks, Director of the FlexGroup at New Ways to Work, a San Francisco research, training, and advocacy organization for flexible work arrangements. "Flexibility is *always* a time-management plus."

Many women echo this phrase when they tell me about their alternative jobs because when you opt for alternatives you can arrange your time to:

- establish a balance between your work and family life

- work during the hours you have time off from family responsibilities

- match your workstyle to your lifestyle
- utilize your skills and training
- stay on your career track even though you can't work full time for a while
- test the waters if you haven't begun a career
- maintain established business contacts and/or develop new ones

Sheila Wellington, the current president of Catalyst, the New York research and advisory organization that studies women and work, agrees that the growing trend toward alternatives has benefits for women.

"The varied demands on women's time—and the fact that they shoulder a disproportionate share of family and home responsibilities—present women with a different set of time management problems in the workplace," she stresses.

"Our study on flexible work arrangements shows that increased use of and interest in flexible work arrangements is an indicator of women's increased value to employers. Among female employees studied, the option of working on a reduced schedule was credited with reducing the amount of time spent on maternity leave."

### SELF-TEST:
#### *Would an Alternative Work for You?*

To evaluate how an alternative would meet your time needs, write your answers to the following questions and considerations. There are no right or wrong answers. But the thoughts you put down will help you see how this workstyle could work in your case.

1.  How could a different work structure help relieve the tension and stress of feeling you never have enough time in your current work arrangement?

_____

_____

_____

2.  In what specific ways would an alternative give you greater control over your time? List where and when you would save or gain time.

_____

_____

_____

3.  Note other positives that would apply to you.

_____

_____

_____

4.  What aspects of your present lifestyle could you cut down on (or give up) if switching to an alternative means you'll earn less money? Could you manage with a reduced income and trade off money to gain the time and flexibility fewer hours at work could afford?

_____

_____

_____

5.  What fringe benefits could you afford to lose if you shifted to an alternative that provided no benefits?

_____

_____

_____

6.  Are there ways that an alternative would force you off the career track and hold you back in your career development? If so, list them.

_____

_____

_____

7. Write down any negatives you can think of to working an alternative schedule.

_____

_____

_____

8. What support will you have at home should there be times when your alternative arrangement may be especially demanding?

_____

_____

_____

Now that you've evaluated how alternatives would affect your lifestyle, let's look at the four main options and the ways women make them work.

## (1) *W*ORKING PART TIME CAN PROVIDE FREEDOM

The number of hours of work required for part-time status varies with the organization setting the criterion.

For instance, New Ways to Work defines part time as anything less than full time. The Bureau of Labor Statistics states "less than 35 hours a week" as the standard. Catalyst indicates that companies usually require part-time professional and managerial employees to work a minimum of 20 hours a week.

In the Catalyst study the most common amount of time worked by part-time employees was three days a week, which can be set up in various ways:

- partial days from 9:00 A.M. to 1:00 P.M. five days a week
- consecutive or alternate days in which an employee might work from 9:00 A.M. to 5:00 P.M.

- a combination of full and partial days where an employee might work from 9:00 to 5:00 on Mondays and Wednesdays and from 9:00 to 1:00 on Thursdays.

## How Successful Women Make Part-Time Employment Work for Them

Pam Kriston, the time management and organizational consultant—and a woman who personifies the growing "less-is-more" lifestyle trend—chooses to work part time because she wants time to herself to explore what's important to her.

"In my entire working life I've probably done 9:00 to 5:00 for only 4 or 5 years," she says. "The values that are important to me, along with my work, are my friends, my outdoors, and nature. I like walking, cross country skiing, and spending stretches of time in the natural environment several times a week.

"If you're comfortable with part-time work and don't have to have the identity of a 9:00 to 5:00 job you can figure out ways to get along and have a *really* different kind of life.

"Because I'm single, I'm able to keep my expenses down so I don't have to work full time," she adds. "The way I've made this work is being frugal, paying off everything I owe, getting rid of credit cards (except one for emergencies) and isolating myself from the consumer loop. Eliminating these things gives you an incredible amount of more time and money."

Like Pam, Penelope Grover uses the part-time alternative to engage in activities that are important to her. But her solution is to pursue multiple part-time jobs—a work arrangement I encounter frequently.

As the mother of four children ranging from 4 to 17, Penelope is a singer/actress/and voice teacher, all on a part-time basis. Along with teaching in her home, she sings in a temple Friday nights and performs as a soloist with choral groups and orchestras. She's also an actress for A Small Company in America, a nonprofit theater company she and her husband founded and own.

"Since I'm involved in teaching, raising funds, advertising, rehearsing, and performing, it sometimes seems as though there are too many things to do," she admits. "But my interests, activities, family and friends are all integrated, so managing work and family time usually works out okay."

More and more women are choosing part-time work schedules not because they're forced to, but because they want to keep a balance between their families and their careers. "I don't work on Fridays because having time to do special things with my family is extremely important to me," says Elaine Gardner. "My husband's work enables him to care for our 7-year-old son and 4-year-old daughter four days a week, and I'm home the other three. I enjoy my work as an attorney, but I feel lucky I can work part time, so we can do many things with our children."

"I work part time because when I worked full time I constantly had the feeling I didn't want my 7-year-old and 9-year-old to miss anything because I was working." says Pat Peters. "I want to be there for my children's after-school care and transportation and for seeing they don't lose out on things—even something as simple as a birthday party."

"When my children are in school I'm at work from 9:30 to 2:30 four days a week," says Sandra Sharp. "When they have days off I juggle my free work day and vacation days. I've arranged my work/family time so that July has been a day-camp month and August is a variety of things—baby sitters at my home, one parent on vacation, and day care when necessary. We also plan our family vacations for when there is absolutely no other child care available."

## (2) FLEXTIME GIVES YOU MORE CONTROL OVER YOUR TIME

A study conducted by the Families and Work Institute shows that a flextime arrangement is a much-sought-after alternative in firms that of it.

"You're on the job a full working day," explains Linda Marks, who has worked at all the alternatives herself. "But the arrangement allows employees to choose their starting and ending time within limits set by management."

## Types of Flextime

Generally flextime allows you to come in anytime between 6:00 and
10:00 A.M. But there are variations within this alternative. They are:

*Flexitour.* You pick your hours and stick with them every day.
For instance, if you choose to come in at 7:00 A.M. then you
come in on that schedule each day.

*Gliding time.* You work a full workday, but each day you can
choose different hours to work. One morning you might come
in at 7:00 and another at 9:00—whatever works for you as long
as you work a full day.

*Variable day.* The length of your day is up to you as long as you
get your week's total hours in over a one or two week's work
period. One day you might work 10 hours, another 6.

*Maxiflextime.* Usually in a flextime schedule there are certain
core hours in which all employees must be at work. But in max-
iflex an employer may say "We're not going to have core hours
on Mondays and Fridays so you can arrange your hours with
that in mind as long as over the two-week pay period you put
in your 40 hours."

### SELF-TEST:
#### *Would Flextime Benefit You?*

Answer Yes or No on this quiz to evaluate whether a flextime arrangement
would help you manage your time better.

|  |  | Yes | No |
|---|---|---|---|
| 1. | Would flextime make your trip to work easier? | ____ | ____ |
| 2. | Would it allow you to be home with your children at the times when you're most needed there? | ____ | ____ |
| 3. | Would it put you on a schedule that would make it easier to contact people whom you need to work? | ____ | ____ |
| 4. | Would it mix-and-match well with your personal time clock and daily energy levels? | ____ | ____ |

There's no scoring on this quiz, but after you check Yes or No, think through the reasons for your answers and evaluate them in more detail. The experiences detailed by other women may help you put your reasons in place.

*Commuting Woes:* "I moved into flextime because of my commute, and the two years I've been on this schedule have been a boon to my time squeeze," says Beverly Konner, an insurance claim examiner. "The freeway I have to travel on is terribly clogged between 8:00 and 9:00 A.M. so I never used to make it to my desk on time. Now I start work at 7:00 and I'm no longer late. Another great advantage is that I can now pick up my toddler from her day care center before the freeway gets clogged again. Formerly, when I left work at 5:00 I was always tardy at the center."

*Child-care Needs:* "A baby sitter who came to my home was always my child care solution," says Sally Evans, a medical records technician. "But as soon as my son became a preteen he wanted no more of that, and we had a real problem with him. Both my husband and I were reluctant to let him be a latchkey kid, so I arranged my time with the hospital so I now go in at 6:30 A.M. and leave at the end of eight hours. In the morning my husband sees our son off to school. When the bus drops him off in the afternoon I'm arriving home."

*Client Contact:* "When my husband's firm moved from the east coast to the west coast, my agency transferred me to its San Diego office, and that was a lucky break for me," says Lucy Berns, an advertising copywriter. "But since most of my clients were still on the east coast, I ran into problems dealing with them because of the three hours' time difference. When I'd get to work at 9:00 A.M. I'd frequently need immediate information from somebody back east, but all too often the person I called had already left for lunch. That meant I was hung up waiting for facts I had to have. Now that I've switched to flextime and come in at 6:00 A.M. my east coast dealings are resolved."

*Personal time Clock:* "I'm a slow starter in the morning," admits Jane Perkins, a secondary-school textbook editor, "so pulling myself together and waiting in line to board a bus with the rest of the early commuters was an everyday hassle for me. Now I arrive at work between 10:00 and 10:30 A.M. which gets me into the office in time for late-morning meetings. I generally stay till 7:00, and I love this flextime arrangement."

# (3) *As* A TEMP, WORK WHEN AND HOW YOUR TIME PERMITS

According to Barbara Schryver, an information specialist for Manpower, the world's largest provider of temporary workers, the fast-growing temporary service industry is one of the most popular alternatives when women want to balance their work with other interests or demands and choose the time when they want to work.

Clerical work, office automation, and technical and medical jobs are the industry's largest occupational segments. However, the number of people in executive temporary jobs has more than doubled in the past few years, and a trend is emerging in which doctors, dentists, lawyers and computer specialists are hired on a temporary basis.[3]

Employers who use temporary workers pay the services directly, so when you work as a temporary employee the service pays you and handles all paperwork. However, you should review your pay stubs to make sure taxes are being deducted (if you've asked for that), so you're not faced with an unpleasant surprise at tax time.

## The Up Side of Temporary Work

- You can work while your children are in school and be free for their holiday and vacation time without being committed to a job.

- You can explore different fields and gain experience and knowledge about several before looking for permanent employment.

- You can obtain free hands-on training for office automation jobs from the services that offer that.

When Lisa Brandon, the single mother of a 5-year-old, needed a job following her divorce she knew she'd have to be computer-savvy to be part of today's business world. But she needed an immediate job so she couldn't afford the time or money to go to a computer school.

Her solution—time wise and money-wise—was a series of short-term temporary assignments and free-of-charge computer training.

"Once I got training through Manpower, I decided to work as a permanent temp," she says. "My first assignment with my new skills was to last 6 weeks. Months later I'm still on that job in a company's benefits department, and two nights a week I go to school for additional training."

"Everything works out for me because my parents pick up my daughter from school and keep her till I finish work. On the evenings I attend school till 10:00 she's bathed and ready for bed—and so fast asleep she doesn't wake up when I pick her up from my parents' house."

Lori Howard is another woman who finds temporary work a beneficial time management arrangement.

"Though I've had permanent jobs I prefer the flexibility of working as a temp," says Lori who works in different secretarial capacities for the same company and who has been a temp for 20 years.

"I like having time not only for working but also for reading, creative writing, oil painting, walking, aerobics and going to college part time," she explains. "My husband shares my interests so we often get up an hour early each morning just to read and write. Then we begin our working day with the feeling we've already had time to do something special for ourselves.

"In the future I plan to take time off to work full time toward my college degree. Temporary work allows this."

## The Down Side of Temporary Work

Though temping is the right time management arrangement for many women I speak to, others find there are disadvantages to be considered, too. Specifically:

- You may be paid a relatively low hourly rate for many of your temporary assignments.

- You may be hired for one type of position, yet find when you get to the job that you're either required to do something else or asked to work beyond the assignment.

- You may receive few or no benefits, though some of the industry leaders, like Manpower, provide health insurance.

## (4) COULD JOB SHARING FIT YOUR TIME NEEDS?

Under this time-gaining option, two people voluntarily share the responsibilities and share of one full-time position. Although the use of job sharing is growing, it's still offered sporadically because managers sometimes, mistakenly, perceive it as the most difficult form of flexible scheduling to implement.

According to research by Catalyst there are three forms of job sharing:

*Unrelated responsibility:* Two employees who perform completely separate and unrelated tasks are matched for purposes of head-count. Though job-sharers in this type of arrangement usually work in the same department, their duties bear no relationship to each other, nor do they provide backup to each other.

*Divided responsibility:* Two employees sharing one full-time position divide the responsibilities of the position, usually by project or client group. Though job-sharers in this type of arrangement perform separate tasks individually, they also provide backup for each other as required.

*Shared responsibility:* Two employees share the responsibilities for one full-time job. The two employees jointly provide the full range of services associated with the single position they fill.

## Two Women Who Benefit by Job Sharing

Anne Binford Allen and Robin Skolnick belong to the third job-sharing category as they split a job as television tape producers for NBC's "Nightly News with Tom Brokaw."

Robin, the mother of a 4-year-old daughter and 11-month-old son works Monday, Tuesday, and every other Wednesday. Anne, the mother of a 14-month-old son, works Thursday, Friday and every other Wednesday. Their days begin with a 9:30 production meeting and end at 7:00 P.M., following the 6:30 air time for the "Nightly News" show.

"It's a wonderful schedule," says Anne, "because it enables me to be completely focused on my job at work and equally focused on my home life at home."

"I also love being totally at home when I'm home and totally at work when I'm at work," adds Robin. "At work we're really 'on' when we're there. But job sharing helps you be 'on' at work because you know, in the next day or two, you'll have home time to take care of needs there. My biggest time management problem at home is keeping up with meal preparation and seeing the house stays in some kind of order—unless you want to count the workday morning when the baby stands by the bathtub throwing toys into the tub while I'm rushing through a shower to get ready for work."

Anne and Robin got into their job-sharing arrangement through their track records at NBC. Both had worked as tape producers (as well as at other jobs), and Robin had held the job they now share before they left on maternity leave. In their work they deal with the topics that will be on the air for the evening's 6:30 broadcast.

"The hours between 4:00 P.M. and the time we go off the air are the most stressful because of the frequent noteworthy news that happens late in the day," explains Anne. "Remember, for instance, the time that infamous attack and mass killing of Palestine worshippers occurred in a mosque in Hebron?

"On the night we had three interviews between 6:00 and 6:30. In addition, the lead story didn't come in till $1^1/_2$ minutes before Tom Brokaw went on the air. Everything had to be done very quickly."

On nights such as those Anne and Robin arrive home hyped up and exhausted. But in balancing their multicommitment lives they still have baby sitters to send home, babies and toddlers to feed, and dinners to fix.

"On my work days the baby has his meal and a bottle after my husband and I arrive home," says Anne. "Then we play with him till he goes to bed. Later we eat our dinner at 9:30 or 10:00.

"But at the end of every day I look at my little boy and can't imagine having a happier life. Everything is worth it. It's truly the best of both worlds."

## QUICK STARTS

Look into the benefit-package situation before you leap into the alternative of your choice. Some alternatives come with no benefits whatever. In others, health insurance (and sometimes other benefits) may be offered. For instance, a survey on Human Resource Issues and Trends conducted by The Olsten Corporation revealed that 41% of United States companies offer health-care benefits to part-time employees. Find out what you can get, when the coverage will start, and if you can be reasonably sure of not being pulled from a job before your benefits begin.

If no benefits are available, make a realistic appraisal of whether you can afford to work without them.

Come to terms with the monetary trade-off for the time-gain of working at an alternative arrangement. Once you decide to go for a reduced income, don't look back and grouse at how much more you could be making if you worked full time. Money isn't everything! Sometimes time is a better payoff.

When temporary work is your choice, (1) be specific about the type of work that interests you; (2) ask the agency to define and clarify the job for which you're hired; (3) see that that is the work you do when you go to the job; (4) take the free computer training agencies offer, and (5) stay in contact with the agency of your choice (whether you're working or not) so the agency won't forget about you and the type of work and time schedule you want.

If part time, flextime, or job sharing is your choice come up with a strong well-thought-out proposal explaining in detail how you could fill a need and the work you could do in that time frame. For a job-share, find another woman with equal skills and background—and an equal interest in and commitment to sharing a job. Point out to management how the job-share could be beneficial to the company.

Be aware of the fact that some employers assume women who choose nontraditional schedules are not as interested in career advancement as women who work 9:00 to 5:00 (and this assumption is okay to some alternative workers). But if you don't want to get off your career track and lose ground, choosing an alternative doesn't *have* to mean giving up career goals if you approach it with your goals in mind.

Speak up about your goals and let your employer know what you're accomplishing in your alternative schedule, what you're capable of accomplishing, and what you hope to achieve in your chosen work option.

Minimize possible problems with co-workers who may be jealous of your time arrangements by cultivating good relationships and being "one of them," despite your different schedules. Socialize and take your breaks at the same time they take theirs. On days when your lunch time coincides with theirs join them for an occasional lunch.

Be flexible—in return for your flexibility—when the job demands it.

 Finally, go the extra mile and expect to be highly productive in the time you are at work.

*Quick Check/Recheck* A time-wise (and timely) job choice that works for many women is an alternative to a 9:00 to 5:00 schedule. Four popular alternatives are part time, flextime, temporary work, and job sharing. All these alternatives provide time benefits and the kind of flexibility many time-pressured women would like. If you feel this flexibility would be beneficial to you—and if your answers to the *Self-Test: Would an Alternative Work for You?* support this feeling—determine which work style would be most effective. Then use this information as a first step to compiling more information on the alternative of your choice. Once you feel you've found the alternative that is right for you, go for it.

# The Mistress of Your Own Time by Working at Home

*I save an hour a day and have the flexibility to fit in my other interests and activities too."*

**—A dress designer/seamstress**

Working at home can produce extra time for you—an hour or two each work day, ten or more hours a week, or according to some women, as much as 500 hours a year.[1]

The key to success is learning to manage the intertwining time problems that arise while working at home. As Purdue University professor Barbara Rowe, who conducted a study on work-at-home business, states, "Home-based women workers are involved in more juggling, planning, and overlapping of duties than men. A woman watches children, does the laundry, and performs her job at the same time."

"Old home habits die hard," says Barbara Brabec. "Often it falls to the woman to do all the things she used to do around the house even though she now has a business there. I still have to do all the cooking, despite the fact my husband is capable of it. But it was never his job to cook just as it was never my job to mow the lawn.

When a home business comes into the picture the clearly defined lines of what each partner has done seldom change."

Because of this, the benefits of *super* time management can't be overstated. Unless you pay attention to this and implement a disciplined work-at-home regimen nothing else falls into line.

"No matter how much knowledge you have, no matter how creative you are, no matter how extensive your network of industry contacts or how much hi-tech equipment you have—it all amounts to nothing if you can't apply an effective time management regimen to make it produce," agrees Allan Cohen, an authority on working at home and publisher of "Working from Home."[2]

Of course, working at home is not an option available to every woman. But neither is it just for entrepreneurs—or mothers of young children. Overall, more than forty-three (43.2) million Americans (roughly one third of the work force) work at least part of the time from an office at home, and 12.7 are primarily self-employed, according to Link Resources Corporation, a New York research and consulting firm that conducts work-at-home surveys. Moreover, Link predicts that the home workforce will increase steadily each year.[3]

The three most common at-home situations are working full or part-time as (1) a business owner, (2) a telecommuter, or (3) an independent contractor, freelancer, or consultant. There's also a "virtual office" potential in which—if you want to put your home office on wheels—you can work in your car and come to the main office only as necessary.

## $\mathcal{Y}$OU GAIN FIVE KEY BENEFITS BY WORKING AT HOME

Over five million women across the country enjoy the varied benefits—in addition to gaining time—that working at home affords.[4] Here are five prime benefits these working women cite.

**(1) You save commuting time and eliminate the day-after-day rat race.** On a weekly basis, Mary-Lynn and Russ Willms, who gave up commuting and working in a city in favor of running an international design studio from their well-equipped electronic seaside cottage on Canada's west coast, estimate they spend at least ten more hours a week with their children now that they work at home.[5]

**(2) You don't have to maintain a dress-for-success wardrobe.** "I devote minimal hours to shopping for clothes," says Dixie Darr. "As a matter of fact, I just bought a whole wardrobe in one trip—a purple sweatsuit, a turquoise sweatsuit, and a black sweatsuit."

Barbara Doyen, a literary agent who, along with her husband-partner, works from a home office on a midwestern farm in a remote location, also clocks up extra hours because she spends minimal time on clothes, make-up, and hair.

"This is a work-at-home plus since I have to get up really early to be available for incoming business calls across several time zones from our 60 clients throughout the U.S. and abroad," she says.

To this, Joan Frangides, who once commuted to an office, adds, "I pick up time by *not* having to iron a blouse before dressing in a suit to get out of the door for work. All of this makes a huge difference in managing my time."

**(3) You can set your own time schedule.** Carol Kuhn, a regional sales manager in direct selling, was formerly an account executive for a large corporation. "But when my husband and I decided to begin a family I wanted flexible work where I could set my own schedule and gain time for family life," she explains. "Now as a regional sales manager for Lady Remington Fashion Jewelry, I have the flexibility to work around my school-age children's day."

Carol lets her answering machine record her messages in the morning while she does home chores. In the afternoon while her daughters are in school, she returns phone calls, answers voice mail messages, and schedules meetings and interviews for the prospective fashion advisors she recruits, trains, manages, and develops. At 3:30 she picks up her daughters, takes them to extracurricular activities, then helps with homework and prepares an early dinner.

"From 6:00 till midnight I go out to do home fashion jewelry shows four to six nights a week while my husband is home with the girls," she says. "The flexibility to arrange my time has made both my work and family life happy and productive."

**(4) You can be a working woman and have time to be with your children.** I'm grateful I had the satisfaction of both working and being with my children since if you miss out on those childhood years they're too soon gone forever. Ann McGee Cooper agrees with that when she talks in *Time Management for Unmanageable People* about missing the richness of this experience.

"I look at my now-grown son and deeply regret the childhood years I missed out on," she writes. "It is a precious part of my life I can never regain. It's easy for us to overlook the day-to-day treasures such as nurturing our children and mates. Then one day, we wake up and it's too late."[6]

**(5) You save money as well as time.** Dollar-wise, working away from home comes with the daily costs of transportation, tolls and parking (if you drive), lunches eaten outside of the office, gift collections for birthdays, and other miscellaneous expenses. At home you have none of these costs—except for the lunches you choose to eat out.

Generally a home office also allows for tax benefits and breaks as long as the allotted home space is used exclusively for business. Among other things you can deduct the cost of advertisements, equipment, supplies and other business expenses as well as a percentage of your annual expenses for water, electricity, home repairs, et cetera.

## SELF-TEST:
### *What's Your Success Potential for at-Home Work?*

On the opposite side from the benefits are the problems that arise if you're not a good time mistress. From a time management view, check yourself on your success potential by marking Never, Sometimes, or Always on this test.

|  | **Never** | **Sometimes** | **Always** |
|---|---|---|---|
| 1. Can you avoid the slow-start syndrome? | ___ | ___ | ___ |

|  | Never | Sometimes | Always |
|---|---|---|---|
| 2. Can you minimize procrastination throughout the day? | ____ | ____ | ____ |
| 3. Can you handle deadlines and get work out on time? | ____ | ____ | ____ |
| 4. Can you keep up with paperwork and filing? | ____ | ____ | ____ |
| 5. Can you stay on a schedule you set for yourself? | ____ | ____ | ____ |
| 6. Can you close your eyes to distractions—TV, new magazines, plants that need to be watered? | ____ | ____ | ____ |
| 7. Can you say "No" to demands on your time when appropriate? | ____ | ____ | ____ |
| 8. Can you refrain from shortchanging your work routine because of interspersing it with too much home routine? | ____ | ____ | ____ |
| 9. Can you manage both child care and your work? | ____ | ____ | ____ |
| 10. Can you call it quits at the end of your work day without feeling you should continue working since your work is only a room away? | ____ | ____ | ____ |

**Scoring:** If you have 8 or more "Always" checkmarks you're a good candidate for working at home. If the majority of checkmarks are "Sometimes" you have at least a 40/60% working-at-home success potential. If you have an abundance of "Nevers," however, think twice (and then think again) before giving up your away-from-home job.

You'll find solutions to the problems you've checked in the Nine Strategies for a Successful Work-at-Home Regimen that begins on page 131.

# OWNING YOUR OWN HOME BUSINESS MAKES TIME-SENSE

Though it admittedly has its risks and isn't for everyone, developing a business of your own makes a great deal of sense at a time when signing on for lifetime employment in a secure 9 to 5 job with a single employer is becoming obsolete. In fact, leaders like Dr. Mary Frame, the dean of Columbia College's Leadership Center for Women, doubts this old-style employment structure will ever be the prevailing way again.

But there's a positive fallout from this trend. Instead of settling for what the corporate structure dictates, we're forced to evaluate our capability for working at home in a business of our own that might be more beneficial to us in the long run.

"As a business coach, I find it makes sense for many women to be in business for themselves because of the circumstances in which they find themselves in corporate America," says Lynn McIntyre Coffee, who evaluated her own business skills and corporate experience and then started her business. In her home-based work she coaches clients from the corporate world who also want to try their skills at working for themselves.

"Except for coaching these clients for a few hours each week outside of my home office, I do the rest of my work at home," she says, "and I make it clear to my clients that I only have *specific* times available for seeing them outside of my home.

"In working at home my biggest problem is that I don't have large blocks of time for work, since I have an infant son. But I solved this by learning to do things in small segments."

"Small-segments-time" and "nibble-time" are practical and workable solutions for mothers of small children—or any other work-at-home women who also have time-consuming caretaking tasks.

## TIME BOOSTERS

- Write out a plan for your goals and note the steps you need to take to do what you want to get done. Then break up your projects into tasks you can do in small increments.

- If you have to see customers, clients, or other contacts (both inside and outside of your home office) establish definite boundaries on when you'll be available.

- Make your availability times clear to people. Then stick to those you've established since you don't have to be available all the time.

- Check your local zoning laws to be sure your type of business meets town ordinance criteria. You can waste time on later legal battles if you don't check into this first.

## TELECOMMUTING LETS YOU LIVE AND WORK ANYWHERE YOU WANT

According to Link's work-at-home survey, telecommuting is growing faster than any other form of working at home. When you're employed outside of a company's office as a telecommuter you're linked to the office electronically through computers, modems, fax machines, and advanced telecommunications and business services. Because of this electronic support, you can live and work anywhere you choose.

Some telecommuters work full time from home. Others telecommute from home one or two days a week rather than working in the company office five days. Engineers, scientists, computer programmers, teachers, managers, salesworkers, and persons in professional-specialty occupations are the most frequent telecommuters—along with information workers who comprise three-fourths of the total 7,600,000 telecommuters.

Donna Cunningham, a media relations manager for AT&T Bell Laboratories in New Jersey, telecommutes full time from her home in the remote mountains of Vermont. Her working day involves balancing half a dozen projects at once as she works with reporters around the world, exchanges electronic mail with her colleagues, prepares and distributes news releases, and flies to the company office once or twice a month.

"Prior to telecommuting I worked 9 years in the company office," she says. "But now, instead of commuting to work, I start each day with a mile-long walk to and from our mailbox. By 7:30 I'm in my office doing exactly what I did in the company office—except that I now have time to get a great deal more done.

"I don't have people trudging up the mountainside to stick their heads into my office to pass the time of day, and there are no cleaning people dumping my wastebasket and vacuuming under my feet while I'm trying to work. A power lunch is picking up a bagel and my portable phone and taking the dog for a walk in the woods."

Across the country from Donna, Jill Feldon, a public relations specialist, works in an office three days a week and telecommutes the other two days.

"This gives me more time with my 6-year-old twins," she says. "On my days at home I walk them to their bus stop. Then I start working in my office checking phone messages and E-mail as soon as I come back.

"At 9:30 I break for half an hour to volunteer at the children's school. Then as soon as I return I maintain a strict work schedule until 5:00 P.M. An au pair cares for the twins when they return from school.

"When I telecommute I still put in the same amount of work time as when I'm in the office," she adds, "but I gain time on those days because I don't have to leave home at 5:45 A.M. and commute three hours a day."

### QUICK STARTS

Get essential routine tasks off your desk early in the day because as the day progresses the pace of your electronic day will progress too.

Avoid the monotony of life at the computer by taking breaks and doing a variety of tasks through the day.

## ℰHOOSE YOUR OWN HOURS AS AN INDEPENDENT CONTRACTOR, FREELANCER, OR CONSULTANT

The Link survey indicates that about a third of all telecommuters are independent contract workers rather than regular employees.

According to the Women's Bureau of the U. S. Department of Labor, an independent contractor is a person who "exercises control over the pacing, execution, and timing of work; has the opportunity to gain or to suffer losses from her/his work; has made an investment in equipment or capital to accomplish the task; has a skill level which allows her/his competitiveness in the marketplace; and is not in an enduring or permanent relationship with the employer."

In simpler language, independent contractors (including free-lancers and consultants) are self-employed outside persons hired to do work that otherwise would be done by in-house employees. As an independent, you're paid by a contract negotiated on an hourly or piece rate or service-rendered basis, and you're paid only for the work you produce—not for any lag time between projects. Over a period of time you can have multiple contracts with different companies.

As an outside contractor, Lynn O'Connell is a fundraising specialist for nonprofit organizations. In her work she helps a variety of organizations initiate and implement such fundraising efforts as

special events, grant proposals, direct solicitations, and annual cam-
paigns. She works at home 60% of her time and travels the other 40%.

"When you work at home you save more than just commuting
and dressing-for-the-office time," she says. "It's great to just walk into
another room and start working without having to pack lunches or
other essentials, prepare the house for your departure, or have coffee and greet everyone when you arrive for work.

"Because I work at home I take time during the day to do
errands or food shopping, then, while everyone else is in cars sitting
still in the Washington, D. C. rush-hour traffic, I use that rush-hour
time to work in my office and accomplish my to-do list items."

Freelancer Lisa Rogak is a writer, editor, and publisher of
*Sticks,* a how-to-move-to-the-country newsletter—a switch she made
when she decided to combine country living with working at home.
This lifestyle/workstyle provides not only control of her time but
also the flexibility to fit in the other interests and activities so many
work-at-home women endorse as a great benefit.

"I have the hours, conveniences, and freedom for more time for
reading, playing the piano, and being outdoors," she says. "I can also
see friends during the day when I go to the town 30 miles from here
to do my research and errands. After that I work at home at night."

Judith Lederman, a public relations consultant and admitted
workaholic, puts in 12 hours daily trying to fit 60-hour weeks around
25 hours of baby sitting help. But Judith still gains time because
when she worked for a corporation she worked 12 hours a day—and
added 3 hours of commuting time getting to and from her job. She
also gains the satisfaction of having time to be with her children
since, when she works at home, her office is next to her kitchen. In
fact, her children are with her so much that her oldest son's first
word was "Fax."

"The kids are always around," she says, "and sometimes they
help out regardless of their young ages. For instance, one time
when my baby sitter cancelled at the last moment on a day when my
7-year-old son was home with a cold and my 3-week-old infant was
fussing, I had an appointment for a meeting away from home with
a new client.

"When the sitter called I had only 45 minutes before the scheduled meeting and there was no time or way to cancel it. My impromptu solution was to take my son and the baby to meet the client at a local diner.

"I put my son and the baby at one table and informed the waiter that my son had carte blanche with the menu in return for watching the baby. Then, with a professional attitude, I conducted my meeting at an adjacent table, stopping only to shoo people away when they asked my son where his mother was as he sat calmly eating by the sleeping baby. The meeting was saved, my son was fed, and my infant got her much-needed sleep."

## TIME   BOOSTER

- Develop creative skills and keep them in top shape. If your backup plans fall through—and there's no one to help in a crisis—you can swing into action on your own when you face situations such as Judith encountered. "It's easy to get stymied when a sitter cancels or a child is home from school," she says. "But you have to take charge, face the fire, put it out, and make absolutely sure people know that even in emergencies you're a professional who will give your work your attention."

# *N*INE STRATEGIES FOR A SUCCESSFUL WORK-AT-HOME REGIMEN

If you're currently working at home (or planning to in the future) take time now to refresh yourself on the 6–D System in Point 4, the 6–P Techniques in Point 5, and the daily, weekly, monthly, and long-term planning basics suggested in earlier chapters. They all will help you considerably. Then add the following strategies for managing your work time at home.

## (1) Be a Self Starter

The Slow-Start-Syndrome in the workplace discussed in an earlier section is an even greater problem when you work at home. When you have no one to crack the whip to get you started on time, it's easy to procrastinate with "waste-of-time puttering." On the other hand, "pleasurable puttering" is *not* a waste of time. Rather, it's a mini-perk that goes with working at home. As I've previously said, I can't really wait to begin my work every day. But I still regard nurturing family and friends with little things they'll enjoy a most pleasant first part of the day. Other home workers who feel this way take before-work breaks to exercise, read, fill in crossword puzzles, or do whatever starts their day in an enjoyable way. These brief interludes are all right when they're pleasures for which you allot a few moments before you get on with the job.

### QUICK STARTS

Discipline yourself to stick to the brief time frame you allot for any before-work pleasures you choose to pursue.

Reread the tips on the Slow-Start Syndrome in Point 2 and apply everything that's relevant to working at home.

Put aside all nonessential routine household chores that keep you from getting to work. No one says you must do them before you begin your *real* work.

Watch out for a slow start after lunch that stretches into an extra hour of reading, napping, watering plants, making personal phone calls, or sitting in front of TV—unless that hour is intentional and adds to instead of detracts from your work-at-home regimen.

## (2) Clarify Your Work-at-Home Goals

Make copies of the sample planning sheets in Point 3 and re-examine how women filled them out. Then fill out the sheets with your own priorities for your at-home work.

"The concept of prioritizing continues to be a viable one," stresses Dr. Larry Baker, a speaker, seminar leader and president of the Time Management Center in St. Louis. "But every activity that's important does not make an equal contribution to the results you want to achieve.

"The challenge is, first, to know and understand what's truly important, based on the results you desire, and second, to make fine distinctions between what's truly important, what's less important, and what's merely urgent."

The "important, less important, and merely urgent" is a concept that work-at-home women always bring up when they're guests on my panel discussions at workshops and seminars.

"I began yearly goal-setting when I was 9 years old," reports Lynn O'Connell. "Admittedly, it's humorous to go back and read those childhood planning lists now!

"But I've continued making them, and as an adult, I organize my goals into sections: career, social, home, financial, family, and interests. Occasionally I'll add a goal or two, rework a goal already listed, or check off a goal completed. But now that I'm in my 30s I've found my goals are less inclined to change as dramatically as they did when I was younger.

"On the 1st and 15th day of each month, I make a to-do list based upon a review of my goals. Then I block off the time on my calendar that I think I will need for each project."

## TIME BOOSTERS

- Write a brief version of your plans for your short- and long-term goals on a 4″ × 6″ index card and carry it in your purse.
- Note the results you want to attain and the "Must-Dos" you have to implement.
- Review your "Must-Dos" regularly and track how well your plans are working.
- As you accomplish old goals and plans and establish new ones make new "carrying cards."

## (3) Schedule Each Day's Work

Once you've clarified your short- and long-term goals and know your overall "Must-Dos," schedule your daily "To-Dos." Again, make copies of the sample formats for the daily planning sheet and to-do list in Point 2. Re-examine the way other working women filled in their forms. Then adapt and fill in the blank formats with your own schedule and daily goals.

"But always write your schedule in pencil and keep an eraser handy," warns Dr. Baker, "because no one's schedule ever works out exactly the way she wrote it the first time. Know when to use the eraser and change or rewrite your schedule."

## Who Says You Don't Need a Schedule!

Some women who choose to work at home have problems with the word "schedule." They say a schedule won't allow the flexible time arrangement they associate with working at home. But most at-home workers generally find it's better to have a schedule whether, as Dixie Darr points out, you're a morning person who likes to start in the wee hours and finish before lunch, a night owl who works till dawn and sleeps until noon, or someone who works a little in the morning, takes the afternoon off, and finishes up after supper.[7]

"Until I have my tasks scheduled on paper I waste time worrying about how to do it all," says Barbara Doyen. "But once everything's in writing, I can forget about the numerous to-dos and concentrate fully on each task at hand. As I schedule I pay attention to the time of day I'm most alert and energetic and do the most critical tasks for the day in those hours."

Scheduling your day with your most productive time in mind is vital for getting your prime to-dos done, because as Odette Pollar, founder of a consulting and training firm that helps business owners manage and organize time, advised in *Business Start-Ups,* "If you spend just 20 minutes per day on something that's critical, then, if your whole day goes down the tubes after that, you're still 20 minutes closer to your goals."[8]

## TIME BOOSTERS

- Identify the time of day when you do your best work and don't let any home interruptions interfere with that block of time.

- When you can't keep on schedule, due to honest-to-goodness lack of time, take an evening or weekend to catch up. Says Barbara Hemphill: "At different times in my life I've had to work what would be the equivalent of a college 'all-nighter.' I'd go into my office and do things that had been bugging me. I think you have to do that every once in a while. It's a way of clearing out the cobwebs."

### (4) Get Time on Your Side in Your Workspace

There's no one blueprint for setting up your home workspace since each woman's needs are different. But you'll get the most from your time in the office if your workspace looks professional and reflects your personality. The more satisfied you are with your surroundings the more you're likely to be productive.

To get time on your side, select a separate area in your home exclusively for your work and set it up with a desk/worktable, filing cabinet, and shelves. It doesn't matter how small it is as long as it's *yours*. One publicist I know works out of a closet that's large enough for a desk and file cabinet. A speechwriter uses her foyer as a compact, attractive, professional-looking office. Other potential workspaces are a corner of a room, basement, or attic—or an unused room, garage loft, or converted garage. For time-saving strategies to use within your workspace, refer to the sections in Point 5 for organizing your desk top and drawers, filing system, and supplies.

Whenever possible, subdivide your space to create specific locations for the various tasks you do. In my own fairly small home office I have all my computer-related equipment at one end; my desk, files, shelves, and work-in-progress worktable in the middle; and my books, research, reference material and office supplies at the other end.

Depending upon the work you do, the time-saving equipment you use may include a computer, printer, fax machine, modem, tape recorder, answering machine, copier, two telephone lines, and a Rolodex. In addition to surrounding yourself with this time-saving equipment, keep your work-in-progress projects in easily accessible spots. When you have to spend too much time pulling them together you waste time getting to work.

Jeff Berner, author of *Your Successful Home Office: Making a Life While Making a Living* suggests using inexpensive vinyl briefcases, available in blue, burgundy and black, to store papers that go with particular projects. By using this method you can save time by going right to the blue briefcases, for example, to get everything relating to a specific project quickly without having to look in a number of places to assemble what you need.[9]

Dottie Walters, a professional speaker and president of Walters International Speakers Bureau, admits her system for finding things quickly is not as sophisticated as Berner's suggestions. But, still, it saves time for her!

"I use the 'cardboard box' system," she says. "I have about 10 boxes, each labeled with a project I'm working on, a trip I'm about to make, or an upcoming speech. Folders are in each box, and on the outside is the name of the project, deadline, lists of what is done, and lists of what remains to be done. I keep adding to and checking each project till it's completed and add new boxes as new projects come in."

## T I M E   B O O S T E R S

- Re-examine everything in your home office every three months since your needs will change as your work changes and grows.

- Straighten your desk regularly by moving everything off the desk—paper stacks, in-baskets, trays, and other items, recommends Michael A. Bechtle in "Straighten Up" in *Business Start-Ups*.[10] Then place the stacks in boxes temporarily. In this way you can start with a clean slate to organize or reorganize your work.

## (5) Train Family and Friends to Respect Your Time

A major time problem in working at home is the way other people fail to take work-at-home-work as seriously as away-from-home-work. Both family and friends too often think you're always accessible simply because you're home!

"There are times when people don't believe I'm 'working' as opposed to being 'at home,'" confirms Carol Painter Campi. "The doorbell rings. Friends drop by. Or people call on my personal phone for casual conversations."

All of this strikes a familiar chord with every at-home worker whose neighbors and friends not only call with "I hate to bother you . . . but who also think *you* have the time to:

- watch for their delivery persons,
- sign for their packages, and
- take their children after school since you're "at home" and they're "at work."

Some families also tend to think that because you work at home it's easy for you to take the time to

- drop off shirts at the laundry,
- pick up the family dry cleaning,
- return books to the library,
- chauffeur the children constantly, and
- attend *every* school event.

You lose productive time when these "myths" prevail, so insulate yourself against them by implementing these tips.

## TIME BOOSTERS

- Set up strict rules for your at-home working hours.

- Explain to your friends—and people who phone—that you're unable to chat because you're involved in doing a job you have to get done right away.

- Offer to call people—or meet with them—after you finish working.

- Tape a note to your front door saying you're unavailable.

- Put a paper and pencil by the note asking people to leave their name, number, and message. Then call them back during nonwork time.

- Create boundaries for your family and let them know, too, that work time isn't family time!

- Make it clear you're not to be interrupted except for real emergencies (and occasionally a few of life's pleasures). Jeff Berner tells the story of a work-at-home mother who tamed her family's impulse to barge into her office any time by using the "only for emergencies" approach. "I instituted a strict rule that they could only interrupt me in case of an emergency," she told Berner. Then with tongue-in-cheek she defined an emergency "as something involving blood or smoke—and a lot of it."[11]

- Let your family know firmly that you're *not* going to run all the family errands just because you work at home.

- Say "Yes" to requests that steal your time *only* when they are vitally urgent and appropriate. Say "No" to all other demands that interrupt your work time.

## What Successful Women Say

"My solution for minimizing interruptions is to have a separate business line and answering machines on both the business and personal line," says Barbara Doyen.

"Just don't answer your personal phone during business hours," she advises. "I've been interrupted many times by church, school, and other organizations, and I've have to say "No" so many times they've finally quit calling and assigning me volunteer tasks during business hours. But this is a problem in a small rural town where women don't run international businesses!"

"My children know to say 'Excuse me' before they interrupt me," says Carol Kuhn, "and when I'm on the phone on a work-related call they write on a note pad what they want to tell me."

"I'm brutally honest," adds Sherry Suib Cohen. "As a result my family and friends have come to respect my time during the day as sacrosanct."

## (6) Establish the Right Balance Between Your Work and Home Life

Another problem that's *always* there when you work at home is the challenge of striking a workable balance in coordinating work and home chores. There is no single solution for how to strike the right balance, but if you let home tasks take over too much, you rob yourself of productive work time. On the other hand, if work starts to dominate all your time, you sell yourself short on the full benefits of working from your home.

Some women are able to switch back and forth and still stay on the work track. But most find they're better off setting up boundary lines.

One woman who sets clear boundaries takes herself out to breakfast (after her morning home routine) and reads her newspaper and writes up her daily schedule in a nearby coffee shop. Later she returns to her office as if it were not in her home and gets right down to work. At the end of her work day she shuts her office door, goes out for a walk or errands, and then returns to her at-home life.

Other women are able to "smart switch" without really missing a beat. Barbara Marsten, an industrial designer/fine artist, is convinced she *gains* time by working at home because she can start to work early and intersperse time at the drawing board with home chores and around-town errands.

"Since I begin work early I'm free to go out for errands, walks, research, or business appointments after 2:30," says Barbara. "Then by late afternoon I'm back home to finish home tasks and continue drawing. I enjoy both working *and* home chores so I like being able to fit in the latter because I work at home."

Like Barbara, many women who work at home mention that they like this flexibility of switching between home and work chores during the day.

"Much of the time fudging boundaries works well for me, and I'm able to bounce back and forth between my kitchen and office," says Caroline Hull, a business consultant who focuses on entrepreneurial work and publishes the journal "ConneXions. "In fact, just prior to talking to you I completed phone calls in my office and then went to the kitchen to bake some bread."

"I often switch *without* wasting time by playing little tricks or mental games," says Barbara Brabec. "In the afternoon when I want a cup of coffee while I work I put water in the microwave for the coffee and head right down to the basement to put a load of laundry in the washer. I can do this while the water is heating—and I haven't wasted time simply waiting for the water to get hot. I also do lots of interspersing between 5:00 and 6:00 P.M. Theoretically, I stop work at 5:00, but when that time comes I put the laser printer to work while I go to the kitchen to fix dinner. I don't waste time in my work day sitting and waiting for the printer, so I run back and forth after 5:00 between the computer and stove."

## Q U I C K   S T A R T S

 Determine through experience and trial and error whether you can "smart switch" between your work and home tasks or whether you need strict boundary lines.

 If you determine you're able to switch, remember the defining word is "smart."

 Keep that work in front of you as you hold back from taking time for *too much* laundry, cleaning, cooking, impromptu trips to the supermarket, and time-wasting one-at-a-time errands.

 When you're tempted to switch back and forth too much, ask and answer truthfully "Is this task something I'd be doing if I worked away from home?"

Evaluate periodically whether you've fallen into the trap of switching to too many home chores during your working hours. Make immediate adjustments if you're doing this.

## (7) Address Child-Care Issues

Even though one key at-home benefit is having more time with your children, having them and your work under one roof can be a challenging problem that's unique to home-based women. You'll probably need some child-care arrangements at least occasionally so provide for contingency helpers in case emergencies arise. Helpers to consider are baby sitters, nannies, au pairs, friends, family members, women from your temple or church, or high school or college students.

Over and above contingency planning, a more regular child-care solution can involve swapping days with other mothers, as one home-based management consultant did.

"We had three or four people, all of whom were working at home, and we rotated the kids," she said, in explaining how the group worked. "We each had the kids one day, which meant three days of freedom and one day of hell. The fifth day each week, we made other arrangements, either with relatives or by hiring someone. That saved my sanity."[12]

### What Successful Work-at-Home Women Say About Child Care

Here are other suggestions from work-at-home women who keep their children on the premises, rather than sending them to day care, preschool or a baby sitter's house.

"My solution is to hire a sitter who comes to the house at 8:30 A.M.," says Joanne Frangides. "When she arrives, I spend half an hour with her talking about by son and what has gone on since the day before. Then I go up to my office, shut the door and begin to work. When the sitter is out walking the baby I go down to the kitchen and make a sandwich to take up to the office. Usually I don't come down again until 5:00 P.M."

"My arrangement is a part-time nanny and a student-helper who comes to the house Tuesday mornings and Thursday after-noons," says Lynn McIntyre Coffee. "I also have a 13-year-old girl come twice a week from 3:30 to 5:00 to play with the baby."

"I work while the older children are in school a full day, the younger ones half a day, and the youngest at home with once-a-week child care," says Caroline Hull, who as a mother of five, suggests the following Time Boosters when your work and your children are under one roof.[13]

## T I M E    B O O S T E R S

- Along with teaching your children you can't be disturbed every 10 minutes with problems they can handle themselves, address the phone issue. A major problem can be children picking up the phone in the middle of a business call and giggling.

- Schedule important business calls during your children's nap time or when they're settled for a while in front of TV.

- Since time management can be particularly hard during the summer months, start planning your summer workload and child-care arrangements early. If you have grade schoolers, check into available summer camp programs. Ask the school, your neighbors, and local child-care providers about other potential activities.

- Be prepared to change your work schedule and hours during the summer so you can spend the time with the children. Make time for enjoyable hours at the pool or in other activities by getting up an hour earlier to work or going to bed an hour later.

- Get your children involved in your work. When I wrote a syndicated newspaper column while my children were young I got tons of daily reader mail requesting brochures and pamphlets. I'd sort the mail and spread it out on my living room floor. Then the children would stuff and seal envelopes "Getting your children involved allows them to feel they're contributing to the business at the same time it helps you," says Caroline Hull. "Besides, it's kind of nice to have them around. My younger children handle stamping and labeling while my older son alphabetizes material."

## (8) Hire Help When You Need It

In addition to child-care help, it pays to hire other help to whom you can delegate some home tasks that take time you could use for work. But according to Coralee Smith Kern, a consultant to home-based business owners and executive director of the National Association for the Cottage Industry, women in a home business don't always hire or get extra help in the same way men in home businesses do.

This is time-foolish for women, so here are some ways to solve this problem.

### QUICK STARTS

Have someone who wants to also work at home come to your home once a week to pick up a batch of work to take home to do. (This system works effectively for me.)

Line up someone to come to your workplace to work in a separate room making and fielding phone calls, filing, and doing work you assign. (I also use this system at times.)

Hire a word-processing person to sit at your computer while you dictate rough or final drafts of correspondence, reports, proposals, and so one.

Employ household helpers for home chores that take too much of your time. Even once a month is a help if your finances are limited. Consider this a gift to yourself. You've earned it. You work hard.

## What Successful Women Say About Hiring Help

"Don't hesitate to hire assistance if it's cost-effective for you," advises Barbara Doyen. "I have a cleaning lady who comes in one day a week. She's well worth the money I pay her since it frees me to accomplish more in the office."

"I buy both cleaning and lawn services—and I'll spend money on buying time before I spend it on anything else," says Lynn

McIntyre Coffee. "I'm also not afraid to ask people who work for me to help in a variety of ways. Along with watching the baby, my nanny helps with office work, cleans up the kitchen, makes the bed and does laundry. The 13-year-old who comes in from 3:30 to 5:00 to play with the baby often walks the dog and prepares a salad for our dinner."

## When You Can't Afford to Pay for Help

When you're short on money as well as time, try finding another home-based woman who'd like to swap chores or services—or babysit while you work—if you do the same for her. Here are a few examples:

- A woman who runs a dried flower business (and hates spending time keeping books) decorates a home-based accountant's office with seasonal dried arrangements in exchange for quarterly bookkeeping services.

- An exercise instructor who does personal training in a basement in her home, coaches the owner of a nurses' registry in return for part-time home-health care for her mother.

- A graphic designer takes care of her own children, along with her neighbor's two girls, every Monday and Tuesday. The neighbor, a jewelry designer, babysits Wednesday and Thursday. On Friday, they both have outside child-care arrangements. This schedule gives both the designers three child-free days to spend full time on their work.

- The owner of a secretarial service and the owner of a bridal shop save an hour a day during summer vacations by alternating driving their children to summer activities. One takes morning duty, the other picks up the children in the afternoon.

## (9) Know When to Stop Working and End Your Day

A special time problem for work-at-home women is a tendency to continue to work beyond their schedules hours because there's always work to do that's only a room away. In fact, most report they continue working when they *wouldn't* thinking of working that long at jobs away from their homes.

## What Successful Work-at-Home Women Say About Working Overtime

"When you're working at home you can jump onto the computer any time of day or night and lose yourself in what you're doing," says Carol Painter Camper. "I would never work until 11:00 P.M. or later if I were at any office away from home, if for no other reason than security or safety."

"I didn't think about work so much when I worked for someone else," agrees Mary Flood. "My office is up a staircase and visually separate from my home, but mentally it's difficult to leave it."

"If I get up at 3:00 A.M. to get a glass of water the computer may beckon to me," admits Judith Lederman. "I find myself playing catch-up when I should be eating, sleeping, or recreating."

"I'm still working on keeping my business life and my private life separate," concludes Barbara Doyen. "But I'm learning to let the answering machine handle calls past normal business hours and I'm going to *make* myself take Sundays off and quit working into the evenings."

### TIME   BOOSTERS

- Refer to the "Pack-It-In-At-the-End-of-the-Day" section in Point 5 and apply the relevant guidelines to working at home.

- Learn to live with the fact that when your work is close at hand there will always be work you feel you *should* continue to do. Then put this in perspective and discipline yourself to end your day, just as you discipline yourself to start it.

- Except for occasional periods when your workload is especially heavy, close the door on the "always there" work without feeling any more guilty than you'd feel if you worked outside of your home.

- Finally, follow the advice of Marcia Yudkin who says: "Know your limits. Learn to recognize and respect the signals that tell you you've done enough for the day. That helps you accomplish more the following day and avoids three humongous time wasters: burnout, sickness, and exhaustion."[14]

***Quick Check/Recheck*** Although working at home is not an option for every working woman, it's becoming an option for many since more than forty-three (43.2) million Americans work at least part of the time from an office in their home. The home-based arrangements they pursue are working full- or part-time as a (1) business owner, (2) telecommuter, or (3) independent contractor, freelancer, or consultant. You can gain time through these arrangements and achieve many benefits when you successfully juggle the intertwining time problems that arise while working at home. The way to do this is to have a workplace of your own set up to save time; schedules and goals you adhere to; and understanding with your family and friends that you're not always accessible for everything and anything; and a good understanding yourself of how to establish the right balance between your work and home life.

# PART TWO

# MANAGING YOUR TIME AWAY FROM THE JOB:
*A 3-Point Program for Dawn-to-Dusk and Beyond*

# Balance the Work/Home Time Crunch and Feel Good About Yourself

*I'm stressed out to the max, but I can't imagine life any other way.*
**—A book editor**

Most working women don't start their day at an arbitrary 9:00 A.M. and stop when 5 o'clock rolls around. For many, a hectic schedule begins as soon as the clock strikes 6:00 A.M. and doesn't come to a halt until the children are asleep and the dinner dishes are cleared away, whatever time that might be.

In a *Reader's Digest* article, "How to Unlock Time," Ralph Keyes tells of a copywriter and mother of two who compares her life to riding a wave, in which she jumps on the surfboard at 6:00 A.M. and washes up on the beach at 10:00 P.M.[1] All over the country women know exactly how this woman feels as they work their way through everything that they have to do.

# $\mathcal{W}$HERE DOES THE TIME GO?

According to a Report on Women prepared by the Roper Organization for the Prodigy Services Company, the women most likely to feel time-starved are working mothers in their 30s and early 40s. Regardless of their age, income, or marital status, they're more likely than men to feel short of time consistently.[2]

Another survey—conducted by Priority Management Systems, Inc. on time and value conflicts—found that working women are more concerned than men about taking time for community affairs, social activities, and spiritual matters. They also care more about spending time with parents. In fact, this survey showed women spend almost three times as much of their day as men do on caring for parents.[3] In addition, Harvard professor Juliet Schor, author of *The Overworked American,* has determined that working women who are also mothers average more than 80 hours a week on their jobs, housework, and child care.

Even children are aware of women's time crunch. A national survey of school-aged children released by Massachusetts Mutual Life Insurance Co. found that almost two out of three children— 65%—said it's their mother who cares for them when they're sick; 83% reported their mother usually prepares their meals, and 78% said she does the laundry.[4]

## Gaining the Best of Both Worlds

Even though they have too much to do and too little time to do it, most working women, with the right time management, do well with their multiple commitments. In fact, a Cornell University sociologist, Elaine Wethington, has found that in many ways the average working mother is doing better at living a balanced and fulfilling life than the average woman who does not work in the labor force. Moreover, a poll which *Working Mother* magazine commissioned from the Gallup Organization found women who combine work and home responsibilities feel good about themselves.[5]

These studies—along with my personal research—convince me that, despite time-crunch problems, most women today need and want the full life of both working and taking care of their families. And most of them tell me repeatedly that regardless of how work-oriented they are, they wouldn't be happy without the balance between their jobs and their merry-go-round home life.

"My husband and I both enjoy our kids so much we want to do the parenting and caretaking along with our other work," says Annie Byerly, a full-time kindergarten teacher whose husband, a screen writer, takes care of their daughters till Annie gets home. Then they switch their roles.

In an Associated Press article "Working Hard and Loving It," Lisa Genasci cites the story of another working mother—the book editor mentioned earlier—who after getting up at 6:45 A.M., caring for her two young children till the nanny takes over, catching the 8:07 A.M. train to work, and returning $10^{1}/_{2}$ hours later for her after-work hours can't imagine life any other way.[6]

If your idea of the good life is working and feathering your nest (or if you *have* to do both whether you like it or not) here are day-to-day tips on how to transfer the time-saving skills you learned in the on-the-job section to your life at home. You'll see how successful women balance their lives, and you'll get to view the real-life home schedules of many of them.

## TAKE CONTROL OF YOUR MORNING AND THE WHOLE DAY GOES MORE SMOOTHLY

Most women feel that mornings are *the* biggest challenge and problem of the day. To find out what your problems are, evaluate yourself with this checklist.

## SELF-TEST:
### *What's Your Biggest Morning Problem?*

Circle the appropriate number for each task. **3** = a constant problem; **2** = sometimes a problem; **1** = usually not a problem.

| | | | |
|---|---|---|---|
| Fixing and eating breakfast | 3 | 2 | 1 |
| Cleaning up from breakfast | 3 | 2 | 1 |
| Making beds | 3 | 2 | 1 |
| Preparing lunches (if not done the previous evening) | 3 | 2 | 1 |
| Getting everyone dressed | 3 | 2 | 1 |
| Coping with children who dawdle | 3 | 2 | 1 |
| Handling children who fake an illness so they can stay home from school | 3 | 2 | 1 |
| Switching child-care gears when children wake up *genuinely* ill | 3 | 2 | 1 |
| Feeding pets and walking dogs | 3 | 2 | 1 |
| Handling elder-care responsibilities | 3 | 2 | 1 |
| Doing last-minute arranging on who's going where | 3 | 2 | 1 |
| Finding misplaced things that are needed for the day | 3 | 2 | 1 |
| Driving children to school, day care, or a sitter's | 3 | 2 | 1 |

**Scoring:** Take a paper and set up three sections. Under each number write the tasks you circled for that numeral.

**3s**

_____

_____

_____

_____

_____

**2s**

_____

_____

_____

_____

_____

**1s**

_____

_____

_____

_____

_____

Now that you've completed this test you can see your greatest problem areas clearly. Here are Quick Starts to help you solve your morning problems. All may not work in your particular situation since every home is different, but give each one a try. They're all strategies that can help you gain control of your mornings and start your day on automatic pilot. Moreover, they'll benefit *everybody* as you'll leave for work with less hassle and your family will start their day's routine with a smoother beginning.

## QUICK STARTS

Establish a workable morning routine and—except for dire emergencies—stick to it. You be the boss! Appoint everyone else to be assistants who help implement your routine.

Set your alarm clock for an hour earlier than necessary. Then get up when it goes off. You'll gain an hour for yourself to prepare for the day in peace before the turmoil begins. This one-hour jump on the day can be worth more than two or three hours of fractured time later on.

 Sneak out of bed and tiptoe your way to the kitchen so children and/or elders who depend on you will think you're still sleeping.

 Rely on easy-to-fix, easy-to-eat, and easy-to-clean-up nutritional breakfasts. Hot instant oatmeal and cold cereals with bananas or other fruits are easy. So are frozen French toast, pancakes, or waffles that you pop in the toaster and serve with applesauce, berries, or cinnamon.

 Make a rule that all family members put their own dishes in the dishwasher.

 Divide bed making between adults in the house or have your husband/partner make beds while you do kitchen duty.

 Enforce a rule that older children don't leave their rooms till they hang up their clothes and make their beds.

 Prepare lunches (if you don't do it the evening before).

 Establish a system for getting everyone dressed. Older children can dress themselves and help the younger ones. Or, your husband/partner can dress small children while you do something else. (For variety, alternate these types of tasks.)

Feed pets and/or walk the dog. If you live alone you have to walk the dog yourself so make this an enjoyable break rather than a one-extra-thing-to-do hassle. If you live with other people have everyone who's old enough take regular turns walking the dog.

Steel yourself to cope with children who dawdle. When my children were small I cut down on dawdling time by filling a glass with x-number of dimes for each child at the start of each week. Throughout the week I removed a dime from each child's glass whenever that particular child held up the morning routine. At the end of the week what was left in the glass became the child's allowance. This motivated the children and saved time for me.

Brace yourself to act firmly and quickly when children fake an illness so they can stay home from school. Go with your gut reaction on whether it's fake or real, and if you're fairly sure it's fake send the child to school and go off to work yourself. You won't be the first working mother to get a phone call from the school that your child *is* really sick, and then to be chastised by the school nurse with "He said he told you he didn't feel well but you made him come to school anyway." Slough off the nurse's comment—and have plans in place for picking up your child and caring for him for the day.

Be prepared with your contingency child-care plans for *real* sick days when a child wakes up genuinely ill, the baby-sitter calls in sick, or the day-care center or school is closed unexpectedly. (See section on contingency plans in Point 5.)

Do a before-the-last-minute check to be sure clothing, knapsacks, homework, keys, your purse, and everything else people need for the day have been put by the door through which you leave.

Have all chauffeuring plans set up for the day. Know who is going where and when—and who is doing the driving.

Allow a little leeway in your morning routine for the inevitable time-losing problems that are bound to occur. A diaper may have to be changed. A live-in elderly parent may require unplanned attention.

## How Four Successful Women Schedule Their Mornings

Here are real-life schedules from four working women.

*Grace Mastalli:* (1 child, single parent)

| | |
|---|---|
| 6:15 to 8:30 A.M. | Rise. Listen to news while showering. Dress in sweats to play with son. Wake Luke, change diaper, and play with him for an hour. Fix breakfast. Feed Luke and self while reading paper and making necessary phone calls. Visit with 85-year-old live-in mother. Empty dishwasher with Luke's help. Change into work clothes. Log onto computer to read and return E-mail while waiting for baby-sitter. |
| 8:45 | Leave for work. Use cellular phone for calls while driving. |

*Eileen Gardner:* (3 children)

| | |
|---|---|
| 6:30 A.M. | Husband gets up and brings me coffee. |
| 6:45 | Get up, bathe, and dress. |
| 7:30 to 8:00 | Wake kids. Get everyone's breakfast. Husband leaves for work. Make lunches. Start load of laundry. |
| 8:00 to 8:15 | Run around and scream a lot. Look for shoes. Make idle threats! |
| 8:20 | Kids to bus. My youngest and I leave for my office. She stays with me till it's time to drive her to baby-sitter's. After driving her to sitter's back to work. |

*Wendy Dixon:* (2 children)

| | |
|---|---|
| 6:00 A.M. | Rise. |
| 6:00 to 6:30 | Walk. |
| 6:30 to 7:00 | Snuggle with children. |
| 7:00 to 7:30 | Everyone gets dressed. |
| 7:30 to 8:00 | Breakfast. |
| 8:00 to 8:15 | My husband or I make lunches. |
| 8:15 to 8:30 | Coats, boots, hats, backpacks, and into car. |
| 8:30 to 8:50 | Drive kids to school and me to work. |
| 8:50 | Start work in shop. |

*Ruthanne Ciotti, co-owner of an aircraft charter and management company:* (2 children)

| | |
|---|---|
| 5:00 A.M. | Rise. |
| 5:15 | Rowing and calisthenics. |
| 5:30 | Start preparing breakfasts and lunches. Take something for dinner from freezer or start preparing dinner. |
| 6:00 | Shower. |
| 6:15 to 7:15 | Family awakens. Breakfast. While children eat I do my make-up and dry my hair. I make children's beds. My husband makes our bed. My husband gets our son dressed, and I give our daughter any help she needs. |
| 7:15 to 7:30 | Leave house and take son to day care. |
| 8:00 | Start work. |

## Plan Your Own Morning Schedule for
## Top Time-Saving Results

Copy and fill out this form for yourself, using the foregoing schedules as guides. Keep working and reworking the schedule till it puts you on automatic pilot.

6:00    _____

        _____

6:30    _____

        _____

        _____

7:00    _____

        _____

        _____

7:30    _____

        _____

        _____

8:00    _____

        _____

        _____

8:30    _____

        _____

        _____

9:00    _____

        _____

        _____

# $\mathscr{E}$ASE THE TRANSITION FROM WORK TO HOME

In Point 5 you received transition tips for switching from job to home. Here are more ways to handle this potentially stressful daily situation and keep it from getting you down.

As one solution, Dr. Ron Taffel, a psychologist and the author of "Parenting by Heart," tells the story in *The New York Times* of a mother who eased her coming-home transition by retraining her family.

"Before, when I came home everyone yelled 'What's for dinner?' before I took off my coat," reported this mother. "Now they have to ask 'How was Mom's day?' I don't do as much yelling and screaming."[7]

Other women hit the ground running when they arrive at home. If they're like Lois Kohan, a public-health nurse with five children, they make the transition a happy-action time.

"When I come home, I'm usually involved with my small children immediately," says Lois. "They have a snack, and then because they're all athletes, it's time for Mom's Taxi Run. I squeeze in making dinner—a little here and a little there—and put it on the stove for the varied times my family has dinner. Because of all the different ages, hours, and schedules in our home, we can't all sit down and eat together, so I'm busy from when I arrive home until late at night."

## What Successful Women Say About Transition Time

"When I commuted to a job, my transition system was to pick a focal point midway between my home and office, and at that point, switch from one role to the other," says Judith Lederman. "My focal point was a big tree. When I passed that tree on my way home at night, I'd dump my work problems at the tree and go back to being a mom. Whether you use a tree, building, or anything else, a focal point can help you separate the working woman from the mom."

"I grew up on a small farm where the women worked beside the men," explains Yvonne Conway, a licensed hair stylist who takes her mobile services to private homes and institutions. "As my dad taught me how to work, he'd say 'You can last for hours if you pace yourself, keep a consistent pace, and rest when your wheelbarrow is empty—or when you're going down hill.' I've always followed this advice so on my drive home from work, I pretend my wheelbarrow is empty or that I'm going down hill."

"Try keeping a battery-operated tape recorder beside you as a transitional technique if you use your drive home to sort out after-work tasks," suggests Andrea Engber, president of an advertising and creative design agency, director of the National Organization of Single Mothers and editor of *SingleMOTHER.*

"Driving in heavy traffic is certainly not the time to risk jotting down reminders to deposit checks or stop for dog food," Andrea says, "so I record things as they come to me. I also enlist the aid of my son who's riding with me to record meal planning, Cub Scout meetings and ball practice."

## TIME  BOOSTERS

- Follow Judith Lederman's example and pick a focal point for switching from your work to home role.

- Coordinate your small errands so that each day you make one stop on the way home instead of running hither and yon and losing time in the rush.

- If you pick up children, consider the drive home to be a beneficial time-out with them. If you meet them head-on when you get home, spend some unhurried time chatting while you change from your suit to sweats. Or share a healthy snack while they talk about their day.

- If you have no child-care responsibilities, reconnect with yourself for 15 minutes. Play with a pet, read, turn on the news, sip a cup of tea, organize yourself for the evening, or relax and do nothing at all.

# MAKE YOUR EVENING HOURS PRODUCTIVE AND ENJOYABLE

The after-dinner part of your day may be taken up with home chores, children's bedtime, and, maybe, catch-up work for your job. One word of advice: avoid the latter whenever you can. Your evenings belong to you.

**SELF-TEST:**
*How Is Your Evening Time Management?*

Answer "Yes" or "No" to each question.

|  | | Yes | No |
|---|---|---|---|
| 1. | Do you preplan your morning as much as possible? | ____ | ____ |
| 2. | Do you listen to the next day's weather report so you can choose appropriate clothes? | ____ | ____ |
| 3. | Do you lay out your children's and your clothes so you won't have to think about them in the morning? | ____ | ____ |
| 4. | Do you examine clothes for stains, missing buttons, loose hems, etc., to eliminate unwelcome A.M. delays? | ____ | ____ |
| 5. | Do you do any necessary lunch preparation at night if your children take, rather than buy, lunches? | ____ | ____ |
| 6. | Do you make sure older children pack their knapsacks and organize their homework before they go to bed? | ____ | ____ |
| 7. | Do you put your purse and everything you need to take with you in the morning in a strategic location by the door through which you leave? | ____ | ____ |
| 8. | Do you set the table for breakfast and put the coffee in the pot so it's ready to turn on? | ____ | ____ |
| 9. | Do you arrange for any anticipated variation in your morning routine in the evening instead of waiting for it to happen in the morning? | ____ | ____ |
| 10. | Do you include some beneficial fun and pleasure in your evenings? | ____ | ____ |
| | **TOTALS** | ____ | ____ |

**Scoring:**   8 to 10 Yes answers:        You have a good handle on your
                                          evening time management.

               5 to 7 Yes answers:        You're headed in the right direc-
                                          tion but you can take better
                                          charge of your after-dinner time.

               1 to 4 Yes answers:        You can't even hope to set yourself
                                          up for automatic pilot in the
                                          morning.

Here are Time Boosters to help you manage your evenings in beneficial ways, regardless of how well or badly you scored. There's *always* room for improvement!

## TIME   BOOSTERS

- Make two or three days' worth of sandwiches in one evening and freeze them (except for mayonnaise or other condiments which you can add at the last moment).

- Let your children make their own lunches, if they're old enough.

- Have one drawer or shelf in your kitchen set up with everything you need for lunch preparation—sandwich bags, spreaders, plastic cutlery, plastic containers, paper napkins, and single-serving packages of healthy snacks.

- Put money for a week of school lunches and expenses in a special envelope in a kitchen cabinet.

- Place change or tokens for buses, tolls, and parking meters in another envelope.

- See that hats, mittens, scarves, and boots are in easily accessible baskets—and have your family put them in the right baskets as soon as they take them off at the end of the day.

- Hang your car and house keys on a prominent hook reserved especially for them.

- Buy an umbrella stand and keep all umbrellas by the door for quick access when you leave home in the morning.

- Make bath-time and story-time with your children a special bedtime ritual instead of a "hurry-up time."

- Help with homework as necessary but don't get too involved. Research has shown that homework can help teach a child time management, so save *your* time and help your children learn how to manage *their* time by not overdoing homework help.

- Keep up with house chores by scheduling just *one* necessary extra task beyond your regular routine per evening rather than jamming *everything* you need to do into one or two evenings.

- Use discretion in taking on too many outside activities on your Monday-through-Friday nights. Enroll in a course. Do volunteer work. Spend time with friends—or whatever. But since you can't do everything, it's usually good time management to limit activities to one or two times a week.

- Retire at least half an hour after everyone else goes to bed. This will give you an end-of-the day breather for yourself.

- Avoid going to bed with your head full of problems.

- Enjoy yourself—and your life!

---

## What Successful Women Say About Evening Hours

"Our ongoing dinnertime is a big part of my evening," says Lois Kohan, who definitely enjoys her life and family and feels good about her work/home balance. "I feed the younger children at 7:00 or 8:00 P.M. when they come home from their athletic events. Then the older ones help themselves to the dinner I leave on the stove. I wait till 9:30 or 10:00 to eat with my husband since he works long hours. Later, after the younger children are in bed my husband and I walk a couple of miles."

"Watch out for the lure of television as a steady thing," warns Yvonne Conway. "It's easy to think you'll just watch one show. But all too often you slip into the routine of watching two, three or more shows until the whole evening is gone. On my daily schedule I check off the TV I'm going to watch and limit myself to no more than one hour per evening."

"When I worked long hours at the office, my husband and I made it a point that both of us would not go out on a week night," says Gail Stewart Hand. "We felt we had too little time with our children, so if we had a meeting or an engagement that we couldn't escape only one of us would attend. The children always had time with one of us at home at night."

"I believe in allowing sufficient time for bedtime talk, reinforcement, and prayers," advises Dr. Maureen Powers, a holistic practitioner and naturopath. "Once my children are tucked in they're 'reinforced' after prayers as they say 'I'm happy, healthy and terrific! I expect the best and I get the best because I do my best.' This is a powerful time for us."

## How Five Successful Women Schedule Their After-Work Hours

Here are schedules from a variety of women. Some listed times on their schedules. Others lumped their evenings together. Look for tips that could benefit you.

*Grace Mastalli:*

| | |
|---|---|
| 7:45 to 8:15 P.M. | Drive home, stopping enroute to pick up necessary items for my son and mother. |
| 8:15 to 9:00 | Chat with mother. Decompress. Change clothes. Play with Luke. Fix dinner and feed Luke bedtime snack while eating my dinner. Read to Luke and put him to bed. |
| 9:00 to 9:30 | Relax. Monitor a TV program. Run dishwasher. |
| 9:30 to 11:30 | Read mail and material brought home from office. Check E-mail message and watch TV and news. Check on Luke, my mother, and our animals. Have tea and cookies. Read chapter of a novel and pull everything together for morning. |

*Eileen Gardner:*

| | |
|---|---|
| 4:45 to 5:00 P.M. | Leave work and drive to baby-sitter's to pick up daughter. |
| 5:15 to 6:00 | Drive to kids' afterschool programs and pick them up. On some days my husband picks them up and starts them on their homework. |

| | |
|---|---|
| 6:15 to 7:15 | Make dinner and eat. |
| 7:15 to 8:45 | Kids' homework and piano practice. Laundry or house chores while husband does dishes. |
| 8:45 to 9:00 | Older kids' baths and to bed. |
| 9:00 to 9:45 | Miscellaneous chores. |
| 9:45 to 10:15 | Set up coffee for morning while husband feeds dog. Get youngest daughter ready for bed. (She goes to bed late because of her schedule during the day.) Husband reads to her while I finish chores. |
| 10:30 to 10:45 | Retire and read a while. |

*Judith Moncrieff Baldwin:* (no children)

| | |
|---|---|
| 6:00 P.M. | Husband meets me at my office. Dine on way home/or go home for dinner. If eating in, fix dinner. While dinner is heating, my husband and I relax, talk, and catch up. |
| | Do dishes, feed cats. |
| | Sort mail. Check answering machine. Exercise. Read. Watch TV. See friends or have friends over. |
| | Retire. |

*Marie Dolce:* (single, no children)

| | | |
|---|---|---|
| 4:00 P.M. | Complete my list of sewing jobs for the day. | |
| 4:00 to 5:00 | Swim or relax and read. | |
| 5:00 to 6:00 | Prepare dinner or go out with friends. | |
| Weeknight Evenings: | Monday: | Singing group |
| | Tuesday: | Bowling |
| | Wednesday: | Fittings or consultations for bridal parties |

*Marie Dolce:* (single, no children) *(cont'd.)*

|            |                    |
|------------|--------------------|
| Thursday:  | Same as Wednesday  |
| Friday:    | Bowling            |

*Vicky Penner Katz, director of news services for a state university:* (married, no children)

On return home
from work:           Let dogs out.

                     Make and serve dinner.

                     Clean up dishes.

                     Play with computer.

                     Do crossword puzzle.

                     Watch David Letterman.

                     Collapse and go to bed.

## SET UP YOUR AFTER-WORK SCHEDULE FOR TIME-SAVING AND FUN

Adapt the foregoing schedules (and Time Boosters) to your after-work needs and fill in each hour below.

5:00 P.M.    _____

             _____

             _____


6:00         _____

             _____

             _____


7:00         _____

             _____

             _____

8:00 _____

_____

_____

9:00 _____

_____

_____

10:00 _____

_____

_____

11:00 _____

_____

_____

## HOW CAN YOU IMPROVE YOUR AFTER-WORK TIME MANAGEMENT?

After you fill out your schedule evaluate what you write and list five things that you could do to take better charge of your after-work time.

1. _____
2. _____
3. _____
4. _____
5. _____

***Quick Check/Recheck*** Determine where your hours go before and after work so you can balance the work/home time crunch and feel good about yourself. Despite your time-crunch problems, most women need and want the full life of working and feathering a nest. Even though there's too much to do and too little time to do it, working women manage to do this often better than women who aren't in the labor force. The secret of managing off-work time effectively is starting your day on automatic pilot, making your end-of-the-day transition from your job to your home a positive rather than a negative time, and then taking charge of your evenings so that they give you pleasure and enjoyment along with benefiting you timewise.

# Make Home-Sweet-Home Life Sweeter with a 7-Step Time-Gaining Plan

*A great time gainer is not being stressed when you can't do everything.*
**—An assistant buyer**

I'll never forget what my husband said when I phoned to tell him I'd just been hired to write a column offering tips for working women who wanted to progress.

It had become a family joke that my idea of progressing was putting my writing first every day—while leaving the dishes in the sink and the beds unmade till noon.

So what was my husband's comment when he heard about the syndicated column?

"Now you'll tell women *everywhere* to stop doing dishes and beds!" he said.

Of course, I never offered that kind of wrongheaded advice, since I *believe* in doing dishes and beds at some point every day. And I *believe* that maintaining home and family life on an even keel gives women more time to be more effective in their jobs and careers.

In our time-locked lives, however, we too often feel there's too little time for our home and family life. A survey by Priority Management Systems found that married women with children want almost one hour more each day to spend with their spouse and children.[1] The Prodigy Services Company Report on Women found that 66% of women between ages 30 and 44 (vs. 62% of men) say they have too little time. From age 45 to 59, time-squeezed women outnumber men by 55% to 41%, and among two-earner married couples, the perception gap is even more striking.[2]

The following 7-Step Time-Gaining Plan will help you:

1. streamline your daily home care,

2. avoid getting stressed when you can't stretch your time to get everything done every day

3. give first-things-first attention to the things that really matter.

## STEP 1: PUT YOUR CHILDREN AHEAD OF HOUSE CHORES

Forget the false perception that your house ought to be as squeaky-clean as your mother's was and use the hours you don't spend on housecleaning for gained time with your children. This will pay long-lasting benefits. After the children are grown and gone away you can always do the house!

### What Successful Women Say About Housework

"Spending time with my family is more important than frustrating myself with household chores," says Ruthanne Ciotti. "Certain things just don't need to get done. It's not that important to do them."

"My son is my top priority," stresses Grace Mastalli. "At the expense of everything else on the homefront, I protect my time with him for breakfast, a late dinner, and a bedtime routine of stories and prayer."

"If choosing to spend time tossing a ball with your son or daughter means not mopping the kitchen floor this weekend, so be it," advises Ann McGee-Cooper. "In the long term, a happy relationship with your children is far more valuable than a clean floor."[3]

## TIME BOOSTERS

- Realize that even though children need plenty of time in their early years for their physical care, they'll need even more in later years for the strong emotional and intellectual support that will see them through school and social issues.

- While your children are young, put your fragile stuff away. "This will make cleaning faster and give you less to dust," advises Kim Bushaw, a family educator who runs a telephone question service called *Parentline.* "You don't need a museum atmosphere and a house so full of irreplaceable things that you end up yelling at your children when they bump into them."[4]

- Similarly, cut down on extraneous furnishings and material possessions that require too much caretaking time. It's not important to be seen by the world in terms of what you own. When you opt for fewer possessions, you gain time for your children that you'd use to take care of possessions.

# *S*TEP 2: STREAMLINE YOUR GROOMING AND DRESSING

There's no getting around taking time in your home life to keep on top of your grooming and clothes, since looking good when you go to your job is a "Must" in your daily schedule. It's even important when you work at home because you feel and work better when you look your best in your work sweats and jeans.

Just because grooming and clothes are daily necessities, however, doesn't mean that these concerns have to take an excessive amount of your time. There are ways to streamline the process, leaving you more time to handle other critical tasks.

## Q U I C K    S T A R T S
## F O R    G R O O M I N G

1.  Speed up your day-to-day grooming by placing all your hair, skin, and make-up supplies on a convenient and accessible tray. In this way you won't lose time digging for supplies.

2.  Program your morning routine so you can do your hair in 10 minutes and your make-up in another 10.

3.  Choose a short or easy-to-handle hairdo that you can manage in the allotted 10 minutes. If you want long hair, save time by wearing it up or tied back when you're in a rush to get out to work.

4.  Use the less-is-more technique for your make-up routine—a quick splash of cold water, minimal moisturizer and foundation, blusher, loose powder, eye shadow, mascara—and, finally, a good lipstick job.

5.  Take 10 minutes at the end of the day to remove your make-up. I doubt there's a woman anywhere who hasn't succumbed to collapsing in bed without taking time to do this at the close of a tiring day. But you save yourself time in the morning if you spread a moisturizing cleanser on your face for one minute a night, remove it with a damp lukewarm washcloth, and splash your face with cold water again.

## How to Organize for Fast Dressing

Take a cue from Ruth Ann Gates, who dresses at 8:30 A.M. (after exercising, showering, and doing chores), eats breakfast 20 minutes later, and leaves for work at 9:10 A.M. sporting the grooming and high-fashion look her job in retailing demands. "I've trained myself to be a fast dresser," she says, "and I have everything in order to do it."

## Q U I C K    S T A R T S
## F O R    D R E S S I N G

 Hang your clothes in categories so you can find what you want quickly.

 Arrange suits with suits, blazers with blazers, pants with pants, skirts with skirts, and tops with tops.

Rotate your suits and accessories from the back to the front (or left to right) of your closet so whatever you wore most recently is in back.

 Store summer and winter clothes in separate closets if you have space. This will save you the time of changing closets.

 Build your wardrobe on one or two main colors so you can match your accessories and clothes quickly.

 Stick to shoes, bags, and accessories in basic colors that will go with your main colors. "I no longer match shoes, handbags, and clothes," says Grace Mastalli. "Instead I wear the same black, brown, and taupe colors in winter and use taupe for summer."

 Keep an always-ready-to-go year-round basic dress in a dark or neutral color in your closet. You can dress it up or down with jackets, scarves or belts.

 Attach two towel racks to the back of your closet door. Hang your belts on one and your scarves on the other. The scarves won't get mussed, and you'll find what you want in a hurry.

 Get rid of clothes you don't wear. If you haven't worn something for a year move it out of your closet.

 Save last-minute pressing time by hanging an outfit that's wrinkled in the bathroom while you shower. The steam from the hot water will help eliminate wrinkles.

 Unstick a zipper by running a lead pencil up and down the zipper.

Sew a button on with dental floss if it pops off clothing you're planning to wear. It will stay on longer and save you future sewing time.

## Four Strategies for Time-Saving Clothes Shopping

Unless you enjoy shopping till you drop:

- Limit your clothes shopping (except for recreational shopping) to four once-a-season shopping trips and buy only one

major complete outfit each season. This strategy has two benefits: (1) you'll save time by setting aside whole Saturdays for
clothes shopping instead of spending many part-time
Saturdays at the mall, and (2) you'll save yourself from buying
more clothes than you need. "You'll soon discover you don't
have to have 10 great outfits," says Joanna Good. "Fewer will be
fine—and the less clothes you have the less time you need to
care for them."

• On each once-a-season spree, pick up the small things you'll
  need for that season, too. Look for washable blouses and
  sweaters. This will save running-to-the-cleaners time.

• Supplement your once-a-season shopping trips with catalogue-
  shopping when necessary. "A great time-saver is buying panty-
  hose in bulk by mail order," says Grace Mastalli.

• Buy your clothes with travel in mind if you travel for business.

## $\mathscr{S}$TEP 3: GET OVER THE "EVERYTHING MUST BE PERFECT" SYNDROME

In talking to women about house chores I don't meet very many
who like coming home to a hovel. But there *is* a happy medium
between perfectionist standards and no standards at all.

Happily, most working women are keeping this in mind. In an
essay in *Time* magazine, Barbara Ehrenreich pointed out that
Harvard economist Juliet Schor's research shows women have been
eliminating half an hour of housework for every hour they work
away from home—or up to 20 hours a week. This, as Barbara
Ehrenreich states, is the equivalent of a 50-foot mound of unfolded
laundry or a dustball as large as a house.[5]

### What Successful Women Say About Housekeeping

"Ask yourself how essential certain home tasks are," suggests Sherry
Sheridan, a divorced mother and part-time librarian. "If I don't fer-
tilize and water my lawn I don't have to mow it very much. The

weeds stay green in the summer anyway, so my lawn is the ecological lawn of the future!"

"Things are never done," says Paula Baum, "so if my house isn't as clean as I would like it to be it's not that important. It doesn't really matter."

"I keep my home at a low-maintenance level," concludes Debra Gallanter, a single mother who works for a nonprofit organization. "I don't cook fancy dinners, and I do very little shopping for *any-thing* other than food. Along with saving time, this saves me money, too."

## TIME BOOSTERS

- Do your best to accomplish the most essential tasks day-by-day. But be flexible and learn to let the rest go.
- Be willing to trade off some undone chores for time and energy to do more of what really matters to you in terms of meaning and long-lasting value.
- Remind yourself that you've never read—and probably never will—an obituary with a punch line that says "She kept a perfect house."

# STEP 4: SPEED UP CLEANING AND LAUNDRY

Even though you practice minimal maintenance, streamline the care of your home, and give first-things-first attention to things that really count, you *still* have the problem of handling really essential housework.

Take cleaning and laundry, for instance. Most of us can't eliminate them, so here are ways to do both as quickly as possible.

## Save Time with Quick Cleaning

Except for occasional thorough top-to-bottom cleanings, settle for clean-enough cleaning.

If you have people to help you, take all the help you can get. If you're solo, allot four hours a week to cleaning and call it quits at the end of that time. By working fast you can:

- keep bathrooms in order
- dust and vacuum throughout the house
- do kitchen floors, counters, refrigerators, and appliances.

Granted, you won't want to eat off of the floor after four hours of cleaning. But who cares? Your house will be clean enough!

Some working women clean on weekend mornings. Others who have energy to spare do it in a four-hour stint one evening. Still others clean in two-hour stints two nights after work. Find out by trial and error what makes the best use of your time.

To make your cleaning quicker and easier, spend some money to set yourself up with good time-and-labor-saving devices. The ones that will save you the most time are a dishwasher, a garbage disposal, a self-cleaning oven, a dust-buster, and a vacuum cleaner with attachments. Keep your devices in good running order, too. (A vacuum that's slow on the pick-up because it needs servicing or a dishwasher you have to coddle wastes time rather than saving it.)

## TIME BOOSTERS

- Save the time it takes to get out your vacuum more than once a week by keeping a colorful and attractive whisk broom at the top of any carpeted stairs and "whisking away" dust or debris in your routine trips up and down the stairs.

- Plug a dust-buster in the most convenient place in your home and use that for five-minute clean-ups here and there.

- Pick up and put away newspapers in the morning as you go from the bedroom to the kitchen. Or do this as the last thing at night to get a head start on the morning.

- Use "in-the-middle time" to do a small portion of the chores you feel you never have time for—such as dusting bookcases or cleaning kitchen cabinets. Instead of viewing those jobs as too time-consuming, break them down into smaller, more manageable tasks. For example, do one shelf in your bookcases or one cabinet in your kitchen when you have some spare time.

- Do chores when you're in the mood. You'll do them faster.

- Make the two-things-at-once system work for you. Says Dottie Walters, "I try to make my actions do double duty. I keep cleaning materials handy on the kitchen sink and in the bathrooms, and while I'm in those rooms for something else I grab a sponge and clean something. I check the waste baskets as I pass them, and if they're full I pull out the plastic bag and put in a clean one. And I *always* leave things at the bottom or top of the stairs ready to take with me on the next trip."

- When you walk in the door with an armload of mail, dry cleaning, briefcase, purchases, library books, or whatever, put each in its appropriate place right away instead of dropping them temporarily on the nearest chair.

- Try to complete one house chore before starting another. This cuts down on surrounding yourself with frustrating, unfinished jobs.

- Finally, set up your house so you have less to clean by putting away or giving away (1) things you don't use or need, and (2) things that give you no pleasure or enjoyment.

---

## Cut Laundry Problems Down to Size

The best antidote for laundry build-up and overflowing hampers is to make laundry a "minutes" rather than an "hours" job. One way to do this is to drop a load in the washer and put it in the dryer as part of your morning routine. Another is to fit it in as part of your after-work routine.

My own solution is a kitchen set-up where my washer and dryer are an arm's length away from my other kitchen chores. With my counter TV, dishwasher, microwave, sink, stove, refrigerator, washer, dryer, and exercise bike all in a horseshoe pattern, I can cook, put bowls and utensils in the dishwasher as soon as I finish with them, catch a glimpse of the 6:00 P.M. news, and load the washer and dryer, all while I'm fixing dinner. If there's time to spare while waiting for dinner I ride the exercise bike.

This arrangement may not be the last word in perfect kitchen design. But it works for me and saves me the time of going to a basement to do laundry at some other time—and that's all I care about!

## QUICK STARTS

 Save the time it takes to pull things out of a hamper by using laundry baskets (one for whites and one for dark colors) and take the baskets with sorted clothes directly to the washer.

 Throw your panty hose and lingerie in a mesh laundry bag at the end of the day and toss the whole bag in the washer when you do your next laundry. (Use the gentle cycle for everything if you're a purist about caring for your personal laundry.)

 Cut down on sorting after taking things from the dryer by having adults and older children wear one-size-fits-all, same-color socks. Do the same for young children, as much as possible.

 Similarly, use permanent markers to differentiate each person's clothing. Mark dots on the seams—a different color for each person.

 Keep no-iron clothes and household items looking good by taking them from the dryer as soon as the dryer stops—or just before it stops. "Putting clothes on a hanger then saves a great deal of time", says Diane Hahnel.

Dampen items that *must* be ironed and put them in a plastic bag in the refrigerator," adds Donna Goldfein. "They'll iron beautifully when you take them out."

Have all family members take their own laundry to their rooms.

When family members are old enough, consider having each person do his or her own laundry. If husbands and children can operate VCRs they can also work washing machines and dryers!

## $\mathcal{S}$TEP 5: FOOD SHOP IN THE EXPRESS LANE

Some women relish saying "I'm always on the go." But I've observed that this usually means they're running around picking up food and stopping hither and yon without accomplishing very much except being "on the go"—a time waster, incidentally, that robs us of time for things we'd do "if we had the time."

Admittedly, putting food on the table is a never-ending home chore. But trying to do it piecemeal or hitting the all-night convenience store for a quart of milk at midnight is *not* the way to do it. Instead there are time-saving ways smart working women use.

### What Successful Women Say About Food Shopping

"I order my meat by phone and have it freezer-wrapped and marked," says Diane Hahnel. "Then I do the rest of my shopping at the same store because I know where everything is."

"I find it helpful to buy in bulk and have a lot of nonperishable items in stock," says Ruthanne Cianni. "This makes it easier and less time-consuming to do the weekly shopping."

"I buy duplicates or triplicates of everything I use frequently so I don't have to rush out to buy them for the emergencies that arise between shopping trips," says Judith Moncrieff Baldwin. "Keep extras of your most-used items—such as coffee and pet food—squirreled away in a logical place."

## TIME BOOSTERS

- Keep a "To-Get" list on your refrigerator door so you and everyone in your household can write down what you need whenever items on hand get low.

- Prepare a "Master Shopping List" set up according to the way products are arranged in the store where you stop. Make photocopies of your list or print them from your computer if you keep your list on a disk.

- Each week either circle what you want on one of the photocopies or copy items from the Master List and add them to the needs listed on your refrigerator door. This time-saver makes writing your list so simple you can do it in no time at all—at the hairdresser's, in a dentist's waiting room, or on a bus or train.

- As an alternative to a Master List, try what Sheri Benjamin, owner of a technology public relations and marketing firm, calls her "Things we are never allowed to run out of in this house" list. "That standard list includes dozens of items we should never be out of—from milk to eggs to deodorant," she explains. "It's an 'evergreen' list, and each week we add special items to it."

- After you make your list, organize your grocery coupons by putting colored Post-its on the front of each group—one color for canned goods, another for soaps and cleansers, another for cereals, and so on. Clip each group together and put coupons in the right group as you accumulate them.

- Avoid supermarket lines by scheduling your once-a-week trip to the store for odd hours. One working woman saves time by shopping at 7:00 A.M. on Saturday mornings. Other women have a late meal one night during the week and shop while other people are having dinner.

- Lay out the best route for your shopping so you can hit necessary stops with a minimum of wasted traveling time.

- If possible, let someone shop for you. "My college-girl helpers shop every week," says Sheri Benjamin. "But be very *specific* about your list if someone else does your shopping!"

### SAMPLE MASTER SHOPPING LIST
*(Personalize to Fit Your Own Needs)*

Cheese (Reduced fat)

Milk

Butter

Margarine

Coffee/cream

Eggs

Canned goods
   Fruits, vegetables, soups,
     tomato sauce

Desserts

Ice cream

Frozen yogurt

Cookies

Frozen goods
   Pizza
   Vegetables
   Pancakes, waffles, French toast

Mayonnaise

Salad dressing

Catsup

Mustard

Peanut Butter

Jelly

Nonstick vegetable spray

Sugar

Oil

Vinegar

Spices and condiments

Cleaning and laundry supplies

Toiletries

Pet food

Meat

Chicken

Fish

Cold cuts

Bread

Rolls

Crackers for soup

Small bags of snacks for lunches

Cold cereal/oatmeal

Fresh fruits

Fresh vegetables

Salad things

Pasta

Rice

Potatoes

Fruit juices

Diet sodas

Coffee/Tea

Sandwich bags

Bags for food storage

Bags for garbage and trash

Aluminum foil

Paper napkins

Paper towels

Toilet tissue

Light bulbs

# $\mathscr{S}$TEP 6: GET A QUICK FIX ON MEALS

Your weekday breakfasts can be standard and simple—with the previously suggested cereals and fruits, along with occasional goodies such as frozen waffles, pancakes, or French toast that you pop in the toaster. Lunches can be fairly standard too, with a different kind of sandwich each day (cold cuts, peanut butter, egg salad, cream cheese) plus beverage, fruit, and a healthy snack.

That leaves you to plan nutritional dinners, based on time-saving menus, instead of opting for a steady diet of Monday-through-Friday fast foods.

What's the best way to do this when you already have so much to do? Here are three quick fixes:

- Since you may be too tired (and, also, too pressed for time) to peel and chop fresh vegetables at the end of your working day, rely on frozen vegetables for most of your dinners during the week.

- Wash and prepare some fresh vegetables on weekends to intersperse with the frozen ones.

- As an alternative to going out for fast foods too often, have a pizza dinner at home on a night you're too weary to cook. You can keep frozen pizzas on hand to serve with a platter of the vegetables you've prepared. Fill the platter with such nutritional favorites as celery, scallions, carrot sticks, radishes, red and green pepper strips, cucumber, zucchini and red onion slices, or whatever you and your family prefer. Top off the meal with frozen ice cream cones from the freezer, and presto, you have a simple meal.

"I find this more relaxing than a fast food place where you have to put up with other people's cranky, hungry children and bad parenting," says Gail Stewart Hand. "At home you can make the meal very easy with everyone working to set the table, get the food on the table, and clear the table. This gives the children a sense of responsibility and provides a way for the family to reconnect."

## Sample Dinner Menus for a Week

Use these suggestions as they fit your needs and mix up the nights to complement your schedule.

| *Monday* | *Tuesday* | *Wednesday* | *Thursday* | *Friday* |
|---|---|---|---|---|
| Broiled hamburgers | Chicken (from Sat.) | Spaghetti with sauce | Broiled flounder | Pizza |
| Mashed potatoes | Rice (from Sat.) | Mixed vegetables | Baked potatoes | Sliced vegetable |
| Peas | Corn on cob | Green salad | Spinach | Ice cream cones |
| Tomatoes and lettuce | Cranberry sauce | Hard bread | Coleslaw | |
| Melon | Cookies | Raspberry yogurt bars | Berries | |

| *Saturday* | *Sunday* |
|---|---|
| Baked chicken (Do double amount to freeze for one dinner during week) | London broil |
| | Parslied boiled potatoes |
| Rice (Make enough to freeze for chicken dinner during week) | Fresh broccoli |
| | Waldorf salad |
| Fresh string beans | Lemon chiffon pie |
| Tossed green salad | |
| Frozen eclairs | |

## Q U I C K   S T A R T S

 Post your week's menus on the refrigerator door and establish a firm rule that the first person home starts dinner.

 Have younger children set the table and older children make a salad or help in other preparations. Involving them in helping makes more time for being together. Even your youngest children can "pretend" they're doing the same chores as you.

 Eliminate dinnertime interruptions by letting an answering machine take calls while you're preparing and eating your meal. Or keep a cordless phone beside you so you can continue with what you're doing when people decide a good time to call is as soon as you get home from work.

 Give everyone a break from meal preparation by planning occasional dinners out.

## What Successful Women Say About Preparing Meals

"As you cook one meal, prepare other cook-ahead meals to take from the freezer and put into the oven," says Donna Goldfein. "A pasta casserole can easily be doubled and frozen. Extra hamburger patties can be stored in the freezer with plastic wrap between them. Roasted chicken can be sliced and put in several foil packets for future meals."

"While I'm cooking I sometimes make 20 quarts of spaghetti sauce and hundreds of meat balls," says Ruthanne Ciotti. "I do the same with soups and stews."

"Dinner preparation can be a drudgery or chore—*or* a time to let your mind rest, to think and be creative, and to talk or play with your children," says Lynn McIntyre Coffee. "I look at it as a time of unwinding."

## STEP 7: KEEP TRACK OF ALL COMMITMENTS ON A HOME-AND-FAMILY CALENDAR

In Point 2 we talked about your personal/work calendar and the benefits of never leaving home or office without it. A home-and-family calendar offers the same time benefits and eliminates cluttering up your mind with home details to remember.

The calendars women choose for home vary with individual needs, but many women like a weekly calendar so they can see at a glance where the whole family needs to be. Here's a blank Sample Weekly Calendar to copy and fill in. Take your cue for filling it in from the Sample Filled-in Calendar.

## SAMPLE WEEKLY CALENDAR

**Monday**        **December 12**

_____

_____

_____

_____

_____

**Tuesday**        **December 13**

_____

_____

_____

_____

**Wednesday**        **December 14**

_____

_____

_____

_____

**Thursday**      **December 15**

_____

_____

_____

_____

_____

**Friday**      **December 16**

_____

_____

_____

_____

_____

**Saturday**      **December 17**

_____

_____

_____

_____

_____

**Sunday**      **December 18**

_____

_____

_____

_____

_____

While a large majority of women choose weekly calendars like the samples, others prefer monthly ones. Sandra Sharp, for instance, uses a giant monthly calendar that fills the whole side of her refrigerator.

"It's conveniently located across from my telephone and has many lines for each day," she says. "For each day I write *everything*—gym days, library due dates, and kids' school activities. In this way I'll never double-book.

"When my church group meets and plans its meetings for the year, I come home and write the whole year down. I also write down 'last swim class' for the end of one session so I'll know that on that day I need a check in hand to pay for the next session. I highlight birthdays in yellow, and if I've arranged for a baby-sitter I write her name and the time I will pick her up.

"Around the edges of my calendar I hang a countless number of little magnets with clips like clothespins. This makes it easy to clip book report instructions, monthly church bulletins, lunch menus, emergency phone numbers, and so forth, to the calendar. Each morning I check my calendar and the papers on my magnets. This saves me from wasting time looking for lost papers."

Whatever calendar format you use make the following Quick Starts part of your at-home routine.

## QUICK STARTS

 Pencil in meetings, activities, and all commitments as soon as you make them.

Add expected social engagements and trips to be made if your business or personal life takes you traveling.

As you do at work, include the phone numbers of contacts for appointments so you won't waste time searching for numbers when you need them.

Post the phone numbers of your emergency child-care people so you can call for help quickly if the school or day care closes or your baby-sitter cancels. (See Point 5 on support-system people.)

Look at the calendar at the start of each week to get a sense of your time schedule and priorities for the week ahead.

Check the calendar again each morning and evening to see what's ahead in the daily time frame.

## SAMPLE FILLED-IN WEEKLY CALENDAR

### 12 MONDAY
DECEMBER

| | |
|---|---|
| Bank Deposit on way to work | Buy dessert for |
| 4:00 Robbie — Soccer practice | Bridge Club |
| Get baby sitter for Sat. night - 931-2744 | Robbie — Cub Scout |
| Call Jane about Sat. night — 444-3232 | project due |
| Call Mom & Daddy at night | Jay — Practice poem for |
| 8:00 Tim — Council Mtg. | X mas play |

### 13 TUESDAY
DECEMBER

| | |
|---|---|
| 8:30 Foot Dr. appointment | Tim — Library Bd. 7145 |
| Call Jack for his birthday 212-644-7840 | 8:00 - Bridge Club |
| Mail Smiths' anniversary card | here |
| Tim - drop off suit for alteration at tailor's | |
| Call glass place for window pane replacement | |
| 3:30 Robbie — Cub Scouts | 5:00 Haircut |

### 14 WEDNESDAY
DECEMBER

| | |
|---|---|
| Tim - get car serviced | |
| Jay - Birthday party after pre-school | |
| (Sitter take & pick up.) | |
| 4:00 Robbie - soccer practice | |
| Call Mayor about speaking at college club | |
| Food shopping after work—Take Chinese food home for dinner | |
| Tim - 8:30 Bowling | |

## THURSDAY DECEMBER 15

9:00 - Robbie's class trip to museum
Tim - Send in insurance claim for towing charge
4:00 - Jay's appointment with neurologist
        Xmas presents ready for kid's teachers
8:00 Committee meeting for Antiques Fair (Barb's House)
Jay - Before bed - Practice poem

## FRIDAY DECEMBER 16

10:00 Attend Jay's pre-school Xmas program & party

7:00 - Robbie's monthly Cub Scout meeting -
        (Tim will go)

8:30 - Tim Bowling
Clean 2 hrs. upstairs

## SATURDAY DECEMBER 17

8:00-10:00 Clean 2 hrs. downstairs
        (Tim do rest of routine)
11:00 Take kids to pick out Xmas
        tree & out to lunch
Finish Xmas shopping
Tim take knives to be sharpened
Kid's library books due
7:00 Jane's Party

## SUNDAY DECEMBER 18

Early A.M. - Pay bills & reconcile checks
11:00 - Scheduled to be Church liturgist
12:00 - Get family pictures taken
        for church directory
2:00 - Kids Xmas party at church
5:00 - Tim and I leave for concert
        in New York, Bess will baby sit

***Quick Check/Recheck*** Maintaining your home-and-family life on an even keel gives you more time to be more effective in your job or career. To achieve this goal you can use a 7-Step Time-Gaining Plan that will help you (1) streamline your daily home care, (2) avoid getting stressed when you can't stretch your time to get everything done every day, and (3) give first-things-first attention to the things that really matter. You can make this plan work on a daily basis by putting your children ahead of house chores; fast tracking your grooming and dressing; overcoming the "Everything Must Be Perfect" syndrome; speeding up cleaning and laundry; food shopping in the express lane; getting a quick fix on meals; and keeping all home-and-family commitments written on one calendar. As you work on implementing and fine tuning each of the 7 Steps, you'll find that your home life offers even greater rewards and benefits despite your busy schedule.

# Share the Workload at Home to Free Up Your Time

*When I found out my husband did his own ironing,*
*I thought to myself, 'Good'!*

**—A business coach**

You may be doing all you can to better manage your home responsibilities in the time you have. But there's no better move you can make than to get the others in your household to share the work with you. Listen to what four spokeswomen say!

- "If I had one thought to offer working women in respect to time, it would be to spend some of their time considering how others can be of assistance," says Sheila Wellington, president of Catalyst.

- "Women still take too much responsibility for child care and running the home instead of protecting their time by setting boundaries and requiring others to do their share," adds Carolyn Bushong, a psychotherapist specializing in relationships. "Since women have been doing this for so long, men often expect women to pick up the slack and are less likely to come through."

- "A main problem of women I've surveyed is that their husbands will 'help' only if asked," reports Dr. Gayle Kimball, an authority on working parents and author of *The 50–50 Parent* and *The 50–50 Marriage.*

- "Many men are still really mother's helpers," agrees Dr. Kathleen Gerson, author of *No Man's Land: Men's Changing Commitments to Family and Work.* "While some men are more involved than in the past, many women say 'He'll do it, but I have to tell him.'"

Across the country women concur that one of their most frustrating problems is that far too often *they* have to say "We need to do this or that" before their husbands pitch in and help.

But forget that four-letter word called "help!"

Today the word is "share"—and all working women need people to *share* in the household chores!

In fairness to men, however, I find in my interviews that growing numbers of couples do share home-work tasks. As Penny Grover told me, "My husband is an unusually generous person. He does things without being asked and often does more than I do. Household and child-care duties are easily divided between us."

So how do you achieve this division of labor? How do you overcome the problem of being the one with too much to do?

Here's a 5-Point Agenda for work-sharing at home. Adapt it to fit your particular needs. Each working woman has her own ideas about "what" and "how" to share, and each family splits the workload in ways that match the personalities of the individual members of the household.

## (1) CHECK WHO DOES WHAT

On this evaluation sheet, mark what jobs you're responsible for and what jobs other people handle. This will give you an overview of your home-work situation. If you do most of a listed task put a check mark by that job. If others do the bulk of a task, check that column.

| *At-Home Jobs* | *You Do* | *Others Do* |
|---|---|---|
| Meal planning | ____ | ____ |
| Food shopping | ____ | ____ |
| Cooking and preparing meals | ____ | ____ |
| Cleaning up after meals | ____ | ____ |
| Picking up the house | ____ | ____ |
| Vacuuming | ____ | ____ |
| Making beds | ____ | ____ |
| Doing laundry | ____ | ____ |
| Cleaning bathrooms | ____ | ____ |
| Putting out garbage and trash | ____ | ____ |
| Recycling | ____ | ____ |
| Child care | ____ | ____ |
| Arranging for baby-sitting | ____ | ____ |
| Taking children to their activities | ____ | ____ |
| Assisting with homework | ____ | ____ |
| Participating in and attending school and community activities for the children | ____ | ____ |
| Shopping for clothes and other items for the family | ____ | ____ |
| Family paperwork, finances, and bill-paying | ____ | ____ |
| Banking | ____ | ____ |
| Post office errands | ____ | ____ |
| Miscellaneous errands | ____ | ____ |
| Clothes to cleaners and laundry | ____ | ____ |
| Car maintenance | ____ | ____ |
| Yardwork | ____ | ____ |
| Household repairs and maintenance | ____ | ____ |
| Contacting repair services | ____ | ____ |
| Watering plants | ____ | ____ |
| Caring for pets | ____ | ____ |
| Planning social activities and entertaining | ____ | ____ |

| *At-Home Jobs* | *You Do* | *Others Do* |
|---|---|---|
| Buying cards and gifts | ____ | ____ |
| Sending cards and thank-you notes | ____ | ____ |
| **TOTALS** | ____ | ____ |

**Scoring:** Total the check marks in each column. If the YOU DO column has far more checks than the OTHERS DO, the division of work isn't equitable in your household. Agenda 2 through Agenda 5 will give you ideas for solving this problem. But, first, here are work-splitting strategies that work for three working women.

## What Successful Women Say About Work-Splitting

"I do all the paperwork, bill-paying, decorating, and liaison work with repair people," says Sheree Bykofsky. "My husband does the laundry, clean-ups, grocery shopping and plant-watering."

"I cook and my husband cleans," says Wendy Dixon. "I market 85% of the time, he 15%. I get the laundry washed and dried. He sorts through it and puts it away."

"Sometimes when I come home from my hospital rounds and office hours, my husband will say 'You're tired, I'll cook,'" says Dr. Violet Master. "Then he'll do whatever needs to be done. Between the two of us, things get accomplished. Sometimes it's 100% one person. Other times, it's 100% the other. In still other situations, we accomplish things together."

## T I M E   B O O S T E R S

- Take each person's needs into account when you make house rules.
- Establish a clear understanding that each of you—when necessary—will shoulder the other's responsibilities during crises and nonnormal periods.
- Know when it's human kindness to pick up the slack for the other person.

# (2) $\mathscr{A}$SK FOR A WORKABLE DIVISION OF LABOR

Cynthia Cohen Turk, a management consultant to consumer industries, *started out* her marriage with an agreement with her husband on the division of labor—an ideal way to protect your time while your marriage is new.

But many women don't split chores when they get married—or even at any time after that. Eventually, they end up stressed when nobody seems to notice how much they have to do.

The way to avoid this problem is to *ask* for work-sharing *directly*—instead of throwing out hints that usually go unnoticed.

"A few years ago I did all the work myself for Thanksgiving dinner for 20 people," says Sheri Benjamin. "But last Thanksgiving I didn't whip myself into a frenzy about all I had to do. In fact, I didn't even do any of the shopping for the 20 people.

"Instead I made a list for my college-student helper and asked her to shop the day before. Then I asked my husband to order and pick up the fresh turkey. I also asked all the friends and family who came to dinner to take on a duty or two.

"And everything went well."

## T I M E  B O O S T E R S

- Sit down with your partner (or whoever shares your home) and make a list of what needs to be done and what each of you think is important to do:

| *What Needs to Be Done* | *What's Important to Me* | *What's Important to My Partner and Others* |
| --- | --- | --- |
| _____ | _____ | _____ |
| _____ | _____ | _____ |
| _____ | _____ | _____ |
| _____ | _____ | _____ |
| _____ | _____ | _____ |
| _____ | _____ | _____ |

- Using these lists as a guide, divide up the workload. People will more readily do the tasks that they think are important. For jobs you both want to do, you can split the tasks. The same is true for things neither of you wants to tackle.

- After the lists are made and an agreed-upon sharing is established, make sure each person knows that in the future he or she is *not* to wait to be asked to do the agreed-upon share.

---

## (3) EXPECT YOUR CHILDREN TO DO THEIR SHARE

In addition to helping you gain more time when you hand over chores to your children, you give them valuable training in taking responsibility that they can carry into adult life.

In a newspaper article "Cleaning Up His Act," Ruth Padawer tells the story of Tim Wright who at age 11—and the eldest of 4 children—had to do his share of laundry, food shopping, dishes, vacuuming, cooking, and yardwork when his mother took over the family business after his father died. Today, Tim is a public policy administrator and he shares the home-work 50/50 with his wife, a designer of computer systems.

"If our life style requires us both to be employed full time outside the home, then it requires the same division of labor inside the home," he states. "If I want clean dishes, clean windows, home-cooked dinners and plants that aren't dead, I can't expect my wife to make more of a time commitment when she's working as much as I am."[1]

Wright learned, through necessity, to do his share of home-work. Your children can learn to do tasks, too. Here's a list of chores they can handle, categorized according to age.

## What Children Can Do to Assist You

### Ages 5, 6, 7:

Put toys away.

Chop or peel vegetables with a blunt knife while you're in the kitchen with them.

Set the table.

Throw their own dirty clothes into your laundry receptacle.

Carry their pile of clean laundry to their rooms and put it away.

Be go-fors and runners when you need things from other parts of the house.

### Ages 8, 9:

Clear the table.

Put dishes in the dishwasher.

Unload the dishwasher and put dishes, pots, and silver away.

Put empty cans in recycling container.

Make their own beds.

Water plants.

Learn to cook simple things.

"I've started to teach my 8-year-old son to cook because I want him to become self-sufficient," says Judith Lederman. "He can make spaghetti and fried chicken breasts."

### Ages 10 and up:

Empty wastebaskets into garbage container.

**Ages 10 and up:** *(cont'd.)*

Clean bathrooms.

Run their own clothes through the washing machine.

Put their clothes in the dryer.

Iron.

Dust and vacuum.

Give you a hand with food shopping and plain cooking.

Take out garbage.

Do lawn and garden work.

### Teenagers

In Utopia teens would do all the above (willingly at that!), along with running household errands and watching younger children.

But in the real world of teens today, you're competing with sports and school activities and after-school part-time jobs—to say nothing of normal teen-aged rebellion. Save your time policing their rooms if your teens are the typical ones who suddenly have no memory of their early childhood training to "pick up and put away." My most time-saving, stress-saving tip: Simply close the bedroom door!

## Should You Pay Children?

Working women have varying views about whether or not to pay children for house chores, though many do pay in one way or another. For example, each Saturday Sandra Sharp gives her children a small allowance for the tasks they do. "The minor responsibilities they have are not really great time-savers to me," she says, "but they're worth it because they're good foundations for later responsibilities."

"My kids do chores daily for money," says Paula Mate, a freelance writer. "For instance, they get $1.00 for setting up the dinner table and clearing the table to the dishwasher. This system helps me because I no longer have to give daily directions."

Q U I C K    S T A R T S

Keep things organized so your children can know *specifically* where everything goes. This makes it easier for them to put things away.

Discuss the tasks children prefer, and as much as possible, divvy up the chores so they can do the work they want to do. "Each Saturday my children choose a laundry or cleaning job," says Maureen Powers. "Then I describe in detail what's expected. In this way the house gets pretty well cleaned with occasional quality-control inspections by me."

Establish a time limit for how long your children will have to complete their chores. Says Gail Stewart Hand: "On Saturdays my husband, children, and I do the household grind. But we set a limit to the time we spend on it and call off the work at noon."

# (4) *U*SE VISUAL AIDS TO GAIN COOPERATION

From her talks with and studies of working parents, Gayle Kimball is thoroughly convinced that charts and lists are a woman's best insurance against being a live-in nag![2]

Since none of us relishes *that* reputation, it benefits everyone if you (1) put tasks in writing under each family member's name, and (2) post the chart or bulletin board in a can't-miss spot. Sandra Sharp recommends the refrigerator as the best spot in the house. "The chart has a check-off space for each child's duties for each day of the week," she says. "At the end of the week the children get their allowance if they fill their chart."

## Using a Bulletin Board for Work-Sharing

Instead of using a chart or calendar (like the Home-and-Family Calendar in Point 9) some women use a bulletin board for their home work-share to-dos. Some even make *doubly* sure no one forgets a task by using both a calendar and/or chart or bulletin board.

# Sample Chart for Children's Duties

| | JAMIE | For check mark ✓ | KAREN | For check mark ✓ | BILL | For check mark ✓ |
|---|---|---|---|---|---|---|
| Monday | Help Karen clear table & Bill load dishwasher Pick up newspapers & put in bin. | | Set dinner table clear table Clear dishwasher from yesterday | | Load dishwasher Feed & walk Buster Take out garbage | |
| Tuesday | Help Karen clear table & Bill load dishwasher Pick up newspapers/put in bin | | Clear dishwasher from yesterday Set dinner table clear table | | Load dishwasher Feed & walk Buster Take out garbage | |
| Wednesday | Help Karen clear table & Bill load dishwasher Pick up newspapers/put in bin | | Clear dishwasher from yesterday Set dinner table clear table | | Load dishwasher Feed & walk Buster Take out garbage | |
| Thursday | Help Karen clear table & Bill load dishwasher Pick up newspapers/put in bin | | Clear dishwasher from yesterday Set dinner table clear table | | Take recycled cans to curb Load dishwasher Feed & walk Buster Take out garbage | |
| Friday | Help Karen clear table & Bill load dishwasher Pick up newspapers/put in bin | | Clear dishwasher from yesterday Set dinner table clear table | | Load dishwasher Feed & walk Buster Take out garbage | |
| Saturday | Help Mom wash salad greens & make salad Pick up newspapers/put in bin | | Help unload groceries from car & Put away Pick up & clean your room | | Empty waste baskets into garbage cans Pick up & clean your room Take out garbage | |
| Sunday | Help weed our rock garden Pick up newspapers/put in bin | | Water plants Take dad's shirts To laundry | | Mow Lawn take out garbage | |

## Weekly Bulletin Board Sample for Week of November 7

| DONNA | KEVIN | ONCE-A-WEEK HOUSEHOLD HELPER |
|---|---|---|
| Plan menu + do shopping list for Sat. night Dinner party | Fill car with gas Monday | Do lampshades Throughout house |
| Shop for Party on way home from work Friday | Bowling – Thurs. night | Clean refrigerator + freezer |
| Buy commutation ticket book Garden Club Thurs. night (EAT OUT) | Dr's appt. Tues. at 5:00 Get new prescription from him + drop off at Druggist | Polish brass Candlesticks |
| Wed. night – pay bills. Get checks ready to mail | GET HAIRCUT | Bathrooms Scrubbed + Chrome shined |
| Borrow wallpaper books from paint store and look for possibilities | Thurs. noon: Mail checks + make bank deposit | Go through house for cobwebs |
| Take Blair to piano lesson Sat. a.m. | Call insurance company about increasing coverage on furnishings Get estimate for painting living room + dining room | Windows in front + back door cleaned Woodwork on staircase scrubbed |
| Sat. After lunch: Set table + fix food for party | MAKE CHEESECAKE FOR PARTY FRIDAY NIGHT | Routine vacuuming + dusting |
| Sort out magazines + get rid of surplus. | SLICE HAM FOR PARTY SATURDAY | |
| | PICK UP CLOTHES FROM CLEANERS SAT. AND PUT AWAY | |

"I have a central bulletin board," says Sheri Benjamin. "It has three listings: one for my husband; one for me; and one for the two part-time college students who help me. I leave nothing to chance. For instance, if someone needs to take the car for an oil change, I assign the project by putting it with a due date under the person's name.

"Sure, people think you're Attila the Hun for the first few weeks," she admits. "But eventually this reminder is easier on everyone."

## (5) DON'T INSIST ALL WORK MUST BE DONE YOUR WAY

As you aim for sharing the home-work, realize that every job you assign won't be a four-star performance. People perform at different levels and work in different ways, so factor in human elements and "hang loose" when people don't do things exactly as you would. Then, for the good of everyone, stick to these Time Boosters.

## TIME BOOSTERS

- Relax your standards (when it doesn't make *that* much difference) if other people don't do a job as thoroughly as you would do it.

- Let people do a job their way. "I've learned from many dads that there's more than one way to powder a baby's butt," says Kim Bushaw. "I'm thinking especially of a disgruntled dad who wanted to be a nurturing half of his child's life but who wasn't allowed to by his wife. Some women believe they should know how to 'do it all' so they develop little rules and strategies when a baby is born. Then, they think there is only one way to handle any given situation."

- Teach your children how to do things "The Right Way." "But also realize there's such a thing as 'good enough,'" points out Gail Stewart Hand. "Teach children to recognize when they've reached 'good enough,' at the same time you teach them that giving a task only half their attention isn't 'good enough.'"

- Avoid being overly critical about how and when jobs are done. "The main complaint of men I've interviewed and surveyed is that women are always critical of the job they do, so why do it!" says Gayle Kimball.

- Never compare one person's efforts in a negative way to those of other persons.

- Fight the temptation to do a job over. "Women who expect only perfection have only one solution," says Donna Goldfein. "They will continue to do the housework alone because only they can clean, cook, and wash in the manner they consider correct."

- Finally, recognize and appreciate the contributions of the people in your life who share the home-work with you.

---

***Quick Check/Recheck*** Protect and add to your time by determining how other people in your home can share the workload with you. Ask for and discuss a work-split with your husband, partner, or live-in—and expect your children to pitch in, too. List everyone's tasks and responsibilities on a chart and/or bulletin board placed in a can't-miss spot. Consider each persons' needs and personalities when you make house rules. Establish an understanding that when necessary you'll all shoulder each other's responsibilities during crises and non-normal periods. Stay aware of the fact that people perform at different levels and work in different ways, and don't insist all work must be done your way. Avoid being overly critical and be sure to show appreciation for what other people do.

# PART THREE

# MANAGING YOUR PERSONAL TIME:
*A 3-Point Program
for Making Time for Yourself
and Time for Others*

# Set Aside Personal Time for Yourself to Recharge Your Batteries

*I always have things I should be doing, so it takes discipline to take time off.*
**—A home business authority**

The only way to take time off for yourself is to *make* the time!

*Making* personal time is vital to our well-being, too, because we *want* more from life than our routine work-and-home life, no matter how good things are. As the following table shows, we *want* to trade some job/household hours for personal time for ourselves.[1]

Taking time to be a friend to yourself and the people in your world is an integral part of good time management—and a special issue for women. Even though both men and women need leisure and personal time, there's never enough for women. In fact, according to The Prodigy Services Company Report on Women, men enjoy one hour more leisure time than women on a daily basis, and employed women are the most time-squeezed of all.[2]

## HOW PEOPLE WOULD LIKE TO CHANGE THE TIME ALLOCATIONS
## OF THEIR WORK WEEK

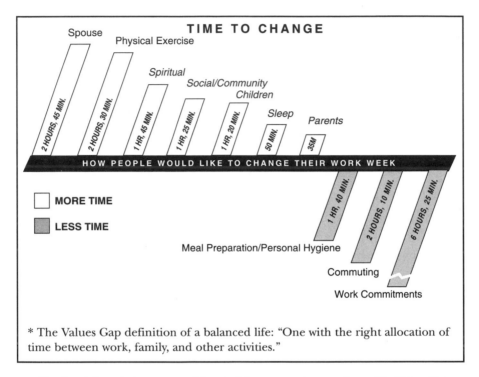

* The Values Gap definition of a balanced life: "One with the right allocation of time between work, family, and other activities."

*Reprinted through the courtesy of Priority Management Systems, Inc.—The Values Gap*

### SELF-TEST:
### *Do You Take Time Off for a Personal Life?*

To see how well you're doing at taking time for yourself, mark "Yes" or "No" to the following questions:

|  |  | Yes | No |
|---|---|---|---|
| 1. | I give up my personal time because there's always so much else I have to do. | ____ | ____ |
| 2. | I feel guilty when I take time for myself at the expense of something else. | ____ | ____ |
| 3. | I put my own needs last. | ____ | ____ |

|  | Yes | No |
|---|---|---|
| 4. I let other people take too much of my time unnecessarily because I often view their needs as more important than mine. | ____ | ____ |
| 5. I have no time for leisure. | ____ | ____ |
| 6. I feel compelled to catch up on housework in my spare time. | ____ | ____ |
| 7. I believe that sacrificing personal time is the only way to cope with job and family demands. | ____ | ____ |
| 8. I don't know how to slow down. | ____ | ____ |
| 9. I get uptight about my multiple roles. | ____ | ____ |
| 10. I'm always saying "Not today—I don't have the time when it comes to doing something for myself." | ____ | ____ |

**Scoring:** If you checked "No" to most statements, you're already taking time off for a personal life, but there are ways you can take even more.

If you have about the same number of "Yes" and "No" answers, you're a sometimes-friend to yourself.

If you answered "Yes" to most of these questions, you're selling yourself short on personal time. You're not being a good friend to yourself.

## Ease Out of Self-Sacrificing Your Time

Sacrificing personal time is penny-wise and pound-foolish. The National Study of the Changing Workforce conducted by the Families and Work Institute found that:

1. personal well-being apparently suffers when workers are more likely to sacrifice time for themselves rather than time for work or family

2. carving out time for yourself represents an investment in mental health that may well offset occasional or modest reductions in attention to work and family.[3]

There will always be time for your other demands, so take your deserved share of personal time to benefit yourself, your relationships, your values, and your interests. You'll find out how to do this using the Ten Master Keys for Unlocking Personal Time that follow.

Each of these keys will provide positive benefits, but because you're so busy—and so pressed for time—you can't realistically expect to do all of them in a single week. Plan on doing a few things each week—or even a few each month. Use the CIRCLE-IN-THE-ROUND WORKSHEET at the end of this chapter as a boost for getting started.

## What Successful Women Say About Personal Time

"If we get in touch with ourselves physically, emotionally, spiritually, and physically, we'll gain working time and be more effective," says Alexis Talbott. "If I don't take some time alone for myself, I become tense. I feel like I'm turning into a martyr because I do so much for others and nothing for me. You should love yourself enough to want to take time for yourself."

"Your belief that you deserve to have time for yourself reflects your self-esteem, self-confidence, self-worth, and understanding of time," says Suzanne Frisse. "If we as women, spouses, mothers, partners, daughters, employees fail to take time for ourselves, that time will surely be taken away."

"Downtime is something that doesn't come easily in our busy lives," agrees Ruthanne Ciotti. "In my case, I sacrifice some sleep for personal time by getting up at 5:00 A.M. when nobody else is up for at least an hour to an hour and a half. Just having that time alone is good, even though I'm also doing things in the kitchen and getting ready for work."

"I always tell my patients 'Take time for you and nurture you. Then you may give to your family from your overflow,'" says Maureen Powers. "If you're empty you have nothing to give."

# $\mathcal{U}$NLOCK PERSONAL TIME WITH THESE TEN MASTER KEYS

## Master Key 1: Make Time for Relationships

From his 30 years of studying relationships, Dr. Clifford Swensen, a Purdue University professor of psychological sciences, has found

that relationships with other people are what really make life worthwhile. "Studying persons who are looking back and assessing their
lives confirms the hypothesis that the most important thing is people," he states.

With this in mind, never let yourself forget that, regardless of
your time constraints, you need people-nourishment—both as a
giver and receiver. "Nothing is so urgent that time for caring should
be forgotten," says Donna Goldfein. "People really never care how
much you know—until they know how much you care."

In making more time for relationships, it's an advantage for
women that *generally* our nature is to assume the greater responsibility for establishing and maintaining personal communication
links. Despite our fragmented lives, women find time to write an
average of 2.5 personal letters per month, compared with 1.6 for
men, according to The Prodigy Services Company Report on
Women. Women also make 4.3 long distance telephone calls in an
average month while men make 3.8. Moreover, women more often
than men pick up the phone to call a friend (by 42% to 27%).[4]

## TIME   BOOSTERS

- Review the things you have to do in a day and determine what's the
  most important. "Is it relationships or dust-bunnies under your bed?"
  asks Suzanne Frisse. "Even when I've got a to-do list that would paper
  my living room, I sift through it quickly and decide what's important."

- Subtract a less important activity in order to do something that will
  further one or more of your relationships.

- Attach as much importance to scheduling that one relationship-
  building thing as you do to scheduling job and home commitments.

- Factor in time for maintaining relationships as you go along. "I do
  this with a phone conversation here, a walk with a friend there, or a
  breakfast together," says Paula Mate. Adds Vicky Penner Katz, "I talk
  to a lot of my friends before 8:00 A.M. and sometimes I even talk at
  6:00 A.M. "The lesson? Cultivate friends who are morning people—
  *real* morning people!"

## Master Key 2: Make Time to Enjoy Your Family

When New Jersey governor Christine Todd Whitman was on the campaign trail she rejected all political advice and made time to go with her family on a two-week vacation. She considered this a top priority, even though it could have cost her the election.

Older people—men and women—looking back later in life often focus their regrets on misspent time—especially time not spent with families. The Prodigy Services Company Report found that of six leisure activities presented (ranging from pursuing personal interests to thinking and reflecting), spending time with one's family was the *only* leisure time pursuit considered "very important" by a majority (72%) of women.[5] Added to that, "The Values Gap" survey published by Priority Management Systems found that married respondents with children want almost one hour more each day to spend with spouse and children.[6]

## QUICK STARTS

Block out family time on your calendar and don't let anything except genuine emergencies interfere with that time.

Create opportunities for spending this blocked-out time together. "Have meals together, plan family outings, go bowling or for walks," says Judith Myers-Wall, associate professor of family studies at Purdue University. "It's in these casual moments that some of the best conversations take place."

Give children a list of projects and activities you can do together and let them pick their favorite. This prevents everyone from wasting time on something no one wants to do.

Make special dates with your children. "Along with our other family activities I have dates with my three children—two hours in length for each one—every week," says Wendy Dixon. "We believe that bringing up children to be healthy, happy, centered, bright human beings takes lots of time. But it's our hope that by spending happy time/money now doing many things with our children we can avoid spending unhappy time/money with therapists or whatever later."

## Master Key 3: Make Time for a Social Life

Most of us need to take a break for occasional social activities. But often because of our time squeeze, social activities get minimal space on our list of things to do. We deserve some pleasant diversion, however, and need to make time for it in whatever way fits our taste and lifestyle.

---

## TIME  BOOSTERS

- Set up specific dates for doing something special once or twice a month. Otherwise, you'll never get around to finding time for it. "My working-women friends and I all love to cook and entertain," says Sandra Sharp, "so we make time for that by scheduling a regular night every other month to hire sitters and enjoy a meal in someone's home. We rotate homes, and each member of our group prepares a gourmet dish assigned by the hostess."

- Include your children in your social life if that works out best for you. "I work all day on Saturday and find it's too much trouble to get baby-sitters Saturday night," says Pat Peters, "so my husband and I socialize with families with similar situations. We usually eat out together, then socialize for a couple more hours while our children amuse themselves all together."

- Involve other people in your social commitments, so you'll carry through with them instead of skipping them at the last moment because you don't have time. A few suggestions are a dutch-treat "Ladies Night Out," an occasional party or buffet dinner, a simple meal in your home with people who are comfortable with your children, or meeting friends for nonbusiness lunches on a regular basis.

---

## Master Key 4: Make Time for Community Service

Volunteering some of your time to churches, schools, and community projects is another way of helping yourself and other people. There are positive benefits for all concerned when you donate some of your time.

Here's a quick look at how five successful women make time for volunteer work:

- Nancy Read, a pediatric visiting nurse (who also attends college two nights a week), sings in her church choir on Sundays and rehearses one night a week (along with her husband and daughter). One other evening a week she's at the church for a committee meeting.

- Dr. Violet Master is active in her church's youth activities and serves as a liturgist and usher.

- Lois Kohan founded and directs a community Food Pantry, and, along with collecting food, collects clothes for needy families.

- Ruthanne Ciotti volunteers two hours every week to a community care program.

- Gail Stewart Hand helps at her children's school on her way to work. "I find out what morning jobs need to be done, such as helping the children get settled and assisting those who need aid with reading," she says. "This is a good way to volunteer if you can schedule it at that time. You're there already, so you're not losing any time driving back and forth."

## TIME BOOSTERS

- Choose one or two church, school, or community organizations as the focus of your volunteer time each year. By concentrating your support this way, you'll make sure your time investment for community service doesn't get out of hand.

- Though some working women (for instance, Nancy Read) are able to handle several nights out, many can make time for just one or two. Keep this in mind, especially if you're a working mother. There's nothing wrong with giving up community-service activities that require too many week nights out.

- Say "No" to requests you can't handle no matter how worthwhile the cause. Kim Bushaw has a reminder by her phone that reads "Saying no to others means saying yes to your family."[7]

- Save time by showing up at meetings a little late instead of ahead of time or right on time. In that way you're there to do your share. But you don't waste a half hour or more on unproductive preliminaries for which you're not really needed.

## Master Key 5: Make Time for Hobbies and Special Interests

If a hobby or special interest is important to you, give it a specific place in your schedule. Music is vital in my life, so I write "Music" in *ink* on my calendar and fight for the time to pursue it.

Here's how three other women make time for hobbies and special interests:

"I set up time slots for short-term interests," says Alexis Talbott. "For instance, I want to select and purchase new curtains and valances for my bedroom windows within three months. I want to study and invest in mutual funds to gain x number of dollars in a year."

"Since two of my hobbies are crafts and cooking I start early each year to make Christmas gifts and jams and jellies," says Diane Hahnel. "Another special interest is communicating with my friends all over the country. I start writing Christmas cards and send them out December 1, so my friends can respond in their Christmas letters to me."

"I love to read stimulating biographies every week," says Dottie Walters, "so I keep books by my bed, in the bathroom, in the car, and in our den and read them in snatches of time."

### QUICK STARTS

Set up goals and time frames for your hobby or special interest. Then, within that time frame, start working toward that goal. For example, if you'd like to sing in a choral group, give yourself a month to watch newspapers for items about various groups. When you see one that interests you call the phone number that's given and ask about membership requirements.

Juggle your interests to make time to pursue several. "I regard juggling interests as an 'art form,'" says Vicky Penner Katz. "I juggle to make time to fit everything in and still manage to garden, sew, read, play the piano, and so on."

Let something else go and give one night a week (or every two or three weeks if that's all the time you have) to your hobby or special interest.

## Master Key 6: Make Time for Exercise

Finding time for exercise is not always easy but don't neglect this all-important activity simply because you're pressed for time. Unless you're physically fit, you won't maintain your energy level and function at your best.

## What Successful Women Say About Exercise

"I use a step platform and minitrampoline for indoor exercising," says Maureen Powers. "Outdoors I swim, hike, and bike in the summer and ski and sled with my children in the winter."

"I walk two miles every morning," says Yvonne Conway. "Immediately upon awakening I'm out of the door so I don't have time to think about it and 'chicken out.' If I wait till later, my exercising doesn't get done. Time runs out. I get tied up. Or a family member needs me for something."

Some of the other exercises women use to stay fit include:

| | |
|---|---|
| aerobics | stationary bikes |
| golf | tennis |
| racquet ball | running |
| rowing machines | treadmills |
| sit-ups | yoga |
| stair climbing | weight training |

### QUICK STARTS

Psych yourself up by thinking of exercise as an investment of time that pays big benefits. As Edwin G. Bliss wrote in *Getting Things Done,* "Aside from the benefits of regular exercise to your lungs, heart, and digestive system, there is an incidental benefit related to time management. The aggressiveness with which you perform tasks throughout the day is closely related to your physical vigor. Being in good physical condition can increase the percentage of your working hours that can be considered 'prime time,' during which your output is maximized."[8]

Set aside a regular time to do a routine exercise (as opposed to a less frequent exercise such as skiing) and discipline yourself to exercise at that time whether, like Yvonne Conway, your choice is walking first thing in the morning or going to a health club after work.

## Master Key 7: Make Time for Relaxation and Rest

Personally, I can think of no worse fate than slowing down my life for full-time relaxation and rest in which golf, shopping, socializing—and sitting around doing nothing—take up the better part of my days!

But even when we *like* to speed up rather than slow down, we all need time for relaxation and rest in our overloaded lives. This is such a common need that in The Prodigy Services Report on Women, 7 in 10 of the working women polled say being able to relax is a significant choice when they have time to themselves.[9]

This Rx for your emotional and physical health is important even if all you can find time for are slow-breathing exercises at intervals throughout the day or occasional Sunday morning rest and relaxation in bed.

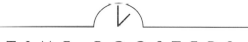

### TIME  BOOSTERS

- Award yourself an hour a day as often as you can to spend in a way that relaxes you. "It requires discipline to take the hour," says Donna Goldfein. "You will not 'find' the hour. It is only with the control of your time that you can routinely give to yourself the hour that is most important to your day and your life."[10]

- Treat yourself during one of "your" hours to a massage, facial, or pedicure.

- Close your eyes and listen to relaxing music for a few moments every day. Aim for the end of the day if there's no other time you can do it.

- Go to bed early for some extra rest when you're tired. Things like work and the house can wait. The world will continue to go on while you make up for too-little sleep.

- Learn to recognize overload and especially use your R and R time allotments when it occurs. Says Marcia Yudkin, "Don't follow the example of one working woman I knew who only slowed down when she actually became sick from her overloaded life. When that happened she'd have to go to bed. Then, as soon as she recovered, she'd pursue the same overloaded cycle till she became ill again."

## Master Key 8: Make Time to Refuel on Weekends

Mathematically speaking, more than two-sevenths of your life is lived from Friday nights till Monday mornings. In that time you have a chance to put back into your life some of the things the work-week necessarily takes away from it.

All of your weekends won't be the same. Depending on each week's situation, different weekends will have different needs. Your options will also depend on your personal circumstances—your budget, obligations, interests, and whether you are single or married. But, whatever your choice for refueling is, the *important* thing is to take a break from the hustle and bustle of your job and the weekday routine of running your home.

## What Successful Women Say About Weekends

"One Sunday a month I put dinner in the crockpot and then do nothing all day but things that keep my mind off business," says Barbara Brabec. "I work on a craft, play the piano, do a puzzle, or pursue anything else that interests me. I find it especially relaxing to work on the teddy bears I make to give to people who've never had a teddy bear."

"On Saturday afternoons my children and I may enjoy a movie or board game together," says Maureen Powers. "Sunday mornings I brunch with friends while the children are with their father."

"During most of the year my children have cultural classes through their school on Saturday mornings," says Sandra Sharp. "My husband and I split the taxi driving, and each of us runs errands during this time. We regroup for lunch and then it's family time the rest of the afternoon. This may entail a trip away—a museum, family visit, and so on—or a stay at home. Sometimes if you ask the kids 'What shall we do today?' they'll just say 'Stay home.' That's fine. With hectic weekday schedules we all need time to unwind. Sunday is church. I also try to make a habit of eating in the dining room with candles and the works at least one evening meal during the weekend."

TIME   BOOSTERS

- Set aside time—and *stick* to that commitment—for such diverse weekend activities as antiquing; backpacking; overnight trips to resorts, inns, or second-home retreats; educational courses; seagoing seminars; sports; cultural events; gardening; entertaining; dining out; resting and relaxing; or anything else that would bring you pleasure and be a change from your workweek.

- Schedule only a short time span for the inevitable household maintenance and upkeep chores you have to do. Short time allotments will serve you well and save time for other things. If you permit yourself only two hours instead of three to do a job you can usually complete the job in that time.

- Reward yourself with something enjoyable as soon as the weekend chores are out of the way—a lunch out or a catch-up phone conversation with a friend.

- Leave time and room for spontaneous happenings. Sometimes they're the best times of all!

## Master Key 9: Make Time for Fun

All work and no play is time management at its lowest ebb, so whatever you do *leave time for fun* as the icing on the cake in your busy life. You need to spend time playing, so schedule "Fun Dates" and "Play Dates" as regularly as you schedule work. If you don't structure in time for fun it gets lost in the other demands of your life and you soon find yourself saying "I never have any fun anymore."

What you define as fun depends on you—and your personal taste—but for many women brief vacations or travel are favorite diversions. For example, an account executive opts for an inexpensive lake-side cabin at $40 a night where part of her fun is listening to fish splashing at dawn and crickets chirping at dusk.

## TIME    BOOSTERS

- Ask yourself "What one thing could I do today (tomorrow or next week) that would be *fun?*"

- Write your answer on your calendar and mark off time for it. A financial consultant who plans three days off for fun every six weeks says, "I note this time on my calendar and say 'This is what I'll do.' Then I go ahead and do it."

- Follow this example and go ahead and do NOW something that fits whatever your idea of fun is. As Ann McGee-Cooper wrote in an article in "Vibrant Life:" "Too often we postpone having fun, trying something new, or taking a risk until all the work is done. In fact, all the work is never done, so we must plan to enrich and enjoy the work by combining work and play . . . Play is critical and essential to maintain abundant energy."[11]

---

### Master Key 10: Make Time for Happiness

You can't afford to wait for a perfect time to make time for happiness. Instead you can make it a state of mind—a choice you make very day. As singer Naomi Judd has said so well, "Happiness is not at the end of the road. It's all along the way."

Missing happiness along the way—or putting it off till time slows up—deprives both you and others of a great psychological benefit. If you take care of yourself and do what makes you happy, the other people in your life will be better off and happier, too.

In her *Happiness Seminars* Sunny Schlenger has people observe what's around them, and then make a list of things they already have that brings them happiness. Here's a sample of one woman's list. Note how little time it takes to enjoy these simple pleasures—and the memories of them.

After you read through this list fill in the blank list with ten things you already have that could put you in a happy frame of mind.

## SAMPLE FILLED-IN HAPPY LIST

Shells from the seashore

Famous people's diaries

Books about cowboys from the old West

Yellow roses

Tapes of James Galway

Bubble bath

Pictures of me snorkeling

Horseshoe from a favorite horse at camp

Raspberry-scented candles

Collection of ceramic dogs

## BLANK HAPPY LIST FOR YOU TO FILL IN

_____

_____

_____

_____

_____

_____

_____

_____

_____

_____

_____

_____

## T I M E   B O O S T E R S

- After you write down your already-in-place happiness list, think about other gratifying things you don't have or aren't doing now that would bring you happiness.

- Make a new list based on this think-through. Set a date for when you can take the first small step to get started on one of the things on this list.

- Don't let the happiness wait that would make you a good friend to yourself and others. "Too few of us resolve to sing or to walk in the snow, to make love or to make someone laugh," wrote columnist Ellen Goodman. "The pursuit of happiness that once carried the moral weight of an American revolution now seems frivolous and has to wait. But happiness is not a banal smiley face to stick on an envelope. It's an option we must exercise or watch atrophy."[12]

# USE A CIRCLE-IN-THE-ROUND WORKSHEET TO START TAKING CHARGE OF YOUR PERSONAL TIME

Make a copy of the following blank circle-in-the-round worksheet and write your work (and all that relates to it) in the smaller circle in the middle since your job consumes the major portion of your time and attention. The labeled spokes going out from the small center circle are the "Make Times" that complement your work and give you a personal life. Write what you want to make time for under the heading on each of the spokes. For guidance in filling out your circle use the sample circle filled in by an artist. Some of your entries may overlap. That's all right. Don't concern yourself.

After you fill in your circle, clip it to your calendar. Review it monthly (1) to keep on top of what you've listed, and (2) to make changes and additions. Make new worksheets as you need them because the fill-ins will be ever-changing as you expand the benefits of taking personal time.

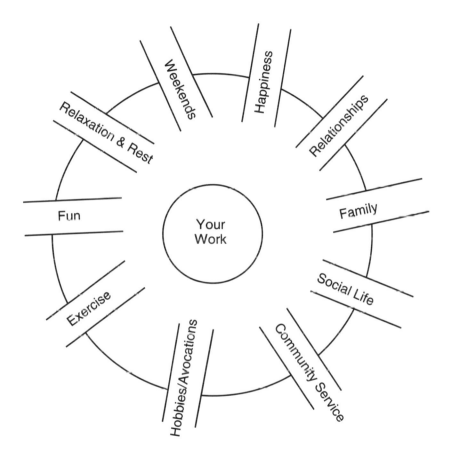

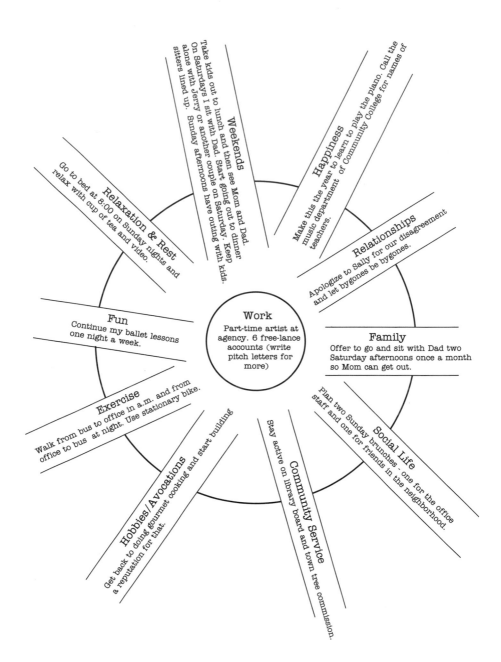

**Work**
Part-time artist at agency. 6 free-lance accounts (write pitch letters for more)

**Weekends**
Take kids out to lunch and then see Mom and Dad. On Saturdays I sit with Dad. Start going out to dinner alone with Jerry or another couple on Saturday. Keep sitters lined up. Sunday afternoons have outing with kids.

**Happiness**
Make this the year to learn to play the piano. Call the music department of Community College for names of teachers.

**Relationships**
Apologize to Sally for our disagreement and let bygones be bygones.

**Family**
Offer to go and sit with Dad two Saturday afternoons once a month so Mom can get out.

**Social Life**
Plan two Sunday brunches - one for the office staff and one for friends in the neighborhood.

**Community Service**
Stay active on library board and town tree commission.

**Hobbies/Avocations**
Get back to doing gourmet cooking and start building a reputation for that.

**Exercise**
Walk from bus to office in a.m. and from office to bus at night. Use stationary bike.

**Fun**
Continue my ballet lessons one night a week.

**Relaxation & Rest**
Go to bed at 8:00 on Sunday nights and relax with cup of tea and video.

***Quick Check/Recheck*** Managing time off for yourself is just as important as managing your work and home time. But with all your other commitments, personal time won't squeeze itself in and announce "I'm here!" The only way to get it is to make time for it. It's important for you to do this, too, no matter how time-starved you are. The way we treat ourselves affects everything else we do, gives us the energy to cope day to day, and helps us be a friend to ourselves and the people in our world. Use the Ten Master Keys for Unlocking Personal Time to make time for yourself, your relationships, your values, and your interests. When you do, you won't run on empty—even when you have too much to do and too little time to do it.

# Stay Focused and You Can Almost "Have It All" Your Way

*Superwoman is dead—and no one is sad. Hardly anyone attended her funeral. No one had the time.*

—**A family educator**

Is there time in your life to have it all? Or enough hours in your day to resurrect Superwoman?

Back in the '70s and '80s we were besieged by the have-it-all blitz. But as baby boomers grew up—and as women made greater strides in business, politics, and education (while simultaneously feeling stressed when trying to do too many things)—the daughters of the '70s and '80s began to look at the day-to-day problems of managing time in more realistic ways.

We've *always* had different cycles than men. But today we're coming to terms with the fact that our time issues relate to the cycle we're in. As such, time doesn't permit having *everything* in every cycle or state, so our childbearing and child-rearing cycles—and our full-time, part-time, or work-at-home stages—are all different segments of "having it all" or almost "having it all."

In fact, in a survey of working women for *Women and the Work/Family Dilemma* Deborah J. Swiss and Judith P. Walker found the top-notch professionals they interviewed said no one *has* it all, even if from all outward appearances they appear to *do* it all.[1] This 21st century reality gives our time management a tremendous, up-to-date boost.

## $\mathcal{W}$HAT'S HAVING IT ALL ANYHOW?

In responding to "What is having it all?"—and that other frequent question "What do women want?"—reporter Susan Reimer wrote, "They, we, would ask for more time, I think. Time to do well all the things that are expected of us at home and at work. And a little more time to ourselves when we are done."[2]

Susan Reimer goes on to say that she and other women also want more time to collect our many-sided selves, and then more time to think about the next step in our lives.

To this, Dr. Mary Frame adds that having it all for today's woman is having that all-important quality of life each woman as an individual wants.

"The way it was presented to women for a while—having a successful career, successful husband, successful children and wonderful house—is a too Cinderella-like, pie-in-the-sky answer that we don't want to perpetuate," she told me. "You give one working woman the finest books and a piano and she's happy. You give another an outdoors setting away from the city and hubbub, and she's happy. Who's to say that one is right and one is wrong?"

The following responses show how ten other women answer the question, "What is having it all?"

Nancy Read: "Having it all means going beyond the pattern of 'married with children' to become the person I was meant to be at the same time I enjoy motherhood, marriage, and my profession. Because of my present career and family responsibilities achieving that goal will take time. But I know that I will get there."

Ingrid Steele, a musician, accompanist, and director of choirs, choral, and theater groups: "Having it all means doing what *you* feel makes you the happiest. I have a supportive husband whose interests parallel mine and who encourages me to pursue my career and home life at my own pace. It might be nice to have more materially. But we have everything we need."

Carolyn Bushong: "Having it all means different things at different times, since our needs and desires change. But, as women give up the superwoman role, they gain more choices without feeling judged or inadequate."

Caroline Hull: "'Having it all' is probably one of the worst phrases that ever entered our language. It's a stupid myth! I was bamboozled by this notion before I had my five children, and it was a tremendous letdown to realize I couldn't hand over my first baby to someone I'd interviewed twice, and then go on with the fast-track career I had. I didn't want to do this and be gone 12 hours a day. What I'm doing now is the closest to having it all for now if that's what I'm after—which I'm not. You don't have to have everything all at one time."

Paula Baum: "I think it's possible and achievable to have *enough* but not possible to have it all and do it all. My goal is to enjoy my work and family and make enough money to pay my bills and have some left over. At this point that's my *enough*—and that's achievable."

Dr. Jane Mattes: "As a therapist, woman, and mother, I don't think you can have it all at once, but you can have pieces of it at different times. Women have to figure out where they're going and then focus on and enjoy those pieces at the different times."

Carol Painter Campi: "Nobody can have it all, and I believe in trying to have it all and live up to some unrealistic expectations touted by the media, women experience higher levels of stress and anxiety. Everything has a price. I have come close in many areas at various times of my life to this having-it-all mystique. Maybe someday I'll have it all together—but I'm not holding my breath."

Judith Moncrieff Baldwin: "I don't think anyone can have it all in any one lifetime—particularly as the individual's definition of "all" will change with time and personal evolution. From that standpoint I've had it all at many given points in my life, but I still haven't reached the point where I can rest in the all that I have. I'm happy with the evolution, though. It's been interesting."

Lynn McIntyre Coffee: "I learned early on when I was in the
corporate world that I could have been president of a corporation.
But it would have cost me *everything*. Instead of that high payoff I
looked for more balance, and now my life is my husband, my child,
my home and my own business. I also have realistic expectations. My
children aren't going to be dressed in hand-sewed clothes. I'm not
going to be on every board. I'm not going to have a booming business practice. But I don't want all that now. My husband, child,
home, and business are like a chord in my life, and it's important to
give enough time to hit each note equally."

Dr. Violet Master: "Balancing my work and family is having it
all in the way I want it. When I was starting out people would say
'What hospitals do you go to?' When I'd mention one they'd ask
'Why don't you go to this or that hospital?' Then they'd say 'How
many hours do you work?' or 'Couldn't you work more hours?' I
made my own decisions. I didn't want the practice and the life they
described. In some people's viewpoints, you may not have it all. But
it's your own satisfaction that counts."

## *E*IGHT WAYS YOU CAN HAVE IT ALL YOUR WAY

The bottom line of having it all is having time for the quality of life
that rewards and benefits you. Here are eight ways to take charge of
your time in whatever stage of life you're in. Each way builds on suggestions highlighted in earlier sections.

### (1) Reinforce Your Goals

Always remember that in your work, home, and personal life managing your time *begins* with planning what *you* want (and can realistically achieve), and then giving priority to the goals that provide
direction for your life.

Barbara Doyen does this by keeping what she calls the 'Gold
Book'—a timetable she uses regularly to review her plans for the
careers and lives she and her husband share.

"Right from the beginning of our marriage we took time to
plan our professional and personal lives and figure out how to

accommodate each other's needs and wants," she says. "Now, at the start of each year, we discuss and write in our 'Gold Book' our specific goals for the next twelve months."

"As a result of this planning, we know where we're heading in 5 years, 10 years, and beyond."

### QUICK STARTS

Put your planning into action by doing at least one task toward meeting one goal in your job, home, or personal life each week.

Revise your planning when your needs and goals change or you feel dissatisfied.

## (2) Look at the Available Choices for Your Current Life Cycle

In order to have it all, you must recognize and choose different options at different times—unless your financial situation rules out having a choice, at least for the time being.

If you have a choice, however, you may want to change from 9:00 A.M. to 5:00 P.M. employment to job sharing, part-time, temporary, flextime—or, maybe, start your own business or service. These are choices some women make in order to have the "all" that satisfies them during the stage in which they're currently living.

In Virginia, Heidi Brennan, the mother of four children, works as Co-Director and Public Policy Director of Mothers at Home, a national nonprofit organization that addresses the nature and work of motherhood through a monthly publication *Welcome Home*. A core group of women like Heidi manage the operation from a family-friendly office where mothers work while their children play in a large sunny playroom.

In Washington, a mother of two works at home 20 hours a week as a copy editor. In New Jersey, a former securities lawyer and mother of a three-year-old works as a bank teller in a special program to fit mothers' needs. In Iowa, the mother of a son and daughter makes and sells hair bows. And in Idaho, the mother of two works one day a week as an occupational therapist.

"This is the way women make choices," stresses Linda Marks, Director of the FlexGroup at New Ways to Work. "They don't need to play out the scenario the way it has always been done."

## TIME BOOSTERS

- Enjoy what you're able to do in your present time frame, since no choice is forever. Keep your eye on the future while thinking ahead to what you want next.

- If your choice is job sharing, part-time, temporary, flextime, or your own business, arrange your schedule to coincide with your children's school hours.

- Consider working late, early, or on weekends if your job field is conducive to that. "When my children were small I worked twelve evening shifts a month," recalls Diane Hahnel, the health-screening nurse. "Four of the shifts were on every other weekend, so my children bonded with their Dad and I kept up with my profession."

## (3) Concentrate on the Values That Enrich Your Life

The search for values continues to be so prevalent, that even in an *international* survey on time and values, Priority Management Systems found people everywhere want time to pay more attention to what's meaningful in their lives.[3] When you make the time to do this (rather than always following what other people expect you to do), you free yourself to manage your time in truly beneficial ways.

"I like to hear what other people feel and think, but I'm not influenced terribly by that," says Ingrid Steele. "When I was doing too many things, I decided I needed more time off, and that's okay. Now, because most of my rehearsals, concerts, and shows are at night, I stay up late after rehearsals to read, do crossword puzzles, and flip around on TV. This is *my* time—and all of these things enrich me and let me taste everything.

"So when people say 'You don't start your day at 8:00 A.M.' or 'You don't answer your phone at 9:00,' I answer, 'That's right—I'm a night person and not on your time schedule.'"

## QUICK STARTS

 Once you sort out your values, write them down. They're less amorphous when they're in black and white.

 Get started on enriching your life and gaining time by acting on the values that are most essential to you first.

 Review your values regularly so you never lose sight of them in your time-squeezed life.

### (4) Balance Your Time Among All Areas of Your Life

In her book *Time Management for Unmanageable People,* Ann McGee Cooper talks a great deal about the two brain hemispheres that play a significant part in the way we look at our time, lives, and work.[4]

Stated simply, left-brain thinkers narrow the picture of their lives to a smaller size and perspective and reduce their lives and time commitments. Right-brain thinkers scan the big picture and enlarge their lives and time commitments.

The best strategy is to find a balanced, whole-brained approach to time and life rather than settling for a left or right extreme. But as you seek a balanced approach, keep in mind that narrowing your life to a smaller perspective is *not* the same as simplifying it and cutting back on nonessentials. The latter opens up opportunities, while narrowing your life to a too-small perspective limits your opportunities.

## Q U I C K   S T A R T S

Keep on top of what needs to be done in all areas of your life each day, week, and month.

If you find you're obsessed with one area for too long a time, watch out. That's when imbalance takes over.

## (5) Be Flexible When Circumstances Change

No time schedule should be so rigid there's no way to change your plans when necessity demands it—or when it's beneficial to shift to another direction.

"You need to be what I call a professional chameleon and have the ability to adapt yourself to the changing environment in which you work," advises Dr. Larry Baker.

"You can't control all the things that impact your time management, so my idea of time management is knowing several ways to accomplish something. Then you can choose the right way under the right conditions. This is adapting, not selling out."

### T I M E   B O O S T E R S

- Be prepared to change your route when obstacles beyond your control make it difficult to continue toward a work goal you've established. Suppose, for instance, your goal has been to earn kudos from your boss by surprising her with a finished job well in advance of the deadline she gave you. You've set up your time to complete the job by a certain date and cleared your calendar to do it. Then along comes your boss with two new jobs she wants immediately. You can't convince her that someone else might have more time for these jobs, so you have to shift gears and abandon your almost-completed work. You're frustrated and disappointed. But be flexible enough to reassign your want-to-earn-kudos-from-the-boss goal to the new tasks on your desk. You'll find that when you're flexible, there's more than one path to an overall goal.

- Reconsider your circumstances when a situation at home takes such an unexpected turn it seems better to change your planned schedule or course. A C.P.A. who worked at home till her two children could enter school was scheduled to take a full-time job with a major corporation as soon as that time came. But by the time the children were ready to enter school she was unexpectedly pregnant. "So it's back to diapers and working at home," she said philosophically. "Under the present circumstances that's my best choice now."

---

## (6) Forgive Yourself When You Make Mistakes

Simply because you're human, there will be times when you make mistakes and fall short of managing time well. But occasional missteps along the way don't mean you'll always fall down. Be kind to yourself when this happens—and as Cynthia Cohen Turk points out—"Learn when to say I did the best I could and that will have to do."

I'll never forget the first speech I gave when I was beginning my career. One of my major goals at the time was to lecture, along with writing, so I said "Yes" to my first invitation to speak to a group of women.

I prepared a speech for working women without taking time to research the audience and find out what their interests were (Mistake No. 1). Unfortunately, when I got to the meeting the audience was *non*working women, and no one cared even remotely about my speech on getting ahead in a job or career.

My time management was as off as my subject, too! Instead of asking what time I was scheduled to speak (Mistake No. 2), I asked what time the meeting began—and in a show of promptness, arrived two hours ahead of speaking to sit through endless committee reports, one of which was how wonderful the previous month's speaker had been!

When I was finally introduced, half the audience went to the kitchen to get the refreshments ready—and the other half showed very clearly they were more interested in coffee and cake than in anything I was saying. But I'd timed by speech to last 30 minutes and

because of my lack of experience I didn't know how to cut it and get
it over with.

It was hard to forget—and forgive—that mistake even though
I'd done my best. But as the years and speeches went on I ultimately
viewed that low point as a four-star learning experience that benefit-
ed me the rest of my life in preparing, giving, and timing speeches.

## T I M E   B O O S T E R S

- When mistakes happen, ask yourself "What did I do wrong?"

- Write down where and when you got off track since it's just as important to know what you're doing wrong as what you're doing right.

- Analyze why and how you got off track and determine the logical
  steps you could have taken to get back on. (In my own case, I could
  have (1) asked to speak earlier as long as I was there, (2) tailored my
  speech to the audience, (3) eliminated the material that didn't
  relate, and above all, (4) cut the speech at least in half.)

- Ease up on yourself and get rid of any guilt and discouragement
  about mistakes. Guilt and discouragement rob you of productive
  time. (I lost the whole next day worrying about my speech disaster.)

- Keep your mistakes in perspective. When it's appropriate to laugh at
  them—and laugh at yourself for making them—lighten up and
  maintain a sense of humor.

## (7) Expect Some Time Management Detours

Just as you need to be flexible and adapt yourself to changes in your
work/life environment you have to expect to face changes in your
personal life. The best timetables fall apart when divorce, family
problems, accidents and illnesses, or the death of a loved one or
friend make it hard to manage time as usual. This goes with the ter-
ritory called life, and no one is immune.

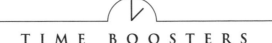

## TIME   BOOSTERS

- When these unforeseen circumstances arise, work and live around them as you do your best with what you *can* do, while the temporary situation lasts.

- Bolster yourself with the knowledge that you will be able to get back on the time management track toward having it all your way when the detour is behind you.

## (8) Be Glad You Have Multiple Roles

Although you may not always recognize the fact, you *benefit* from having multiple roles. Research has indicated that women who work:

- do well with their multiple commitments

- feel better about themselves than the average woman who is not in the workforce

- are happier than nonworking women.

Current research continues to show that the juggling act should not be viewed in negative terms. For instance, Dr. Pepper Schwartz, author of *Peer Marriage: How Love Between Equals Really Works,* wrote in an article in *The New York Times* that rather than being unhealthily stressed by their having too much to do and too little time, women who juggle many roles are *blessedly* stressed.

"Give them the complicated life and these determined jugglers maintain their equilibrium—rather like a table with four legs," she stated. "One element of their lives can support them when the other aspects appear to be falling apart (assuming, of course, that everything doesn't crash at once)."

The article goes on to point out that Dr. Rosalind Barnett of the Wellesley College Center for Research on Women found in a random sample of 300 women in dual-earner couples over two years that most women viewed their jobs as more rewarding than problematic, were generally pleased with their marriages, and felt good about their mother-child relationships. In fact, the more roles women had the better they rated their own mental health.[5]

I like the blessedly stressed idea because even though you're bound to have occasional feelings of stress, the self-esteem, income, and satisfaction from meaningful multiple roles are benefits not only for you, but also for everyone around you. Remember this on those time-crunched days when it seems you'll never catch up.

## T I M E    B O O S T E R S

- Splurge on occasional outside help when things pile up in your work/home/personal life and you question whether "having-it-all-your-way" isn't too much after all.

- Recognize the value of the juggling act and know that having multiple roles is lifetime insurance for having it all in the combination that's right for you.

# $\mathcal{C}$HECK YOUR HAVING-IT-ALL-YOUR-WAY STATUS

Throughout this book you've worked on improving your use of time through a 13-Point Program for managing your 9:00 A.M. to 5:00 P.M. on-the-job hours, your before-and-after work life, and your personal time for yourself and others. You've picked up solutions to your problems from the Quick Starts, Time Boosters, and What Successful Women Say features, and you've also answered a variety of questionnaires and self-evaluation exercises.

Here's a comprehensive checklist to show you where you're standing now, and what you still need to do to apply these time-saving strategies in your work, home, and personal life so you can have it all your way. Mark a check under the appropriate headings.

| | What I'm Doing Now | What I Still Need to Do |
|---|---|---|

**YOUR TIME AT WORK**

1. I'm making the most of my trip to work and arriving at my job on time. ____ ____

2. I start work when I arrive and don't procrastinate—either upon arrival or during the rest of the day. ____ ____

3. I use a calendar/calendars. ____ ____

4. I do daily, weekly, monthly, and long-term planning. ____ ____

5. I'm organizing my time with to-do lists and everyday file sorters. ____ ____

6. I'm keeping day-logs and time journals to check where my time goes. ____ ____

7. I'm learning to say "No" when "No" is in order. ____ ____

8. I'm doing better at meeting deadlines. ____ ____

9. I've upgraded my decision-making skills. ____ ____

10. I delegate some of my tasks. ____ ____

11. I'm factoring in some leeway for interruptions and the unexpected. ____ ____

12. I'm *starting* to keep paperwork and filing from piling up. ____ ____

13. I'm becoming more assertive about passing up waste-of-time meetings I don't have to attend. ____ ____

14. I'm restraining myself from detouring from my main goals to less important ones. ____ ____

15. I'm realistic about what I can and can't accomplish. ____ ____

16. I know when to end my workday and go on to the rest of my life. ____ ____

|  | What I'm Doing Now | What I Still Need to Do |
|---|---|---|

**YOUR TIME AT HOME**

17. I'm beginning my days with a smoother morning routine and getting everyone out of the house with less hassle. ___ ___

18. I've arranged my family's and my clothes, closets, and drawers for speed-up dressing in the morning. ___ ___

19. I've set up more than one child-care contingency plan so I always have an alternative if one arrangement falls through. ___ ___

20. I'm putting time with my family/children as a first-things-first commitment before and after work. ___ ___

21. I streamline home care and house chores to give my first-things-first attention to things that really matter. ___ ___

22. I save time and stress by not being a perfectionist. ___ ___

23. I'm gaining time by organizing my shopping and errands so I make fewer trips to the stores. ___ ___

24. I ask for and expect help from others. ___ ___

25. I don't always insist other people do things exactly as I'd do them. ___ ___

26. I have a calendar or bulletin board for home and family activities. ___ ___

27. I try to relax a few moments after leaving work, and before starting dinner. ___ ___

28. I'm decreasing the "Hurry up" approach to my home life. ___ ___

29. I preplan and prepare for mornings at night as much as I possibly can. ___ ___

|  | *What I'm Doing Now* | *What I Still Need to Do* |
|---|---|---|

**YOUR TIME FOR YOU**

30. I'm paying attention to *my* values and simplifying my life to include them when I plan my time. ____ ____

31. I'm leaving more breathing space for *me* in my life. ____ ____

32. I've stopped feeling guilty when I make time for myself. ____ ____

33. I take good care of my health and slow down when I need to. ____ ____

34. I spend some time alone getting in touch with myself emotionally, spiritually, and psychically. ____ ____

35. I'm taking more time to nurture my relationships with people. ____ ____

36. I have outside interests beyond my work and home life. ____ ____

37. I spend some time relaxing and having fun on weekends. ____ ____

38. I'm enjoying my day-to-day life more. ____ ____

39. I'm increasing my self-esteem. ____ ____

40. I'm beginning to feel I can control my own destiny at least to some degree. ____ ____

There's no score to tally on this checklist, but copy your completed list and keep it available as an ongoing memo to yourself. It will apply indefinitely whether you're single without children, single with children, married without children, or married with children.

***Quick Check/Recheck*** Time doesn't permit you to have *every-thing* in every cycle or stage. You'll take a giant step toward gaining control of your time by coming to terms with the 21st century real-

ity that most working women can't (and don't choose to) have
everything at one time. For most women today having it all is having time for the quality of life that rewards and benefits them in the
choices they make. The concept of having it all is different for different women and depends on each woman's values and the stage
of life you're in. But as you practice time management based on
women's special issues, you'll learn by trial and error how to find
time for your many-sided life and have it all *your* way with the time
you have.

POINT THIRTEEN

# Let Your Individual Situation Guide Your Time Management Choices

*I've been married/I've been single. . . .*
**—A writer, editor, publisher**

Whether we're single/single with children, or married/married with children, *all* working women have commonalities as well as differences that influence the way they manage time.

The Number 1 *commonality* is having too much to do and too little time. The *differences* evolve from our individual marital and family situations. It goes without saying, for example, that a single woman without children doesn't have the same time-management problems as a married woman with a husband and children.

Most of the time management techniques presented in the previous sections apply to all working women, regardless of their marital status. But there are special considerations unique to single/single with children lifestyles, or married/married with children lifestyles that we'll discuss in this section. Some of the what's useful for one category is also valid for others, so keep each strategy in mind as you read.

# $\mathscr{S}$INGLE WITHOUT CHILDREN: TAKE ADVANTAGE OF THE TIME BUT WATCH FOR THE PITFALLS

When you're single and live alone (without obligations to plan your time around other people's needs), you can devote more hours to your career objectives.

This situation offers many advantages for taking control of your time. For example, Elizabeth Randall, the New Jersey Banking Commissioner and member of many boards, uses her single status as bonus time to work well beyond the usual working day.

"As a single woman, I have no need to hurry home to keep up with home demands and make sure my house is shipshape," she says. "This isn't a first priority with me."

Along with the benefits, however, being single brings its own problems if you become so involved in your job you leave too little time for a home or personal life. Time management expert Jeff Davidson relates the story of a working woman/student who followed such a hard-and-fast daily schedule she had no breathing space.

"I trip through a day like this," she told Davidson. "Wake up at 6:00 A.M.; eat breakfast and get out of the door by 7:30; run to the subway to commute to my job; work from 8:00 A.M. till noon; take classes from 1:00 to 5:00 P.M.; exercise from 6:00 to 7:00 P.M.; eat and regain my sanity from 7:30 to 8:00 P.M.; and devote the strength I have left to homework till 12:30 A.M.

"If I watch television or go to a party, my mind is plagued with the thoughts of what I could and should be doing."

This do-do-do and go-go-go can be common for a single woman who has neither marriage nor child-care commitments. "Unless that woman is in a relationship with someone saying 'Make some time for me,' her biggest time problem may be allowing no time for her personal life while she puts all her efforts into work," warns psychologist Dr. Michael Broder, author of *The Art of Living Single*. "Sometimes this may be an antidote for loneliness. Other times it's because she hasn't thought of doing things differently.

"For her the key advice is to set priorities beyond work so her personal life won't go by the board and bring regrets later on."

Here's what one successful woman has to say about time management and her single status.

"Because I don't have many demands on my time from other people, I *savor* time instead of *managing* it," says Dixie Darr. "I pare my life down to doing only those things I truly want to do. And since I simply love my work, I may work on weekends or in the middle of the night when I have trouble sleeping.

"But no one would call me a workaholic. In fact, I sometimes wake in the morning consumed with happiness that I've been given another day to use time exactly as I wish and to have the freedom to spend time with friends and family whenever I want to."

"I've been married and I've been single," says Lisa Rogak who makes time to write, publish a newsletter, help renovate an old house, enjoy the outdoors, and see friends. As a divorced mother with a son who stays with his father I live with my boyfriend in the country. Both of us work at home and my boyfriend makes me feel I have more time to do things now than when I was married *or* single and living by myself.

"I take care of shopping and food and ignore small things around the house until they're intolerable. Then I do them all at once and forget about them for a while. My boyfriend works on the house and yard, and each of us does our own laundry.

"And since we both work on our jobs in the evening we never have to ask each other 'Why aren't you spending time with me?'"

## QUICK STARTS

If you have no family (or are far removed from one) take time to make the kind of friends who can become your extended family. This beats keeping your nose to the grindstone on holidays—and celebrating your birthday by yourself.

Involve yourself in a variety of nonwork interests or hobbies, so your work won't become your only identity.

Take full advantage of the time that's your own to invest in and round out your personal growth.

# $\mathscr{S}$INGLE WITH CHILDREN: WHAT YOU CAN DO TO OVERCOME THE HARSH REALITIES

Single women with children have a far different story than women who are single and living alone. Barbara Duncan wrote in *The Single Mother's Survival Manual,* "As a single working mother you will find yourself short on both time and energy each day."[1]

The way single mothers resolve the complicated problems of working, parenting, running the house, and (if there's no help from the father) supporting their children and themselves depends on each woman's time frame.

"But many of the single mothers I see live at a frantic pace and function with what amounts to survival techniques as they try to maintain an acceptable lifestyle, adhere to high standards of parenting, and put in long hours at work because of their qualms about job security," says Dr. Mary Frame.

When you add this kind of job pressure to never-ending home responsibilities, you're well on your way to major stress unless you:

- figure out what's really essential for a good combination work and lifestyle for you and your child/children

- let go of what's nonessential

- take time for yourself in between

## What Successful Women Say About Single Motherhood

"When I became a single mother, my initial priorities were to (1) minimize the hours I'd have to be away from my son, (2) make enough money to support us, and (3) do as little as possible of anything else," says Dr. Jane Mattes. "My mother baby-sat while I worked, and for some of my evening hours a teenager in our building helped out.

"My outside interests went by the wayside except for founding Single Mothers By Choice, and I cooked and cleaned as minimally as possible. If the house got messy, I didn't care—and neither did my young son. For quite a while my entertaining was bringing in playmates for my son and serving peanut butter and jelly sandwiches."

"One of my biggest problems is being responsible for 99% of the 100% it takes to run a house," reports Paula Baum. "I get only limited help from my teenagers except for what I insist on, so during the week I plod through the 'Musts' and leave what I can for weekends.

"But before I get to the weekend chores I do something for me. I take an hour to read in bed and have my morning coffee every Saturday and Sunday. I sip my coffee and savor that hour, and even when other things don't get done I enjoy that respite."

"Every day I have 24 hours, so I make choices about what to do with that time," says Sherry Sheridan. "An important choice for me is to 'be there' for my 9- and 12-year-old children so the extra money I could make by working full time, rather than part time, is not worth the stress and time that would require.

"My idea of what is required economically has changed a great deal as a result of this arrangement, but I'm grateful the arrangement gives me enough money to provide us with food, clothing and shelter and allows me the time and energy to keep growing as a mother and person.

"So my windows need washing. There are dishes in the sink. The kitchen should be painted. The yard is overgrown. There are piles everywhere. But we are alive and well—and I hesitate to say it—happy."

## T I M E   B O O S T E R S

- Form a support system of relatives and friends whom you can call on for help, advice, and understanding.

- Be your own woman and don't attempt to follow the suggestions and systems of well-meaning relatives and friends who never held a job or who have husbands to pitch in and help.

- Trade off some driving chores and baby-sitting and child care responsibilities with other single mothers. Even though you have baby-sitters for hire on tap, this exchange will save everyone money and time.

- Set aside some non-hurry-up-let's-go time for connecting with your children and attending to their needs at the beginning and end of each day, no matter how stressed, impatient, or tired you are. Even though this is difficult at times, both you and your children will feel better.

- Spend time each week, if possible, on a one-to-one activity with each of your children. One single mother accomplishes this—and gets other tasks done in the bargain—by taking one child with her on her after-work weekly supermarket trip. "We choose food together, talk in the car, and stop for a snack," she says. "My children love 'our time' so much they can't wait for their turn."

- Realize you don't have to spend all your time with your children. You don't deprive them of their "due" when you take time to socialize with friends. This outlet—and time to do things on your own—is important for *you.*

- Similarly reserve quiet time for yourself each day—even if it's only half an hour. "After 9:00 P.M. is *my* time and I'm available only for emergencies," says Sherry Sheridan. "My bedroom is *my* space—and knocking at the door is required."

---

## $\mathscr{M}$ARRIED WITHOUT CHILDREN: GAIN CONTROL OF YOUR TIME WHILE AVOIDING THE TIME TRAPS

If you and your husband don't have children, you're much more likely to have more time to devote to your work and away-from-work-life. Your time management issues are not the same as those of a married woman who's also raising children.

But still, you're probably responsible for home and hearth. And you still have your own brand of problems in balancing your 9:00 A.M. to 5:00 P.M. life with the other demands of multiroles.

In her research on working women, Dr. Pepper Schwartz found that a great many women like you are deeply involved in multiple roles and a complicated life. As one woman told her, "I'd like to cut back—it's too much really. But what would I cut out? I need my friends, I love my work, I love choir, I'd miss any of it. What can I say, It makes me nuts—but it keeps me sane."[2]

## What Successful Married-Without-Children Women Say About Managing Time

"Since I like to do many things besides working and keeping up with the house, I devote a lot of my time to being a church organist and soloist and singing in choral groups," says Ruth Ann Gates. "I also plan outings for my family and friends at least once a month. But there are *still* things to do at home, so the old adage 'A woman's work is never done' is true. I get up early to fix dinner and straighten up. Later, before I get home from work at 6:45, my husband sets the table and puts dinner in the oven."

"When I want to recharge my batteries I like 'quiet time' with my husband since he travels 50% of the time," says Judith Moncrieff Baldwin. "My favorite treat for myself is gardening or a 20-minute bubble bath with a good book, good music, and a glass of champagne when there's time for that. I don't really know how women with children manage. I just have one large black cat, and he interrupts me all the time!"

"I haven't combined having children with working because I don't believe in the myth of having it all," says Sheree Bykofsky. "I hire people to help me do everything possible that doesn't require me to do it. Even though I don't have children, I take the time to keep my nurturing instincts alive and well in working with people in my business practices. At home, my husband is an equal partner and a considerate, easy person to live with. We generally eat out or order in to give us more time together."

"My work is a priority," says Mary Flood, "and I'm another woman who doesn't believe that I can have it all, so my decision not to have children was made for a number of complex reasons. But I also believe both men and women can make time to be nurturers, even though they're not parents. A woman may nurture in different ways than men, but in his own way my husband is a great nurturer. He gives me space for myself and often brings home surprise dinners.

"And when I needed a new car, he selected it, tuned it up and had it ready to go when I came back from a business trip."

## Beware of Three Common Time Traps

While your no-children life can give you more time to devote to your work and away-from-work-activities, you can also encounter time traps. Here are three common problems.

1. You can become so involved in your work that (like a single woman without children) you have too little time for anything else.

   "With kids not there, you're less likely to have some anchor point that pulls you back to the family for dinner time, for family time," points out psychologist Steven E. Hobfoll who with Ivonne Heras Hobfoll wrote *Work Won't Love You Back: The Dual Career Couple's Survival Guide*. "You're more likely to have the ships-passing-in-the-night phenomenon."[3]

2. Since no children compete for your attention you may have a mate who wants extra time and attention from you. If his demands are unreasonable, it takes away time for your own needs.

3. Between the time you spend on your work and the time you spend with your husband you may fall into the habit of never having time to see your friends and maintain those relationships.

## TIME   BOOSTERS

• Use the time you gain by having no child-care responsibilities not only for being more involved in your work, but also for putting high value on time to do other things. Some of the favorites of women who use time they'd spend on child care for other activities are reading, music, art, taking courses, acting in theatre groups, gardening, volunteering, home decorating, gourmet cooking, crafts, traveling, camping, working out, yoga, walking, running, racquet ball, swimming, and skiing.

- Talk out your time problems and issues with your husband (especially if he expects unreasonable amounts of your time). Make sure you're each empathetic to the other's needs.

- Have "dates" with your husband and do things together on weekends if you see little of each other during the week. But try to spend at least a small amount of time together during the week—preferably when the two of you aren't exhausted. Plan for quiet times together as well as joint activities that you both enjoy.

- Set aside specific times to be with your friends—say, every Wednesday or Friday evening. If you don't make these plans and stick with them, you probably won't maintain real relationships with your friends.

---

# ᴹARRIED WITH CHILDREN: JUGGLING MULTIPLE RESPONSIBILITIES IN A CONSTANT TIME CRUNCH

In the last decades of the 20th century, married women with children have accounted for a tremendous growth in employment, since most of today's families depend on dual incomes.

But along with this employment growth came a growth in daily time problems, since married women with children face day-after-day juggling acts in managing their time.

As opposed to a single mother (who has everything heaped on her shoulders), you have a husband to share part of your tasks. But in most situations, you are the partner with the greatest time crunch in integrating family and work.

Your days *are* fragmented with small tasks, and generally, the segments of your life are less clearly defined than your husband's. You're also probably the person who has to adjust your schedule to meet your children's needs and the one who most often must ask for time off when the children are sick or on vacation.

Your challenge is combining *everything* and matching your 24 hours to the many aspects of your life. But when you *expect* to be flexible—and commit yourself to enjoying everything you have—this multiduties/multipeople life is one many women cherish.

## What Successful Women Say About Married-with-Children Life

"I'm flexible, and as a 50/50 team, my husband and I enjoy the beautiful life going on in our house," says Lois Kohan. "I choose to work close to my home because—even though I've had great job offers farther from home—I want quick availability should any of my five children need me. With both older and younger children in the house, people are constantly in and out. It *is* a beautiful life."

"Flexibility is a constant," emphasizes Pat Peters. "I used to set up my schedule to work before my son got out of school because I wanted to devote from 12:30 on to any needs he had before his sister came home at 3:00. But now I must juggle my schedule again because my son is in school till 3:00. I love my work and feel better about myself after my time on the job, but my kids are my first priority which is why I work part time. In addition, my husband depends on me to schedule *all* family arrangements. I feel like I'm the director, and he's coproducer and financial backer."

"Structuring your work life around family needs is a never-ending juggling act, whether you have one child or several children," concludes Caroline Hull. "I find I go through stages where I seem to have everything under control. Then something will happen in my work or one of my children will be going through some kind of stage, and suddenly everything is all out of balance again. You simply have to be flexible and learn, evolve, and change."

## QUICK STARTS

 Ask for support—and understanding—both at work and at home. There will be times when you have to miss work due to a child's illness, and there will be nights when you come home too tired to want to do anything.

 Remind yourself at those times that you don't have to attend to everything personally. You're not the only one able to do things. Remember the Big D—and delegate.

Write down all your responsibilities at work and home and have your husband do the same. As you do this you may also want to review the *Check Who Does What* evaluation sheet in Point 10. This will show you, first, how well you're sharing the workload, and second, where you can make some changes. One husband and wife who did this kind of evaluation now alternate cooking and clean-up nights.

 Invest some of your two-income paychecks in hiring people and household services to help you. Or, if your funds are too limited for that, swap tasks with other working women. A travel agent I know who detests sewing but who finds ironing relaxing ironed two banquet-size tablecloths for a nurse. In return the nurse made curtains for the travel agent's kitchen.

 Cut out unnecessary time-taking activities that provide you with only ambivalent satisfaction. I'm seriously considering getting rid of my live plants so I don't have to take time to water and care for them when I'd rather read a book

 Combine personal and family activities — say jogging or biking— with your husband or children. In that way, you'll be exercising for yourself while simultaneously enjoying time with your family.

 Maintain your health and sense of humor.

 Above all, don't make time management such a grim fast-forward, cast-in-iron burden that you don't leave time to just "be."

# ＵSE THIS FINAL WORKSHEET FOR CONTINUING TO MANAGE YOUR JOB, YOUR LIFE, AND YOURSELF

In Point 12 you evaluated where you're standing now on the *Check Your Having-It-All-Your-Way Status* sheet. Now, as a final push toward

gaining the greatest benefits from the 13-Point Plan, you learned to
(1) go back and review all the worksheets and exercises to which
you wrote responses, (2) compare where you are now to where you
were when you started this book and did the initial exercises, (3)
think through and update your answers, and (4) write them on this
final worksheet. When you complete this final worksheet keep it in
a prominent spot in your personal time management notebook and
refer to it regularly.

Here are six send-off questions to answer:

1.  What do you see *now* as the most important, significant, meaningful
    things you'd like time for in your life?

    a. _____

    b. _____

    c. _____

    d. _____

    e. _____

    f. _____

2.  Which of these things do you value most?

    a. _____

    b. _____

    c. _____

    d. _____

    e. _____

    f. _____

3.  What can you subtract from your present life to be part of the "vol-
    untary simplicity" movement so that, along with having more time for
    the things you've listed, you'll also enjoy a greater quality of life?

    a. _____

    b. _____

    c. _____

      d. _____

      e. _____

      f. _____

4.  What are the internal things (as opposed to external ones) that would make you happier and more satisfied?

      a. _____

      b. _____

      c. _____

      d. _____

      e. _____

      f. _____

5.  Where and when can you find one-hour-at-a-time (or one-day-at-a-time) to start doing just one of the things you have listed?

      a. _____

      b. _____

      c. _____

      d. _____

      e. _____

      f. _____

6.  After you start one activity, which one on your list do you want to do next? How can you begin planning time for that now?

      a. _____

      b. _____

      c. _____

      d. _____

      e. _____

      f. _____

***Quick Check/Recheck*** Whether you're single or single with children, or married or married with children the way to make your juggling act work—and lead a less breathless life—is managing time *women's way* as you take care of your job and your life, and also of yourself.

Simplify. Enjoy. And stay in touch with how you can use your time to blend the work, home, family, personal, physical, emotional, and spiritual aspects of your life into a satisfying whole.

When you do this at every stage of life for the cycle in which you find yourself, you'll manage both your time and your life—and live your life to the fullest.

So wherever you are in your work and your life, the time to do this is now.

# $\mathcal{W}$HO'S WHO:

# A Quick-Check Guide to the Women in the Book

*Anne Binford Allen,* television tape producer

*Judith Moncrieff Baldwin,* inventor of products in the time management field

*Dr. Rosalind Barnett,* senior research associate at the Wellesley College Center for Research on Women

*Paula Baum,* assistant buyer for a large department store

*Sheri Benjamin,* owner of a technology public relations and marketing firm

*Lucy Berns,* advertising copywriter

*Barbara Brabec,* author of *Homemade Money* and publisher of "Barbara Brabec's Self-Employment Survival Letter" and the former "National Home Business Report"

*Lisa Brandon,* temporary service worker in a company's benefits department

*Heidi Brennan,* Codirector and Public Policy Director of Mothers at Home

*Kim Bushaw,* family educator who handles a telephone questionline called *Parentline*

*Carolyn Bushong,* psychotherapist specializing in relationships

*Annie Byerly,* kindergarten teacher

*Sheree Bykofsky,* book producer, literary agent, and author of *500 Terrific Ideas for Organizing Everything*

*Carol Painter Campi,* management consultant

*Ruthanne Ciotti,* co-owner of an aircraft charter and management company

*Lynn McIntyre Coffee,* business coach

*Sherry Suib Cohen,* journalist

*Yvonne Conway,* hair stylist who takes mobile services to private homes and institutions

*Ann McGee Cooper,* business consultant, creativity expert, and author of *Time Management for Unmanageable People*

*Donna Cunningham,* media relations manager/telecommuter

*Dixie Darr,* former director of a Women's Center at a community college and publisher of "The Accidental Entrepreneur," a newsletter for people who work on their own

*Wendy Dixon,* owner of a toy/book shop

*Marie Dolce,* dress designer/seamstress

*Barbara Doyen,* literary agent

*Andrea Engber,* president of an advertising and creative design agency, director of the National Organization of Single Mothers and editor of "SingleMOTHER"

*Sally Evans,* medical records technician

*Jill Feldon,* public relations specialist

*Mary Flood,* workshop leader and publisher of the "Wasatch Letter", a financial newsletter

*Dr. Mary Frame,* consultant on leadership and time management and dean of South Carolina's Columbia College Leadership Center for Women

*Joanne Frangides,* advertising space saleswoman

*Suzanne Frisse,* seminar leader and trainer

*Debra Gallanter,* staff member in county office of a national nonprofit organization

*Dr. Eileen Gardner,* college biology professor

*Elaine Gardner,* attorney and advocate for the deaf

*Ruth Ann Gates,* retailing selling specialist

*Dr. Kathleen Gerson,* professor of sociology at New York University, an expert in gender and family issues and author of *Hard Choices: How Women Decide About Work, Careers and Motherhood*

*Donna Goldfein,* time management consultant and author of *Every Woman's Guide to Time Management*

*Dr. Joanna Good,* psychologist and therapist for a state-run consulting group

*Penelope Grover,* singer/actress and voice teacher

*Diane Hahnel,* health-screening nurse

*Gail Stewart Hand,* newspaper editor and columnist

*Barbara Hemphill,* time management and organization expert and past president of the National Association of Professional Organizers

*Lori Howard,* temporary service worker in a variety of secretarial capacities for the same company

*Caroline Hull,* business consultant and publisher of "ConneXions," a journal that focuses on entrepreneurial work

*Vicky Penner Katz,* director of news services for a state university

*Coralee Smith Kern,* consultant to home-based business owners and executive director of the National Association for the Cottage Industry

*Dr. Gayle Kimball,* authority on working parents and author of *The 50–50 Parent* and *The 50–50 Marriage*

*Lois Kohan,* public health nurse

*Beverly Konner,* insurance claims examiner

*Pam Kriston,* time management and organizational consultant

*Carol Kuhn,* regional sales manager in direct-selling field

*Judith Lederman,* public relations consultant

*Linda Marks,* Director of the FlexGroup at New Ways to Work, a San Francisco research, training, and advocacy organization for flexible work arrangements.

*Barbara Marsten,* industrial designer/fine artist

*Grace Mastalli,* Deputy Assistant Attorney General, U. S. Department of Justice

*Dr. Violet Master,* internist with a private practice

*Paula Mate,* freelance writer

*Dr. Jane Mattes,* psychotherapist and founder of Single Mothers by Choice

*Dr. Judith Myers-Wall,* associate professor of family studies at Purdue University

*Lynn O'Connell,* fundraising specialist for nonprofit organizations

*Helen Pastorino,* owner of a large real estate company

*Jane Perkins,* secondary-school textbook editor

*Pat Peters,* hairdresser

*Odette Pollar,* founder of a consulting and training firm that helps business owners manage and organize time

*Dr. Maureen Powers,* holistic practitioner and naturopath

*Elizabeth Randall,* State of New Jersey Banking Commissioner

*Nancy Read,* pediatric visiting nurse

*Lisa Rogak,* freelance writer and publisher of "Sticks," a newsletter on country living

*Dr. Barbara Rowe,* Purdue University professor who conducted a study on home-based businesses

*Sunny Schlenger,* consultant on personal management and my coauthor of *How to Be Organized in Spite of Yourself*

*Barbara Schryver,* information specialist for Manpower Temporary Services

*Felice Schwartz,* founder and former president of Catalyst, a New York City research and advisory organization that studies women in the workplace

*Dr. Pepper Schwartz,* professor of sociology at the University of Washington

*Sandra Sharp,* bank manager

*Alice Shephard,* professional organizer

*Sherry Sheridan,* librarian

*Robin Skolnick,* television tape producer

*Ingrid Steele,* accompanist, organist, and director of choirs, choral, and theater groups

*Alexis Talbott,* United Methodist Church minister

*Cynthia Cohen Turk,* management consultant

*Karen Walden,* magazine editor

*Dottie Walters,* professional speaker and president of Walters International Speakers Bureau

*Sheila Wellington,* current president of Catalyst

*Dr. Elaine Wethington,* Cornell University sociologist

*Mary-Lynn Willms,* co-owner of an international design studio in an electronic equipped seaside cottage

*Stephanie Winston,* founder of The Organizing Principle and author of *Getting Organized* and *The Organized Executive*

*Diane Wolverton,* editor of "Home Office Opportunities"

*Marcia Yudkin,* creativity consultant and publisher of "The Creative Glow"

# OTHER EXPERTS AND CONTRIBUTORS

*Dr. Larry Baker,* speaker, seminar leader, and president of a time management center

*Edwin C. Bliss,* author of *Getting Things Done*

*Dr. Michael Broder,* psychologist and author of *The Art of Living Single.*

*John Campi,* management consultant

*Allan Cohen,* authority on working at home and publisher of "Working from Home"

*Jeff Davidson,* management consultant and author of *Breathing Space: Living and Working at a Comfortable Pace in a Sped Up Society*

*Merrill E. Douglass,* president of a time management center and coauthor of *Time Management for Teams*

*Alec Mackenzie,* internationally known time management expert and author of *The Time Trap* and *Time for Success*

*Hyrum W. Smith,* CEO of Franklin Quest, a time management system and author of *The 10 Natural Laws of Successful Time and Life Management*

# $\mathcal{N}$OTES

## Introduction

1. National Home Business Report. P.O. Box 2137, Naperville, IL, Summer 1993, p. 4.

2. Families and Work Institute, "National Study of the Changing Workforce." New York, 1993, p. 56.

3. The Bureau of National Affairs, "The BNA Special Report Series on Work and Family." Washington, DC, May 1991.

4. The Bureau of National Affairs, "Daily Labor Report." Washington, DC, June 4, 1993.

5. Leight, Warren, "Why Can't a Man Tell Time Like a Woman?" *Mademoiselle*, July 1991, p. 122.

6. Brouillard Communications. *The Bergen Record*, Sept. 15, 1994.

## Point 1

1. USA Today Study reported in The Prodigy Services Report on Women prepared by The Roper Organization. May 1990, p. 73.

2. National Home Business Report. P.O. Box 2137, Naperville, IL, Summer 1993, p. 3.

## Point 2

1. McGee, Kelly Good, "How to Beat the Time Crunch." *New Woman*, Jan. 1993, p. 44.

2. McGee-Cooper, Ann, *Time Management for Unmanageable People*. New York, Bantam, 1994, p. 112.

3. Yudkin, Marcia, "News . . . from Marcia Yudkin." Creative Ways, Boston, 1993.

4. Ibid.

5. Bittel, Lester R., *Right on Time*. New York, McGraw-Hill, 1991.

## Point 3

1. Genasci, Lisa, *Associated Press* interview, "Grandmother, firebrand, feminist." *The Bergen Record,* June 20, 1993.

2. Keyes, Ralph, "Do You Have the Time?" *Parade* Magazine, Feb. 16, 1992, p. 22.

3. Quiz reprinted by permission of The Priority Management and Atheneum Network, "Choices." Issue 3, 1993.

4. Mackenzie, Alec, Alec Mackenzie's Time Tactics. 5 Broadway, Suite 202, Troy, NY.

5. Boardroom Reports, "Bottom Line." Sept. 30, 1993.

## Point 4

1. National Home Business Report. P.O. Box 2137, Naperville, IL, Winter 1994, pp. 5, 6.

2. Priority Management Systems, Inc., "The 21st Century Workplace Survey 1990." p. 10.

3. Bliss, Edwin C., *Getting Things Done.* New York, Charles Scribner's Sons, 1976 (Rev. 1983).

4. Cave, Kathryn, "The Lunch Gene." *The Bergen Record,* Sept. 25, 1994.

5. Mack, Patricia, "Desktop Cuisine." *The Bergen Record,* Sept. 22, 1993.

6. Ibid.

## Point 5

1. Bliss, Edwin C., *Getting Things Done.* New York, Charles Scribner's Sons, 1976 (Rev. 1983).

2. Schabacker, Kirsten, "A Short Snappy Guide to Meaningful Meetings." *Working Woman,* June 1991.

3. Communication Publications and Resources, *communication briefings,* "The Best Ideas in Time Management." Blackwood, NJ, 1993, p. 18.

4. Research findings from Ethel Klein, EDK Associates, a New York City public opinion research firm.

5. Uchitelle, Louis, "Lacking Child Care, Parents Take Their Children to Work." *The New York Times,* Dec. 23, 1994, p. A–1.

6. Yudkin, Marcia, "News .. from Marcia Yudkin." Creative Ways, Boston, 1993.

## Point 6

1. Findings from a Catalyst Study on "Flexible Work Arrangements for Managers and Professionals" conducted by Catalyst, the New York City research and advisory organization that studies women and work. Catalyst, New York, 1990.

2. U. S. Department of Labor, Women's Bureau, "Flexible workstyles: A Look at Contingent Labor." 1988, pp. 46–53.

3. Tergensen, Anne E., "A Time to Temp." *The Bergen Record,* Nov. 15, 1993, p. C–1.

## Point 7

1. McGee, Kelly McGee, "How to Beat the Time Crunch." *New Woman,* Jan. 1993, p. 44.

2. Cohen, Allan, "Working from Home" Newsletter. Hallandale, FL, June 1993.

3. Research from Link Resources Corporation. *The New York Times,* Sept. 29, 1994, p. C–1.

4. Luciano, Lani, "When Mom Works at Home." *Money Magazine,* Oct. 1994, p. 126.

5. Priority Management and Atheneum Network, "Choices." Issue 3, 1993.

6. McGee-Cooper, Ann, *Time Management for Unmanageable People.* New York, Bantam, 1994, p. 214.

7. Darr, Dixie, "The Accidental Entrepreneur" Newsletter. Denver, July/Aug. 1993, p. 4.

8. Pollar, Odette, "Perfect Timing." Business Start-Ups, Sept. 1993, p. 58.

9. Berner, Jeff, "Your Successful Home Office: Making a Life While Making a Living." Office Depot, Inc., 1993.

10. Bechtle, Michael A., "Straighten Up." Business Start-Ups, Aug. 1993, p. 80.

11. Berner, Jeff, "Your Successful Home Office: Making a Life While Making a Living." Office Depot, Inc., 1993.

12. Amoroso, Mary, "The Pressured Parent." *The Bergen Record,* Jan. 15, 1995.

13. Hull, Caroline, "ConneXions." Manassas, VA, Vol. No. 3, Summer 1993.

14. Yudkin, Marcia, "News . . . from Marcia Yudkin." Creative Ways, Boston, 1993.

## Point 8

1. Keyes, Ralph, "How to Unlock Time." *Readers Digest,* Oct. 1991, p. 111.

2. The Prodigy Services Company Report on Women, prepared by The Roper Organization, May 1990, p. 144.

3. Priority Management Systems, "Choices." Special Edition, Volume 8, Issue 1 (no date given), pp. 7, 8.

4. Massachusetts Mutual Life Insurance Co. study reported in *The Bergen Record,* May 8, 1994, p. A–10.

5. Gallop Poll. Reported in *Working Mother,* May 1994.

6. Genasci, Lisa, "Working Hard and Loving It." (*Associated Press*), *The Bergen Record,* April 14, 1994, p. D–1.

7. Lawson, Carol, "The Elements of Stress in Parenting, 101." *The New York Times,* May 6, 1993, p. C–2.

## Point 9

1. Priority Management Systems, "Choices." Special Edition, Volume 8, Issue 1 (no date given).

2. The Prodigy Services Company Report on Women, prepared by The Roper Organization, May 1990, p. 144.

3. McGee-Cooper, Ann, *Time Management for Unmanageable People.* New York, Bantam, 1994, p. 204.

4. Hand, Gail Stewart, "Time Crunch." *The Bergen Record,* May 20, 1993.

5. Ehrenreich, Barbara, "Housework Is Obsolescent." *Time,* Oct. 25, 1993, p. 92.

## Point 10

1. Padawer, Ruth, "Cleaning Up His Act." *The Bergen Record,* June 16, 1994, p. L–1.

2. Hand, Gail Stewart, "Time Crunch." *The Bergen Record,* Sept. 30, 1993.

## Point 11

1. Priority Management Systems, "Choices." Special Edition, Volume 8, Issue 1 (no date given).

2. The Prodigy Services Company Report on Women, prepared by The Roper Organization, May 1990, p. 121.

3. Families and Work Institute, "National Study of the Changing Workforce." New York, 1993, pp. 73, 76.

4. The Prodigy Services Company Report on Women, prepared by The Roper Organization, May 1990, p. 118.

5. The Prodigy Services Company Report on Women, prepared by The Roper Organization, May 1990, p. 52.

6. Priority Management Systems, "Choices." Special Edition, Volume 8, Issue 1 (no date given).

7. Hand, Gail Stewart, "Time Crunch." *The Bergen Record,* May 20, 1993.

8. Bliss, Edwin C., *Getting Things Done.* New York, Charles Scribner's Sons, 1976 (Rev. 1983).

9. The Prodigy Services Company Report on Women, prepared by The Roper Organization, May 1990, p. 123.

10. Goldfein, Donna, *Everywoman's Guide to Time Management.* Celestial Arts, Berkeley, CA, 1977.

11. McGee-Cooper, Ann, "Don't Go Home Exhausted." *Vibrant Life,* March/April 1992, pp. 22, 23.

12. Goodman, Ellen, "Joy Is Also a Habit." *The Bergen Record,* Jan. 7, 1994, p. D–7.

## Point 12

1. Swiss, Deborah J. & Walker, Judith P., *Women and the Work/Family Dilemma.* New York, John Wiley & Sons, 1993.

2. Reimer, Susan, "Do-Me Feminism? Give Us a Break." *The Bergen Record,* Jan. 30, 1994, p. L–3.

3. Priority Management Systems, "Choices." Special Edition, Volume 8, Issue 1 (no date given).

4. McGee-Cooper, Ann, *Time Management for Unmanageable People.* New York, Bantam, 1994, p. 63.

5. Schwartz, Pepper, "Me Stressed? No Blessed." *The New York Times,* Nov. 17, 1994, p. C–1.

## Point 13

1. Duncan, Barbara, *The Single Mother's Survival Manual.* Saratoga, CA R & E Publishers, 1984.

2. Schwartz, Pepper, "Me Stressed? No Blessed." *The New York Times,* Nov. 17, 1994, p. C–1.

3. Mezger, Roger, "When Flowers Don't Cut It: Love and the Two-Career Family." *The Bergen Record,* Nov. 17, 1994, p. C–1. (Article is based on views of Steven E. Hobfoll and Ivonne Heras Hobfoll, authors of *"Work Won't Love You Back: The Dual Career Couple's Survival Guide.* New York, W. H. Freeman and Co., 1994.)

# RECOMMENDED READING

**Bliss, Edwin.** *Getting Things Done.* New York: Scribner's, 1976 (Rev. 1983).

**Bond, William J.** *Home-Based Newsletter Publishing.* New York: McGraw-Hill, 1992.

**Brabec, Barbara.** *Homemade Money.* Cincinnati: Writer's Digest Books, 1994.

**Broder, Dr. Michael.** *The Art of Living Single.* New York: Avon, 1990.

**Broder, Dr. Michael.** *The Art of Staying Together.* New York: Hyperion, 1993.

**Bykofsky, Sheree.** *500 Terrific Ideas for Organizing Everything.* New York: Fireside, 1993.

**Communication briefings.** *The Best Ideas in Time Management.* Blackwood NJ: Communication Publications and Resources, 1993.

**Covey, Stephen R.** *The 7 Habits of Highly Effective People.* New York: Fireside, 1990.

**Covey, Stephen, Merrill Roger A., and Merrill, Rebecca R.** *First Things First.* New York: Simon & Schuster, 1994.

**Crosby, Faye J.** *Juggling.* New York: The Free Press, 1991.

**Davidson, Jeff.** *Breathing Space: Living and Working at a Comfortable Pace in a Sped Up Society.* New York: MasterMedia Limited, 1991.

**Douglass, Merrill E. and Donna N.** *Time Management for Teams.* New York: American Management Association, 1992.

**Duncan, Barbara.** *The Single Mother's Survival Manual.* Saratoga, CA: R & E Publishers, 1984.

**Gerson, Dr. Kathleen.** *No Man's Land: Men's Changing Commitments to Family and Work.* New York: Basic Books, 1993.

**Gerson, Dr. Kathleen.** *Hard Choices: How Women Decide About Work, Careers and Motherhood.* Berkeley, CA: University of California Press, 1985.

**Goldfein, Donna.** *Everywoman's Guide to Time Management.* Berkeley, CA: Celestial Arts, 1977.

**Hemphill, Barbara.** *Taming the Paper Tiger.* Washington, D.C.: Kiplinger Books, 1992.

**Hochschild, Arlie.** *The Second Shift: Working Parents and the Revolution at Home.* New York: Viking, 1989.

**Keyes, Ralph.** *Timelock: How Life Got So Hectic and What You Can Do About It.* New York: HarperCollins, 1991.

**Kimball, Gale.** *50–50 Marriage.* Chico, CA: Equality Press, 1988.

**Kimball, Gale.** *50–50 Parenting.* Chico, CA: Equality Press, 1988.

**Lakein, Alan.** *How to Get Control of Your Time and Your Life.* New York: New American Library, 1973.

**Louv, Richard.** *FatherLove.* New York: Pocket Books, 1994.

**Mackenzie, Alec.** *The Time Trap.* New York: American Management Association, 1991.

**Mackenzie, Alec.** *Time for Success.* New York: McGraw-Hill, 1989.

**Mackenzie, Alec and Waldo, Kay Cronkite.** *About Time!* New York: McGraw-Hill, 1981.

**Mattes, Dr. Jane.** *Single Mothers by Choice.* New York: Times Books, 1994.

**McGee-Cooper, Ann.** *Time Management for Unmanageable People.* New York: Bantam Books, 1994.

**McGee-Cooper, Ann.** *You Don't Have to Go Home Exhausted.* New York: Bantam Books, 1992.

**McWilliams, Peter and John-Roger.** *Do it! Let's Get Off Our Buts.* Los Angeles: Prelude Press, 1991.

**Roesch, Roberta.** *Smart Talk: The Art of Savvy Business Conversation.* New York: American Management Association, 1989.

**Schlenger, Sunny and Roesch, Roberta.** *How to Be Organized in Spite of Yourself.* New York: New American Library, 1989.

**Schor, Juliet B.** *The Overworked American: The Unexpected Decline of Leisure.* New York: Basic Books, 1992.

**Scott, Dru.** *How to Put More Time in Your Life.* New York: Dutton, 1984.

**Shaevitz, Marjorie Hansen.** *The Superwoman Syndrome.* New York: Warner Books, 1984.

**Shreve Anita and Lone, Patricia.** *Working Woman: A Guide to Fitness and Health.* St. Louis: Mosby Co., 1986.

**Swiss, Deborah J. and Walker, Judith P.** *Women and the Work/Family Dilemma.* New York: John Wiley & Sons, 1993.

**Winston, Stephanie.** *The Organized Executive.* New York: Warner Books, Revised Edition 1994.

**Winston, Stephanie.** *Getting Organized.* New York: Warner Books, Revised Edition 1990.

# $\mathscr{I}$NDEX

## *R*

## *S*

*S*

Turk, Cynthia Cohen, 195, 235

## $\mathcal{U}$

*Up the Organization,* 92
*USA Today,* 5

## $\mathcal{V}$

Values important to you, concentrating on, 232-33
Variable day, 112
Visual aids, using to ease workload sharing, 199-202

## $\mathcal{W}$

Walker, Judith P., 228
Walters, Dottie, 136, 177
Walters International Speakers Bureau, 136
Weekends, using to refuel, 218-19
Weekly plan, creating, 43-47
*Welcome Home,* 231
Wellesley College Center for Research on Women, 237-38
Wellington, Sheila, 107, 191
Wethington, Elaine, 150
Whitman, Christine Todd, 212
Winston, Stephanie, 69, 88, 90
Wolverton, Diane, 5
  self-test, 4

*Women and the Work/Family Dilemma,* 228
Women's Bureau of U.S. Department of Labor, 129
Work space, planning to save time, 85-88
  efficiency essential for working at home, 135-36
*Work Won't Love You Back: The Dual Career Couple's Survival Guide,* 250
"Working Hard and Loving It," 151
Working at home, 121-46
  benefits of, five, 122-24
  freelancer, independent contractor or consultant, 129-31
  owning home business, 126-27
  quick check/recheck, 146
  self-test, 124-25
  strategies for, nine, 131-45
    balance between work and home life, 139-41
    child-care issues, 141-42
    family's respect for your time, instilling, 137-39
    goals, clarifying, 132-33
    hiring help, 143-44
    scheduling day's work, 134-35
    self-starter essential, 132
    "smart switch," 140
    when to stop, 144-45
    workspace efficiency, 135-36
  telecommuting. 127-29
*Working from Home,* 122
Working late, preparing for, 96-97